THE POETICAL WORKS

OF

JAMES RUSSELL LOWELL.

THE

POETICAL WORKS

OF

JAMES R. LOWELL.

COMPLETE IN TWO VOLUMES.

VOLUME II.

BOSTON:
TICKNOR AND FIELDS.
M DCCC LXVI.

CONTENTS OF VOLUME II.

READER! *walk up at once (it will soon be too late) and buy at a perfectly ruinous rate*

A

FABLE FOR CRITICS;

OR, BETTER,

(I like, as a thing that the reader's first fancy may strike, an old-fashioned title-page, such as presents a tabular view of the volume's contents)

A GLANCE

AT A FEW OF OUR LITERARY PROGENIES

(Mrs. Malaprop's word)

FROM

THE TUB OF DIOGENES;

A VOCAL AND MUSICAL MEDLEY,

THAT IS,

A SERIES OF JOKES

By A Wonderful Quiz,

who accompanies himself with a rub-a-dub-dub, full of spirit and grace, on the top of the tub.

Set forth in October, the 31st day,
In the year '48, G. P. Putnam, Broadway.

TO

CHARLES F. BRIGGS,

THIS VOLUME IS AFFECTIONATELY INSCRIBED.

It being the commonest mode of procedure, I premise a few candid remarks

To the Reader:

This trifle, begun to please only myself and my own private fancy, was laid on the shelf. But some friends, who had seen it, induced me, by dint of saying they liked it, to put it in print. That is, having come to that very conclusion, I consulted them when it could make no confusion. For, (though in the gentlest of ways,) they had hinted it was scarce worth the while, I should doubtless have printed it.

I began it, intending a Fable, a frail, slender thing, rhyme-ywinged, with a sting in its tail. But, by addings and alterings not previously planned,—digressions chance-hatched, like birds' eggs in the sand,—and dawdlings to suit every whimsy's demand, (always freeing the bird which I held in my hand, for the two perched, perhaps out of reach, in the tree,)—it grew by degrees to the size which you see. I was like the old woman that carried the calf, and my neighbors, like hers, no doubt, wonder and laugh, and when, my strained arms with their grown burthen full, I call it my Fable, they call it a bull.

Having scrawled at full gallop (as far as that goes) in a style that is neither good verse nor bad prose, and being a person whom nobody knows, some people will say I am rather more free with my readers than it is becoming to be, that I seem to expect them to wait on my leisure in following wherever I wander at pleasure, that, in short, I take more than a young author's lawful ease, and laugh in a queer way so like Mephistopheles, that the public will doubt, as they grope through my rhythm, if in truth I am making fun *at* them or *with* them.

So the excellent Public is hereby assured that the sale of my book is already secured. For there is not a poet throughout the whole land, but will purchase a copy or two out of hand, in the fond expectation of being amused in it, by seeing his betters cut-up and abused in it. Now, I find, by a pretty exact calculation, there are something like ten thousand bards in the nation, of that special variety whom the Review and Magazine critics call *lofty* and *true*, and about thirty thousand (*this* tribe is increasing) of the kinds who are termed *full of promise* and *pleasing*. The Public will see by a glance at this schedule, that they cannot expect me to be over-sedulous about courting *them*, since it seems I have got enough fuel made sure of for boiling my pot.

As for such of our poets as find not their names mentioned once in my pages, with praises or blames, let them SEND IN THEIR CARDS, without further DELAY, to my friend G. P. PUTNAM, Esquire, in Broadway, where a LIST will be kept with the strictest regard to the day and the hour of receiving the card. Then, taking them up as I chance to have time, (that is, if their names can be twisted in rhyme,) I will honestly give each his PROPER POSITION, at the rate of ONE AUTHOR to each NEW EDITION. Thus a PREMIUM is offered sufficiently HIGH (as the magazines say when they tell their best lie) to induce bards to CLUB their resources and buy the balance of every edition, until they have all of them fairly been run through the mill.

One word to such readers (judicious and wise) as read books with something behind the mere eyes, of whom in the country, perhaps, there are two, including myself, gentle reader, and you. All the characters sketched in this slight *jeu d'esprit*, though, it may be, they seem, here and there, rather free, and drawn from a Mephistophelian stand-point, are *meant* to be faithful, and that is the grand point, and none but an owl would feel sore at a rub from a jester who tells you, without any subterfuge, that he sits in Diogenes' tub.

A PRELIMINARY NOTE TO THE SECOND EDITION,

though it well may be reckoned, of all composition, the species at once most delightful and healthy, is a thing which an author, unless he be wealthy and willing to pay for that kind of delight, is not, in all instances, called on to write. Though there are, it is said, who, their spirits to cheer, slip in a new title-page three times a year, and in this way snuff up an imaginary savor of that sweetest of dishes, the popular favor,—much as if a starved painter should fall to and treat the Ugolino inside to a picture of meat.

You remember (if not, pray turn over and look) that, in writing the preface which ushered my book, I treated you, excellent Public, not merely with a cool disregard, but downright cavalierly. Now I would not take back the least thing I then said, though I thereby could butter both sides of my bread, for I never could see that an author owed aught to the people he solaced, diverted, or taught; and, as for mere fame, I have long ago learned that the persons by whom it is finally earned, are those with whom *your* verdict weighed not a pin, unsustained by the higher court sitting within.

But I wander from what I intended to say— that you have, namely, shown such a liberal way of thinking, and so much aesthetic perception of anonymous worth in the handsome reception you gave to my book, spite of some private piques, (having bought the first thousand in barely two weeks,) that I think, past a doubt, if you measured the phiz of your's most devotedly, Wonderful Quiz, you would find that its vertical section was shorter, by an inch and two tenths, or 'twixt that and a quarter.

You have watched a child playing—in those wondrous years when belief is not bound to the eyes and the ears, and the vision divine is so clear and unmarred, that each baker of pies in the dirt is a bard? Give a knife and a shingle, he fits out a fleet, and, on that little mudpuddle over the street, his invention, in purest good faith, will make sail round the globe with a puff of his breath for a gale, will visit, in barely ten minutes, all climes, and find Northwestern passages hundreds of times. Or, suppose the young Poet fresh stored with delights from that Bible of childhood the Arabian Nights, he will turn to a crony and cry, "Jack, let's play that I am a Genius!" Jacky straightway makes Aladdin's lamp out of a stone, and, for hours, they enjoy each his own supernatural powers. This is all very pretty and pleasant, but then suppose our two urchins have grown into men, and both have turned authors,—one says to his brother, "Let's play we're the American somethings or other, (only let them be big enough, no matter what.) Come, you shall be Goethe or Pope, which you choose; I'll be Coleridge, and both shall write mutual reviews." So they both (as mere strangers) before many days, send each other a cord of anonymous bays. Each, in piling his epithets, smiles in his sleeve to see what his friend can be made to believe; each, in reading the other's unbiased review, thinks—Here's pretty high praise, but no more than is true. Well, we laugh at them both, and yet make no great fuss when the same farce is acted to benefit us. Even I, who, if asked, scarce a month since, what Fudge meant, should have answered, the dear Public's critical judgment, begin to think sharpwitted Horace spoke sooth when he said, that the Public *sometimes* hit the truth.

In reading these lines, you perhaps have a vision of a person in pretty good health and condition, and yet, since I put forth my primary edition, I have been crushed, scorched, withered, used up and put down, (by Smith with the cordial assistance of Brown,) in all, if you put any faith in my rhymes, to the number of ninety-five several times, and, while I am writing—I tremble to think of it, for I may at this moment be just on the brink of it—Molybdostom, angry at being omitted, has begun a critique,—am I not to be pitied ?*

Now I shall not crush *them* since, indeed, for that matter, no pressure I know of could render them flatter; nor wither, nor scorch them,—no action of fire could make either them or their articles drier; nor waste time in putting them down—I am thinking not their own self-inflation will keep them from sinking; for there's this contradiction about the whole bevy—though without the least weight, they are awfully heavy. No, my dear honest bore, *surdo fabulam narras*, they are no more to me than a rat in the arras. I can walk with the Doctor, get facts from the Don, or draw out the Lambish quintessence of John, and feel nothing more than a half-comic sorrow, to think that they all will be lying to-morrow tossed carelessly up on the waste-paper shelves, and forgotten by all but their half-dozen selves. Once snug in my attic, my fire in a roar, I leave the whole pack of them outside the door. With Hakluyt or Purchas I wander away to the black northern seas or barbaric Cathay; get *fou* with O'Shanter, and sober me then with that builder of brick-kilnish dramas, rare Ben; snuff Herbert, as holy as a flower on a grave; with Fletcher wax tender, o'er Chapman grow brave; with Marlowe or Kyd take

* The wise Scandinavians probably called their bards by the queer-looking title of Scald, in a delicate way, as it were, just to hint to the world the hot water they always get into.

a fine poet-rave; in Very, most Hebrew of Saxons, find peace; with Lycidas welter on vext Irish seas; with Webster grow wild, and climb earthward again, down by mystical Browne's Jacob's-ladder-like brain, to that spiritual Pepys (Cotton's version) Montaigne; find a new depth in Wordsworth, undreamed of before,—that divinely-inspired, wise, deep, tender, grand,—bore. Or, out of my study, the scholar thrown off, nature holds up her shield 'gainst the sneer and the scoff; the landscape, forever consoling and kind, pours her wine and her oil on the smarts of the mind. The waterfall, scattering its vanishing gems; the tall grove of hemlocks, with moss on their stems, like plashes of sunlight; the pond in the woods, where no foot but mine and the bittern's intrudes; these are all my kind neighbors, and leave me no wish to say aught to you all, my poor critics, but—pish! I have buried the hatchet; I am twisting an allumette out of one of you now, and relighting my calumet. In your private capacities, come when you please, I will give you my hand and a fresh pipe a-piece.

As I ran through the leaves of my poor little book, to take a fond author's first tremulous look, it was quite an excitement to hunt the *errata*, sprawled in as birds' tracks are in some kinds of strata, (only these made things crookeder.) Fancy an heir, that a father had seen born well-featured and fair, turning suddenly wry-nosed, club-footed, squint-eyed, hare-lipped, wapper-jawed, carrot-haired, from a pride become an aversion,—my case was yet worse. A club-foot (by way of a change) in a verse, I might have forgiven, an *o*'s being wry, a limp in an *e*, or a cock in an *i*,—but to have the sweet babe of my brain served in *pi!* I am not queasy-stomached, but such a Thyestean banquet as that was quite out of the question.

In the edition now issued, no pains are neglected, and my verses, as orators say, stand corrected. Yet some blunders remain of the public's own make, which I wish to correct for my personal sake. For instance, a character drawn in pure fun and condensing the traits of a dozen in one, has been, as I hear by some persons applied to a good friend of mine, whom to stab in the side, as we walked along chatting and joking together, would not be *my* way. I can hardly tell whether a question will ever arise in which he and I should by any strange fortune agree, but meanwhile my esteem for him grows as I know him, and, though not the best judge upon earth of a poem, he knows what it is he is saying and why, and is honest and fearless, two good points which I have not found so rife I can easily smother my love for them, whether on my side or 'tother.

For my other *anonymi*, you may be sure that I know what is meant by a caricature, and what by a portrait. There *are* those who think it is capital fun to be spattering their ink on quiet unquarrelsome folk, but the minute the game changes sides and the others begin it, they see something savage and horrible in it. As for me I respect neither women or men for their gender, nor own any sex in a pen. I choose just to hint to some causeless unfriends that, as far as I know, there are always two ends (and one of them heaviest, too) to a staff, and two parties also to every good laugh.

A FABLE FOR CRITICS.

Phœbus, sitting one day in a laurel-tree's shade,
Was reminded of Daphne, of whom it was made,
For the god being one day too warm in his wooing,
She took to the tree to escape his pursuing;
Be the cause what it might, from his offers she shrunk,
And, Ginevra-like, shut herself up in a trunk;
And, though 'twas a step into which he had driven her,
He somehow or other had never forgiven her;
Her memory he nursed as a kind of a tonic,
Something bitter to chew when he'd play the Byronic,
And I can't count the obstinate nymphs that he brought over,
By a strange kind of smile he put on when he thought of her.
"My case is like Dido's," he sometimes remark'd,
"When I last saw my love, she was fairly embark'd,
In a laurel, as *she* thought—but (ah how Fate mocks!)
She has found it by this time a very bad box;
Let hunters from me take this saw when they need it,

—You're not always sure of your game when
you've treed it.
Just conceive such a change taking place in one's
mistress!
What romance would be left?—who can flatter or
kiss trees?
And for mercy's sake, how could one keep up a
dialogue
With a dull wooden thing that will live and will
die a log,—
Not to say that the thought would forever intrude
That you've less chance to win her the more she is
wood?
Ah! it went to my heart, and the memory still
grieves,
To see those loved graces all taking their leaves;
Those charms beyond speech, so enchanting but
now,
As they left me forever, each making its bough!
If her tongue *had* a tang sometimes more than was
right,
Her new bark is worse than ten times her old
bite."

Now, Daphne,—before she was happily treei-
fied,—
Over all other blossoms the lily had deified,
And when she expected the god on a visit,
('Twas before he had made his intentions ex-
plicit,)
Some buds she arranged with a vast deal of care,
To look as if artlessly twined in her hair,
Where they seemed, as he said, when he paid his
addresses,
Like the day breaking through the long night of
her tresses;
So whenever he wished to be quite irresistible,

Like a man with eight trumps in his hand at a
whist-table,
(I feared me at first that the rhyme was untwist-
able,
Though I might have lugged in an allusion to
Cristabel,)—
He would take up a lily, and gloomily look in it,
As I shall at the ——, when they cut up my book
in it.

Well, here, after all the bad rhyme I've been
spinning,
I've got back at last to my story's beginning:
Sitting there, as I say, in the shade of his mistress,
As dull as a volume of old Chester mysteries,
Or as those puzzling specimens, which, in old
histories,
We read of his verses—the Oracles, namely,—
(I wonder the Greeks should have swallowed them
tamely,
For one might bet safely whatever he has to risk,
They were laid at his door by some ancient Miss
Asterisk,
And so dull that the men who retailed them out-
doors
Got the ill name of augurs, because they were
bores,)—
First, he mused what the animal substance or
herb is
Would induce a moustache, for you know he's
imberbis;
Then he shuddered to think how his youthful posi-
tion
Was assailed by the age of his son the physician;
At some poems he glanced, had been sent to him
lately,
And the metre and sentiment puzzled him greatly

"Mehercle! I'd make such proceedings felonious,—
Have they all of them slept in the cave of Trophonius?
Look well to your seat, 'tis like taking an airing
On a corduroy road, and that out of repairing;
It leads one, 'tis true, through the primitive forest,
Grand natural features—but, then, one has no rest;
You just catch a glimpse of some ravishing distance,
When a jolt puts the whole of it out of existence,—
Why not use their ears, if they happen to have any?"
—Here the laurel-leaves murmured the name of poor Daphne.

"O, weep with me, Daphne," he sighed, "for you know it's
A terrible thing to be pestered with poets!
But, alas, she is dumb, and the proverb holds good,
She never will cry till she's out of the wood!
What wouldn't I give if I never had known of her?
'Twere a kind of relief had I something to groan over;
If I had but some letters of hers, now, to toss over,
I might turn for the nonce a Byronic philosopher,
And bewitch all the flats by bemoaning the loss of her.
One needs something tangible, though to begin on—
A loom, as it were, for the fancy to spin on;
What boots all your grist? it can never be ground
Till a breeze makes the arms of the windmill go round,
(Or, if 'tis a water-mill, alter the metaphor,

And say it won't stir, save the wheel be well wet
afore,
Or lug in some stuff about water "so dreamily,"—
It is not a metaphor, though, 'tis a simile;)
A lily, perhaps, would set *my* mill agoing,
For just at this season, I think, they are blowing,
Here, somebody, fetch one, not very far hence
They're in bloom by the score, 'tis but climbing a
fence;
There's a poet hard by, who does nothing but fill
his
Whole garden, from one end to t'other, with lilies;
A very good plan, were it not for satiety,
One longs for a weed here and there, for variety;
Though a weed is no more than a flower in dis-
guise,
Which is seen through at once, if love give a man
eyes."

Now there happened to be among Phœbus's
followers,
A gentleman, one of the omnivorous swallowers,
Who bolt every book that comes out of the press,
Without the least question of larger or less,
Whose stomachs are strong at the expense of their
head,—
For reading new books is like eating new bread,
One can bear it at first, but by gradual steps he
Is brought to death's door of a mental dyspepsy.
On a previous stage of existence, our Hero
Had ridden outside, with the glass below zero;
He had been, 'tis a fact you may safely rely on,
Of a very old stock a most eminent scion,—
A stock all fresh quacks their fierce boluses
ply on,
Who stretch the new boots Earth's unwilling to
try on,

Whom humbugs of all shapes and sorts keep their
eye on,
Whose hair 's in the mortar of every new Zion,
Who, when whistles are dear, go directly and buy
one,
Who think slavery a crime that we must not say
fie on,
Who hunt, if they e'er hunt at all, with the lion,
(Though they hunt lions also, whenever they spy
one,)
Who contrive to make every good fortune a wry
one,
And at last choose the hard bed of honor to die on,
Whose pedigree traced to earth's earliest years,
Is longer than any thing else but their ears;—
In short, he was sent into life with the wrong key,
He unlocked the door, and stept forth a poor
donkey.
Though kicked and abused by his bipedal betters,
Yet he filled no mean place in the kingdom of
letters;
Far happier than many a literary hack,
He bore only paper-mill rags on his back;
(For it makes a vast difference which side the mill
One expends on the paper his labor and skill;)
So, when his soul waited a new transmigration,
And Destiny balanced 'twixt this and that station,
Not having much time to expend upon bothers,
Remembering he'd had some connexion with
authors,
And considering his four legs had grown paraly-
tic,—
She set him on two, and he came forth a critic.

Through his babyhood no kind of pleasure he
took
In any amusement but tearing a book;

For him there was no intermediate stage,
From babyhood up to straight-laced middle age;
There were years when he didn't wear coat-tails behind,
But a boy he could never be rightly defined;
Like the Irish Good Folk, though in length scarce a span,
From the womb he came gravely, a little old man;
While other boys' trowsers demanded the toil
Of the motherly fingers on all kinds of soil,
Red, yellow, brown, black, clayey, gravelly, loamy,
He sat in the corner and read Viri Romæ.
He never was known to unbend or to revel once
In base, marbles, hockey, or kick up the devil once;
He was just one of those who excite the benevolence
Of your old prigs who sound the soul's depths with a ledger,
And are on the look out for some young men to "edger-
cate," as they call it, who won't be too costly,
And who'll afterward take to the ministry mostly;
Who always wear spectacles, always look bilious,
Always keep on good terms with each *mater-familias*
Throughout the whole parish, and manage to rear
Ten boys like themselves, on four hundred a year;
Who, fulfilling in turn the same fearful conditions,
Either preach through their noses, or go upon missions.

In this way our hero got safely to college,
Where he bolted alike both his commons and knowledge;
A reading-machine, always wound up and going,
He mastered whatever was not worth the knowing,

Appeared in a gown, and a vest of black satin,
To spout such a Gothic oration in Latin,
That Tully could never have made out a word in it,
(Though himself was the model the author pre-
ferred in it,)
And grasping the parchment which gave him in
fee,
All the mystic and-so-forths contained in A. B.,
He was launched (life is always compared to a
sea,)
With just enough learning, and skill for the using
it,
To prove he'd a brain, by forever confusing it.
So worthy Saint Benedict, piously burning
With the holiest zeal against secular learning,
Nesciensque scienter, as writers express it,
Indoctusque sapienter â Româ recessit.

'Twould be endless to tell you the things that he
knew,
All separate facts, undeniably true,
But with him or each other they'd nothing to do;
No power of combining, arranging, discerning,
Digested the masses he learned into learning;
There was one thing in life he had practical knowl-
edge for,
(And this, you will think, he need scarce go to
college for,)
Not a deed would he do, nor a word would he
utter,
Till he'd weighed its relations to plain bread and
butter.
When he left Alma Mater, he practised his wits
In compiling the journals' historical bits,—
Of shops broken open, men falling in fits,
Great fortunes in England bequeathed to poor
printers,

And cold spells, the coldest for many past winters,—
Then, rising by industry, knack, and address,
Got notices up for an unbiased press,
With a mind so well poised, it seemed equally made for
Applause or abuse, just which chanced to be paid for;
From this point his progress was rapid and sure,
To the post of a regular heavy reviewer.

And here I must say he wrote excellent articles
On the Hebraic points, or the force of Greek particles,
They filled up the space nothing else was prepared for;
And nobody read that which nobody cared for;
If any old book reached a fiftieth edition,
He could fill forty pages with safe erudition;
He could gauge the old books by the old set of rules,
And his very old nothings pleased very old fools;
But give him a new book, fresh out of the heart,
And you put him at sea without compass or chart,—
His blunders aspired to the rank of an art;
For his lore was engraft, something foreign that grew in him,
Exhausting the sap of the native and true in him,
So that when a man came with a soul that was new in him,
Carving new forms of truth out of Nature's old granite,
New and old at their birth, like Le Verrier's planet,
Which, to get a true judgment, themselves must create
In the soul of their critic the measure and weight,
Being rather themselves a fresh standard of grace,

To compute their own judge, and assign him his
place,
Our reviewer would crawl all about it and round
it,
And, reporting each circumstance just as he found
it,
Without the least malice,—his record would be
Profoundly æsthetic as that of a flea,
Which, supping on Wordsworth, should print, for
our sakes,
Recollections of nights with the Bard of the Lakes,
Or, borne by an Arab guide, ventured to render a
General view of the ruins at Denderah.

As I said, he was never precisely unkind,
The defect in his brain was just absence of mind;
If he boasted, 'twas simply that he was self-made,
A position which I, for one, never gainsaid,
My respect for my Maker supposing a skill
In his works which our hero would answer but ill;
And I trust that the mould which he used may be
cracked, or he
Made bold by success, may enlarge his phy-
lactery,
And set up a kind of a man-manufactory,
An event which I shudder to think about, seeing
That Man is a moral, accountable being.

He meant well enough, but was still in the way
As a dunce always is, let him be where he may;
Indeed, they appear to come into existence
To impede other folks with their awkward assist
ance;
If you set up a dunce on the very North pole,
All alone with himself, I believe, on my soul,
He'd manage to get betwixt somebody's shins,
And pitch him down bodily, all in his sins,

To the grave polar bears sitting round on the ice,
All shortening their grace, to be in for a slice;
Or, if he found nobody else there to pother,
Why, one of his legs would just trip up the other,
For there's nothing we read of in torture's inventions,
Like a well-meaning dunce, with the best of intentions.

A terrible fellow to meet in society,
Not the toast that he buttered was ever so dry at tea;
There he'd sit at the table and stir in his sugar,
Crouching close for a spring, all the while, like a cougar;
Be sure of your facts, of your measures and weights,
Of your time—he's as fond as an Arab of dates;—
You'll be telling, perhaps, in your comical way,
Of something you've seen in the course of the day;
And, just as you're tapering out the conclusion,
You venture an ill-fated classic allusion,—
The girls have all got their laughs ready, when, whack!
The cougar comes down on your thunderstruck back!
You had left out a comma,—your Greek's put in joint,
And pointed at cost of your story's whole point.
In the course of the evening, you venture on certain
Soft speeches to Anne, in the shade of the curtain;
You tell her your heart can be likened to *one* flower,
"And that, oh most charming of women, 's the sunflower,
Which turns"—here a clear nasal voice, to your terror,

From outside the curtain, says "that's all an error."
As for him, he's—no matter, he never grew tender,
Sitting after a ball, with his feet on the fender,
Shaping somebody's sweet features out of cigar smoke,
(Though he'd willingly grant you that such doings are smoke;)
All women he damns with *mutabile semper*,
And if ever he felt something like love's distemper,
'Twas towards a young lady who spoke ancient Mexican,
And assisted her father in making a lexicon;
Though I recollect hearing him get quite ferocious
About Mary Clausum, the mistress of Grotius,
Or something of that sort,—but, no more to bore ye
With character-painting, I'll turn to my story.

Now, Apollo, who finds it convenient sometimes
To get his court clear of the makers of rhymes,
The *genus*, I think it is called, *irritabile*,
Every one of whom thinks himself treated most shabbily,
And nurses a—what is it?—*immedicabile*,
Which keeps him at boiling-point, hot for a quarrel,
As bitter as wormwood, and sourer than sorrel,
If any poor devil but look at a laurel;—
Apollo, I say, being sick of their rioting,
(Though he sometimes acknowledged their verse had a quieting
Effect after dinner, and seemed to suggest a
Retreat to the shrine of a tranquil siesta,)
Kept our Hero at hand, who, by means of a bray,
Which he gave to the life, drove the rabble away,
And if that wouldn't do, he was sure to succeed,
If he took his review out and offered to read;

Or, failing in plans of this milder description,
He would ask for their aid to get up a subscription,
Considering that authorship wasn't a rich craft,
To print the "American drama of Witchcraft."
"Stay, I'll read you a scene,"—but he hardly began,
Ere Apollo shrieked "Help!" and the authors all ran:
And once, when these purgatives acted with less spirit,
And the desperate case asked a remedy desperate,
He drew from his pocket a foolscap epistle,
As calmly as if 'twere a nine-barrelled pistol,
And threatened them all with the judgment to come,
Of "A wandering Star's first impressions of Rome."
"Stop! stop!" with their hands o'er their ears screamed the Muses,
"He may go off and murder himself, if he chooses,
'Twas a means self-defence only sanctioned his trying,
'Tis mere massacre now that the enemy's flying;
If he's forced to 't again, and we happen to be there,
Give us each a large handkerchief soaked in strong ether."

I called this a "Fable for Critics;" you think it's
More like a display of my rhythmical trinkets;
My plot, like an icicle, 's slender and slippery,
Every moment more slender, and likely to slip awry,
And the reader unwilling *in loco desipere*,
Is free to jump over as much of my frippery
As he fancies, and, if he's a provident skipper, he

May have an Odyssean sway of the gales,
And get safe into port, ere his patience all fails;
Moreover, although 'tis a slender return
For your toil and expense, yet my paper will burn,
And, if you have manfully struggled thus far with me,
You may e'en twist me up, and just light your cigar with me:
If too angry for that, you can tear me in pieces,
And my *membra disjecta* consign to the breezes,
A fate like great Ratzau's, whom one of those bores,
Who beflead with bad verses poor Louis Quatorze,
Describes, (the first verse somehow ends with *victoire*,)
As *dispersant partout et ses membres et sa gloire;*
Or, if I were over-desirous of earning
A repute among noodles for classical learning,
I could pick you a score of allusions, I wis,
As new as the jests of *Didaskalos tis;*
Better still, I could make out a good solid list
From recondite authors who do not exist,—
But that would be naughty: at least, I could twist
Something out of Absyrtus, or turn your inquiries
After Milton's prose metaphor, drawn from Osiris;—
But, as Cicero says he won't say this or that,
(A fetch, I must say, most transparent and flat,)
After saying whate'er he could possibly think of,—
I simply will state that I pause on the brink of
A mire, ankle-deep, of deliberate confusion,
Made up of old jumbles of classic allusion,
So, when you were thinking yourselves to be pitied,
Just conceive how much harder your teeth you'd have gritted,
An 'twere not for the dulness I've kindly omitted.

I'd apologize here for my many digressions,
Were it not that I'm certain to trip into fresh
ones,
('Tis so hard to escape if you get in their mesh
once;)
Just reflect, if you please, how 'tis said by Horatius,
That Mæonides nods now and then, and, my gracious!
It certainly does look a little bit ominous
When he gets under way with *ton d'apameibomenos.*
(Here a something occurs which I'll just clap a
rhyme to,
And say it myself, ere a Zoilus have time to,—
Any author a nap like Van Winkle's may take,
If he only contrive to keep readers awake,
But he'll very soon find himself laid on the shelf,
If *they* fall a nodding when he nods himself.)

Once for all, to return, and to stay, will I,
nill I—
When Phœbus expressed his desire for a lily,
Our hero, whose homœopathic sagacity
With an ocean of zeal mixed his drop of capacity,
Set off for the garden as fast as the wind,
(Or, to take a comparison more to my mind,
As a sound politician leaves conscience behind,)
And leaped the low fence, as a party hack jumps
O'er his principles, when something else turns up
trumps.

He was gone a long time, and Apollo meanwhile,
Went over some sonnets of his with a file,
For of all compositions, he thought that the sonnet

Best repaid all the toil you expended upon it;
It should reach with one impulse the end of its
course,
And for one final blow collect all of its force;
Not a verse should be salient, but each one should
tend
With a wave-like up-gathering to burst at the
end;—
So, condensing the strength here, there smoothing
a wry kink,
He was killing the time, when up walked Mr. ——;
At a few steps behind him, a small man in glasses,
Went dodging about, muttering "murderers!
asses!"
From out of his pocket a paper he'd take,
With the proud look of martyrdom tied to its
stake,
And, reading a squib at himself, he'd say, "Here I
see
'Gainst American letters a bloody conspiracy,
They are all by my personal enemies written;
I must post an anonymous letter to Britain,
And show that this gall is the merest suggestion
Of spite at my zeal on the Copyright question,
For, on this side the water, 'tis prudent to pull
O'er the eyes of the public their national wool,
By accusing of slavish respect to John Bull,
All American authors who have more or less
Of that anti-American humbug—success,
While in private we're always embracing the
knees
Of some twopenny editor over the seas,
And licking his critical shoes, for you know 'tis
The whole aim of our lives to get one English
notice;
My American puffs I would willingly burn all,

(They're all from one source, monthly, weekly,
diurnal,)
To get but a kick from a transmarine journal!"

So, culling the gibes of each critical scorner
As if they were plums, and himself were Jack
Horner,
He came cautiously on, peeping round every
corner,
And into each hole where a weasel might pass in,
Expecting the knife of some critic assassin,
Who stabs to the heart with a caricature,
Not so bad as those daubs of the Sun, to be sure,
Yet done with a dagger-o'-type, whose vile por-
traits
Disperse all one's good, and condense all one's poor
traits.

Apollo looked up, hearing footsteps approach-
ing,
And slipped out of sight the new rhymes he was
broaching,—
"Good day, Mr. ——, I'm happy to meet,
With a scholar so ripe, and a critic so neat,
Who through Grub-street the soul of a gentleman
carries,—
What news from that suburb of London and Paris
Which latterly makes such shrill claims to monopo-
lize
The credit of being the New World's metropo-
lis?"

"Why, nothing of consequence, save this attack
On my friend there, behind, by some pitiful hack,
Who thinks every national author a poor one,
That isn't a copy of something that's foreign,
And assaults the American Dick—"

"Nay, 'tis clear
That your Damon there 's fond of a flea in his ear,
And, if no one else furnished them gratis, on tick
He would buy some himself, just to hear the old click;
Why, I honestly think, if some fool in Japan
Should turn up his nose at the 'Poems on Man,'
Your friend there by some inward instinct would know it,
Would get it translated, reprinted, and show it;
As a man might take off a high stock to exhibit
The autograph round his own neck of the gibbet;
Nor would let it rest so, but fire column after column,
Signed Cato, or Brutus, or something as solemn,
By way of displaying his critical crosses,
And tweaking that poor transatlantic proboscis,
His broadsides resulting (and this there's no doubt of,)
In successively sinking the craft they're fired out of.
Now nobody knows when an author is hit,
If he don't have a public hysterical fit;
Let him only keep close in his snug garret's dim ether,
And nobody'd think of his critics—or him either;
If an author have any least fibre of worth in him,
Abuse would but tickle the organ of mirth in him,
All the critics on earth cannot crush with their ban,
One word that's in tune with the nature of man."

"Well, perhaps so; meanwhile I have brought you a book,
Into which if you'll just have the goodness to look,
You may feel so delighted, (when you have got through it,)

As to think it not unworth your while to review it,
And I think I can promise your thoughts, if you
do,
A place in the next Democratic Review."

"The most thankless of gods you must surely
have thought me,
For this is the forty-fourth copy you've brought me,
I have given them away, or at least I have tried,
But I've forty-two left, standing all side by side,
(The man who accepted that one copy, died,)—
From one end of a shelf to the other they reach,
'With the author's respects' neatly written in
each.
The publisher, sure, will proclaim a Te Deum,
When he hears of that order the British Museum
Has sent for one set of what books were first
printed
In America, little or big,—for 'tis hinted
That this is the first truly tangible hope he
Has ever had raised for the sale of a copy.
I've thought very often 'twould be a good thing
In all public collections of books, if a wing
Were set off by itself, like the seas from the dry
lands,
Marked *Literature suited to desolate islands*,
And filled with such books as could never be read
Save by readers of proofs, forced to do it for
bread,—
Such books as one's wrecked on in small country-
taverns,
Such as hermits might mortify over in caverns,
Such as Satan, if printing had then been invented,
As the climax of woe, would to Job have pre-
sented,
Such as Crusoe might dip in, although there are
few so

Outrageously cornered by fate as poor Crusoe;
And since the philanthropists just now are banging
And gibbeting all who're in favor of hanging,—
(Though Cheever has proved that the Bible and Altar
Were let down from Heaven at the end of a halter,
And that vital religion would dull and grow callous,
Unrefreshed, now and then, with a sniff of the gallows,)—
And folks are beginning to think it looks odd,
To choke a poor scamp for the glory of God;
And that He who esteems the Virginia reel
A bait to draw saints from their spiritual weal,
And regards the quadrille as a far greater knavery
Than crushing His African children with slavery,—
Since all who take part in a waltz or cotillion
Are mounted for hell on the Devil's own pillion,
Who, as every true orthodox Christian well knows,
Approaches the heart through the door of the toes,—
That He, I was saying, whose judgments are stored
For such as take steps in despite of his word,
Should look with delight on the agonized prancing
Of a wretch who has not the least ground for his dancing,
While the State, standing by, sings a verse from the Psalter
About offering to God on his favorite halter,
And, when the legs droop from their twitching divergence,
Sells the clothes to a Jew, and the corpse to the surgeons;—

Now, instead of all this, I think I can direct you all

To a criminal code both humane and effectual;—
I propose to shut up every doer of wrong
With these desperate books, for such term, short or
long,
As by statute in such cases made and provided,
Shall be by your wise legislators decided;
Thus:—Let murderers be shut, to grow wiser and
cooler,
At hard labor for life on the works of Miss ———;
Petty thieves, kept from flagranter crimes by their
fears,
Shall peruse Yankee Doodle a blank term of
years,—
That American Punch, like the English, no doubt—
Just the sugar and lemons and spirit left out.

"But stay, here comes Tityrus Griswold, and
leads on
The flocks whom he first plucks alive, and then
feeds on,—
A loud-cackling swarm, in whose feathers warm-
drest,
He goes for as perfect a—swan, as the rest.

"There comes Emerson first, whose rich words,
every one,
Are like gold nails in temples to hang trophies
on,
Whose prose is grand verse, while his verse, the
Lord knows,
Is some of it pr——No, 'tis not even prose;
I'm speaking of metres; some poems have welled
From those rare depths of soul that have ne'er
been excelled;
They're not epics, but that doesn't matter a pin,
In creating, the only hard thing's to begin;
A grass-blade 's no easier to make than an oak,

If you've once found the way, you've achieved the
grand stroke;
In the worst of his poems are mines of rich matter,
But thrown in a heap with a crush and a clatter;
Now it is not one thing nor another alone
Makes a poem, but rather the general tone,
The something pervading, uniting the whole,
The before unconceived, unconceivable soul,
So that just in removing this trifle or that, you
Take away, as it were, a chief limb of the statue;
Roots, wood, bark, and leaves, singly perfect may
be,
But, clapt hodge-podge together, they don't make
a tree.

"But, to come back to Emerson, (whom by the
way,
I believe we left waiting,)—his is, we may say,
A Greek head on right Yankee shoulders, whose
range
Has Olympus for one pole, for t'other the Ex-
change;
He seems, to my thinking, (although I'm afraid
The comparison must, long ere this, have been
made,)
A Plotinus-Montaigne, where the Egyptian's gold
mist
And the Gascon's shrewd wit cheek-by-jowl co-
exist;
All admire, and yet scarcely six converts he's got
To I don't (nor they either) exactly know what;
For though he builds glorious temples, tis odd
He leaves never a doorway to get in a god.
'Tis refreshing to old-fashioned people like me,
To meet such a primitive Pagan as he,
In whose mind all creation is duly respected
As parts of himself—just a little projected;

And who's willing to worship the stars and the sun,
A convert to—nothing but Emerson.
So perfect a balance there is in his head,
That he talks of things sometimes as if they were dead;
Life, nature, love, God, and affairs of that sort,
He looks at as merely ideas; in short,
As if they were fossils stuck round in a cabinet,
Of such vast extent that our earth's a mere dab in it;
Composed just as he is inclined to conjecture her,
Namely, one part pure earth, ninety-nine parts pure lecturer;
You are filled with delight at his clear demonstration,
Each figure, word, gesture, just fits the occasion,
With the quiet precision of science he'll sort 'em,
But you can't help suspecting the whole a *post mortem*.

"There are persons, mole-blind to the soul's make and style,
Who insist on a likeness 'twixt him and Carlyle;
To compare with Plato would be vastly fairer,
Carlyle's the more burly, but E. is the rarer;
He sees fewer objects, but clearlier, truelier,
If C.'s as original, E.'s more peculiar;
That he's more of a man you might say of the one,
Of the other he's more of an Emerson;
C.'s the Titan, as shaggy of mind as of limb,—
E. the clear-eyed Olympian, rapid and slim;
The one's two-thirds Norseman, the other half Greek,
Where the one 's most abounding, the other 's to seek;
C.'s generals require to be seen in the mass,—

E.'s specialties gain if enlarged by the glass;
C. gives nature and God his own fits of the blues,
And rims common-sense things with mystical hues,—
E. sits in a mystery calm and intense,
And looks coolly around him with sharp common-sense;
C. shows you how every-day matters unite
With the dim transdiurnal recesses of night,—
While E., in a plain, preternatural way,
Makes mysteries matters of mere every day;
C. draws all his characters quite *à la* Fuseli,—
He don't sketch their bundles of muscles and thews illy,
But he paints with a brush so untamed and profuse,
They seem nothing but bundles of muscles and thews;
E. is rather like Flaxman, lines strait and severe,
And a colorless outline, but full, round, and clear;—
To the men he thinks worthy he frankly accords
The design of a white marble statue in words.
C. labors to get at the centre, and then
Take a reckoning from there of his actions and men;
E. calmly assumes the said centre as granted,
And, given himself, has whatever is wanted.

"He has imitators in scores, who omit
No part of the man but his wisdom and wit,—
Who go carefully o'er the sky-blue of his brain,
And when he has skimmed it once, skim it again;
If at all they resemble him, you may be sure it is
Because their shoals mirror his mists and obscurities,
As a mud-puddle seems deep as heaven for a minute,
While a cloud that floats o'er is reflected within it.

"There comes ——, for instance; to see him 's rare sport,
Tread in Emerson's tracks with legs painfully short;
How he jumps, how he strains, and gets red in the face,
To keep step with the mystagogue's natural pace
He follows as close as a stick to a rocket,
His fingers exploring the prophet's each pocket.
Fie, for shame, brother bard; with good fruit of your own,
Can't you let neighbor Emerson's orchards alone?
Besides, 'tis no use, you'll not find e'en a core,—
—— has picked up all the windfalls before.
They might strip every tree, and E. never would catch 'em,
His Hesperides have no rude dragon to watch 'em;
When they send him a dishfull, and ask him to try 'em,
He never suspects how the sly rogues came by 'em;
He wonders why 'tis there are none such his trees on,
And thinks 'em the best he has tasted this season.

"Yonder, calm as a cloud, Alcott stalks in a dream,
And fancies himself in thy groves, Academe,
With the Parthenon nigh, and the olive-trees o'er him,
And never a fact to perplex him or bore him,
With a snug room at Plato's, when night comes, to walk to,
And people from morning till midnight to talk to,
And from midnight till morning, nor snore in their listening;—

So he muses, his face with the joy of it glistening,
For his highest conceit of a happiest state is
Where they'd live upon acorns, and hear him talk
gratis;
And indeed, I believe, no man ever talked better—
Each sentence hangs perfectly poised to a letter;
He seems piling words, but there's royal dust hid
In the heart of each sky-piercing pyramid.
While he talks he is great, but goes out like a
taper,
If you shut him up closely with pen, ink, and
paper;
Yet his fingers itch for 'em from morning till night,
And he thinks he does wrong if he don't always
write;
In this, as in all things, a lamb among men,
He goes to sure death when he goes to his pen.

"Close behind him is Brownson, his mouth very
full
With attempting to gulp a Gregorian bull;
Who contrives, spite of that, to pour out as he
goes
A stream of transparent and forcible prose;
He shifts quite about, then proceeds to expound
That 'tis merely the earth, not himself, that turns
round,
And wishes it clearly impressed on your mind,
That the weather-cock rules and not follows the
wind;
Proving first, then as deftly confuting each side,
With no doctrine pleased that's not somewhere
denied,
He lays the denier away on the shelf,
And then—down beside him lies gravely himself.
He's the Salt River boatman, who always stands
willing

To convey friend or foe without charging a shilling,
And so fond of the trip that, when leisure's to spare,
He'll row himself up, if he can't get a fare.
The worst of it is, that his logic's so strong,
That of two sides he commonly chooses the wrong;
If there *is* only one, why, he'll split it in two,
And first pummel this half, then that, black and blue.
That white's white needs no proof, but it takes a deep fellow
To prove it jet-black, and that jet-black is yellow.
He offers the true faith to drink in a sieve,—
When it reaches your lips there's naught left to believe
But a few silly-(syllo-, I mean,) -gisms that squat 'em
Like tadpoles, o'erjoyed with the mud at the bottom.

"There is Willis, so *natty* and jaunty and gay,
Who says his best things in so foppish a way,
With conceits and pet phrases so thickly o'erlaying 'em,
That one hardly knows whether to thank him for saying 'em;
Over-ornament ruins both poem and prose,
Just conceive of a Muse with a ring in her nose!
His prose had a natural grace of its own,
And enough of it, too, if he'd let it alone;
But he twitches and jerks so, one fairly gets tired,
And is forced to forgive where he might have admired;
Yet whenever it slips away free and unlaced,
It runs like a stream with a musical waste,
And gurgles along with the liquidest sweep;—

'Tis not deep as a river, but who'd have it deep?
In a country where scarcely a village is found
That has not its author sublime and profound,
For some one to be slightly shoal is a duty,
And Willis's shallowness makes half his beauty.
His prose winds along with a blithe, gurgling error,
And reflects all of Heaven it can see in its mirror
'Tis a narrowish strip, but it is not an artifice,—
'Tis the true out-of-doors with its genuine hearty phiz;
It is Nature herself, and there's something in that,
Since most brains reflect but the crown of a hat.
No volume I know to read under a tree,
More truly delicious than his A l' Abri,
With the shadows of leaves flowing over your book,
Like ripple-shades netting the bed of a brook;
With June coming softly your shoulder to look over,
Breezes waiting to turn every leaf of your book over,
And Nature to criticize still as you read,—
The page that bears that is a rare one indeed.

"He's so innate a cockney, that had he been born
Where plain bare-skin's the only full-dress that is worn,
He'd have given his own such an air that you'd say
'T had been made by a tailor to lounge in Broadway.
His nature's a glass of champagne with the foam on't,
As tender as Fletcher, as witty as Beaumont;
So his best things are done in the flush of the moment,

If he wait, all is spoiled; he may stir it and shake it,
But, the fixed air once gone, he can never re-make it.
He might be a marvel of easy delightfulness,
If he would not sometimes leave the *r* out of sprightfulness;
And he ought to let Scripture alone—'tis self-slaughter,
For nobody likes inspiration-and-water.
He'd have been just the fellow to sup at the Mermaid,
Cracking jokes at rare Ben, with an eye to the barmaid,
His wit running up as Canary ran down,—
The topmost bright bubble on the wave of The Town.

"Here comes Parker, the Orson of parsons, a man
Whom the Church undertook to put under her ban,—
(The Church of Socinus, I mean)—his opinions
Being So- (ultra) -cinian, they shocked the Socinians;
They believed—faith I'm puzzled—I think I may call
Their belief a believing in nothing at all,
Or something of that sort; I know they all went
For a general union of total dissent:
He went a step farther; without cough or hem,
He frankly avowed he believed not in them;
And, before he could be jumbled up or prevented,
From their orthodox kind of dissent he dissented.
There was heresy here, you perceive, for the right
Of privately judging means simply that light
Has been granted to *me*, for deciding on *you*,

And in happier times, before Atheism grew,
The deed contained clauses for cooking you, too.
Now at Xerxes and Knut we all laugh, yet our foot
With the same wave is wet that mocked Xerxes and Knut;
And we all entertain a sincere private notion,
That our *Thus far!* will have a great weight with the ocean.
'Twas so with our liberal Christians: they bore
With sincerest conviction their chairs to the shore;
They brandished their worn theological birches,
Bade natural progress keep out of the Churches,
And expected the lines they had drawn to prevail
With the fast-rising tide to keep out of their pale;
They had formerly dammed the Pontifical See,
And the same thing, they thought, would do nicely for P.;
But he turned up his nose at their murmuring and shamming,
And cared (shall I say?) not a d— for their damming;
So they first read him out of their church, and next minute
Turned round and declared he had never been in it.
But the ban was too small or the man was too big,
For he recks not their bells, books, and candles a fig;
(He don't look like a man who would *stay* treated shabbily,
Sophroniscus' son's head o'er the features of Rabelais;)—
He bangs and bethwacks them,—their backs he salutes
With the whole tree of knowledge torn up by the roots

His sermons with satire are plenteously verjuiced,
And he talks in one breath of Confutzee, Cass,
Zerduscht,
Jack Robinson, Peter the Hermit, Strap, Dathan,
Cush, Pitt (not the bottomless, *that* he's no faith
in,)
Pan, Pillicock, Shakspeare, Paul, Toots, Monsieur
Tonson,
Aldebaran, Alcander, Ben Khorat, Ben Jonson,
Thoth, Richter, Joe Smith, Father Paul, Judah
Monis,
Musæus, Muretus, *hem,—μ* Scorpionis,
Maccabee, Maccaboy, Mac—Mac—ah! Machia-
velli,
Condorcet, Count d'Orsay, Conder, Say, Ganga-
nelli,
Orion, O'Connell, the Chevalier D'O,
(See the Memoirs of Sully) *το παν*, the great toe
Of the statue of Jupiter, now made to pass
For that of Jew Peter by good Romish brass,—
(You may add for yourselves, for I find it a bore,
All the names you have ever, or not, heard before,
And when you've done that—why, invent a few
more.)
His hearers can't tell you on Sunday beforehand,
If in that day's discourse they'll be Bibled or Ko-
raned,
For he's seized the idea (by his martyrdom fired,)
That all men (not orthodox) *may be* inspired;
Yet though wisdom profane with his creed he may
weave in,
He makes it quiet clear what he *doesn't* believe in,
While some, who decry him, think all Kingdom
Come
Is a sort of a, kind of a, species of Hum,
Of which, as it were, so to speak, not a crumb
Would be left, if we didn't keep carefully mum,

And, to make a clean breast, that 'tis perfectly
plain
That *all* kinds of wisdom are somewhat profane;
Now P.'s creed than this may be lighter or darker,
But in one thing, 'tis clear, he has faith, namely—
Parker;
And this is what makes him the crowd-drawing
preacher,
There's a background of god to each hard-working
feature,
Every word that he speaks has been fierily fur-
naced
In the blast of a life that has struggled in earnest:
There he stands, looking more like a ploughman
than priest,
If not dreadfully awkward, not graceful at least,
His gestures all downright and same, if you will,
As of brown-fisted Hobnail in hoeing a drill,
But his periods fall on you, stroke after stroke,
Like the blows of a lumberer felling an oak,
You forget the man wholly, you're thankful to
meet
With a preacher who smacks of the field and the
street,
And to hear, you're not over-particular whence,
Almost Taylor's profusion, quite Latimer's sense.

"There is Bryant, as quiet, as cool, and as
dignified,
As a smooth, silent iceberg, that never is ignified,
Save when by reflection 'tis kindled o' nights
With a semblance of flame by the chill Northern
Lights.
He may rank (Griswold says so) first bard of your
nation,
(There's no doubt that he stands in supreme ice-
olation,)

Your topmost Parnassus he may set his heel on,
But no warm applauses come, peal following peal
on,—
He's too smooth and too polished to hang any zeal
on:
Unqualified merits, I'll grant, if you choose, he
has 'em,
But he lacks the one merit of kindling enthusiasm;
If he stir you at all, it is just, on my soul,
Like being stirred up with the very North Pole.

"He is very nice reading in summer, but *inter*
Nos, we don't want *extra* freezing in winter;
Take him up in the depth of July, my advice is,
When you feel an Egyptian devotion to ices.
But, deduct all you can, there's enough that's right
good in him,
He has a true soul for field, river, and wood in
him;
And his heart, in the midst of brick walls, or
where'er it is,
Glows, softens, and thrills with the tenderest
charities,—
To you mortals that delve in this trade-ridden
planet?
No, to old Berkshire's hills, with their limestone and
granite.
If you're one who *in loco* (add *foco* here) *desipis*,
You will get of his outermost heart (as I guess) a
piece;
But you'd get deeper down if you came as a
precipice,
And would break the last seal of its inwardest
fountain,
If you only could palm yourself off for a moun-
tain.
Mr. Quivis, or somebody quite as discerning,

Some scholar who's hourly expecting his learning,
Calls B. the American Wordsworth; but Words-
worth
Is worth near as much as your whole tuneful herd's
worth.
No, don't be absurd, he's an excellent Bryant;
But, my friends, you'll endanger the life of your
client,
By attempting to stretch him up into a giant:
If you choose to compare him, I think there are
two per-
-sons fit for a parallel—Thomson and Cowper;*
I don't mean exactly,—there's something of each,
There's T.'s love of nature, C.'s penchant to
preach;
Just mix up their minds so that C.'s spice of crazi-
ness
Shall balance and neutralize T.'s turn for laziness,
And it gives you a brain cool, quite frictionless,
quiet,
Whose internal police nips the buds of all riot,—
A brain like a permanent strait-jacket put on
The heart which strives vainly to burst off a but-
ton,—
A brain which, without being slow or mechanic,
Does more than a larger less drilled, more vol-
canic;
He's a Cowper condensed, with no craziness bitten,
And the advantage that Wordsworth before him
has written.

"But, my dear little bardlings, don't prick up
your ears,

* To demonstrate quickly and easily how per-
-versely absurd 'tis to sound this name *Cowper*,
As people in general call him named *super*,
I just add that he rhymes it himself with horse-trooper

Nor suppose I would rank you and Bryant as peers;
If I call him an iceberg, I don't mean to say
There is nothing in that which is grand, in its way
He is almost the one of your poets that knows
How much grace, strength, and dignity lie in Repose;
If he sometimes fall short, he is too wise to mar
His thought's modest fulness by going too far;
'Twould be well if your authors should all make a trial
Of what virtue there is in severe self-denial,
And measure their writings by Hesiod's staff,
Which teaches that all has less value than half.

"There is Whittier, whose swelling and vehement heart
Strains the strait-breasted drab of the Quaker apart,
And reveals the live Man, still supreme and erect,
Underneath the bemummying wrappers of sect;
There was ne'er a man born who had more of the swing
Of the true lyric bard and all that kind of thing;
And his failures arise, (though perhaps he don't know it,)
From the very same cause that has made him a poet,—
A fervor of mind which knows no separation
'Twixt simple excitement and pure inspiration,
As my Pythoness erst sometimes erred from not knowing
If 'twere I or mere wind through her tripod was blowing;
Let his mind once get head in its favorite direction
And the torrent of verse bursts the dams of reflection,

While, borne with the rush of the metre along,
The poet may chance to go right or go wrong,
Content with the whirl and delirium of song;
Then his grammar's not always correct, nor his rhymes,
And he's prone to repeat his own lyrics sometimes,
Not his best, though, for those are struck off at white-heats
When the heart in his breast like a trip-hammer beats,
And can ne'er be repeated again any more
Than they could have been carefully plotted before:
Like old what's-his-name there at the battle of Hastings,
(Who, however, gave more than mere rhythmical bastings,)
Our Quaker leads off metaphorical fights
For reform and whatever they call human rights,
Both singing and striking in front of the war
And hitting his foes with the mallet of Thor;
Anne haec, one exclaims, on beholding his knocks,
Vestis filii tui, O, leather-clad Fox?
Can that be thy son, in the battle's mid din,
Preaching brotherly love and then driving it in
To the brain of the tough old Goliah of sin,
With the smoothest of pebbles from Castaly's spring
Impressed on his hard moral sense with a sling?

"All honor and praise to the right-hearted bard
Who was true to The Voice when such service was hard,
Who himself was so free he dared sing for the slave
When to look but a protest in silence was brave;
All honor and praise to the women and men

Who spoke out for the dumb and the down-trodden then!
I need not to name them, already for each
I see History preparing the statue and niche;
They were harsh, but shall *you* be so shocked at hard words
Who have beaten your pruning-hooks up into swords,
Whose rewards and hurrahs men are surer to gain
By the reaping of men and of women than grain?
Why should *you* stand aghast at their fierce wordy war, if
You scalp one another for Bank or for Tariff?
Your calling them cut-throats and knaves all day long
Don't prove that the use of hard language is wrong;
While the World's heart beats quicker to think of such men
As signed Tyranny's doom with a bloody steel-pen,
While on Fourth-of-Julys beardless orators fright one
With hints at Harmodius and Aristogeiton,
You need not look shy at your sisters and brothers
Who stab with sharp words for the freedom of others;—
No, a wreath, twine a wreath for the loyal and true
Who, for sake of the many, dared stand with the few,
Not of blood-spattered laurel for enemies braved,
But of broad, peaceful oak-leaves for citizens saved!

"Here comes Dana, abstractedly loitering along,
Involved in a paulo-post-future of song,
Who'll be going to write what'll never be written

Till the Muse, ere he thinks of it, gives him the mitten,—
Who is so well aware of how things should be done,
That his own works displease him before they're begun,—
Who so well all that makes up good poetry knows,
That the best of his poems is written in prose;
All saddled and bridled stood Pegasus waiting,
He was booted and spurred, but he loitered debating,
In a very grave question his soul was immersed,—
Which foot in the stirrup he ought to put first;
And, while this point and that he judicially dwelt on,
He, somehow or other, had written Paul Felton,
Whose beauties or faults, whichsoever you see there,
You'll allow only genius could hit upon either.
That he once was the Idle Man none will deplore,
But I fear he will never be any thing more;
The ocean of song heaves and glitters before him,
The depth and the vastness and longing sweep o'er him,
He knows every breaker and shoal on the chart,
He has the Coast Pilot and so on by heart,
Yet he spends his whole life, like the man in the fable,
In learning to swim on his library-table.

"There swaggers John Neal, who has wasted in Maine
The sinews and chords of his pugilist brain,
Who might have been poet, but that, in its stead, he
Preferred to believe that he was so already;
Too hasty to wait till Art's ripe fruit should drop,

He must pelt down an unripe and colicky crop;
Who took to the law, and had this sterling plea
for it,
It required him to quarrel, and paid him a fee for
it;
A man who's made less than he might have, because
He always has thought himself more than he was,—
Who, with very good natural gifts as a bard,
Broke the strings of his lyre out by striking too
hard,
And cracked half the notes of a truly fine voice,
Because song drew less instant attention than
noise.
Ah, men do not know how much strength is in
poise,
That he goes the farthest who goes far enough,
And that all beyond that is just bother and stuff.
No vain man matures, he makes too much new
wood;
His blooms are too thick for the fruit to be good;
'Tis the modest man ripens, 'tis he that achieves,
Just what's needed of sunshine and shade he receives;
Grapes, to mellow, require the cool dark of their
leaves;
Neal wants balance; he throws his mind always
too far,
Whisking out flocks of comets, but never a star;
He has so much muscle, and loves so to show it,
That he strips himself naked to prove he's a poet,
And, to show he could leap Art's wide ditch, if he
tried,
Jumps clean o'er it, and into the hedge t'other
side.
He has strength, but there's nothing about him in
keeping;

One gets surelier onward by walking than leap
ing;
He has used his own sinews himself to distress,
And had done vastly more had he done vastly
less;
In letters, too soon is as bad as too late,
Could he only have waited he might have been
great,
But he plumped into Helicon up to the waist,
And muddied the stream ere he took his first taste.

"There is Hawthorne, with genius so shrinking
and rare
That you hardly at first see the strength that is
there;
A frame so robust, with a nature so sweet,
So earnest, so graceful, so solid, so fleet,
Is worth a descent from Olympus to meet;
'Tis as if a rough oak that for ages had stood,
With his gnarled bony branches like ribs of the
wood,
Should bloom, after cycles of struggle and scathe,
With a single anemone trembly and rathe;
His strength is so tender, his wildness so meek,
That a suitable parallel sets one to seek,—
He's a John Bunyan Fouqué, a Puritan Tieck;
When nature was shaping him, clay was not
granted
For making so full-sized a man as she wanted,
So, to fill out her model, a little she spared
From some finer-grained stuff for a woman pre-
pared,
And she could not have hit a more excellent plan
For making him fully and perfectly man.
The success of her scheme gave her so much de-
light,
That she tried it again, shortly after, in Dwight;

Only, while she was kneading and shaping the clay,
She sang to her work in her sweet childish way,
And found, when she'd put the last touch to his soul,
That the music had somehow got mixed with the whole.

"Here's Cooper, who's written six volumes to show
He's as good as a lord: well, let's grant that he's so;
If a person prefer that description of praise,
Why, a coronet's certainly cheaper than bays;
But he need take no pains to convince us he's not
(As his enemies say) the American Scott.
Choose any twelve men, and let C. read aloud
That one of his novels of which he's most proud,
And I'd lay any bet that, without ever quitting
Their box, they'd be all, to a man, for acquitting.
He has drawn you one character, though, that is new,
One wildflower he's plucked that is wet with the dew
Of this fresh Western world, and, the thing not to mince,
He has done naught but copy it ill ever since;
His Indians, with proper respect be it said,
Are just Natty Bumpo daubed over with red,
And his very Long Toms are the same useful Nat,
Rigged up in duck pants and a sou'-wester hat,
(Though once in a Coffin, a good chance was found
To have slipt the old fellow away underground.)
All his other men-figures are clothes upon sticks,
The *derniere chemise* of a man in a fix,
(As a captain besieged, when his garrison's small,

Sets up caps upon poles to be seen o'er the wall;)
And the women he draws from one model don't
vary,
All sappy as maples and flat as a prairie.
When a character's wanted, he goes to the task
As a cooper would do in composing a cask;
He picks out the staves, of their qualities heedful,
Just hoops them together as tight as is needful,
And, if the best fortune should crown the attempt,
he
Has made at the most something wooden and
empty.

"Don't suppose I would underrate Cooper's abil-
ities,
If I thought you'd do that, I should feel very ill at
ease;
The men who have given to *one* character life
And objective existence, are not very rife,
You may number them all, both prose-writers and
singers,
Without overrunning the bounds of your fingers,
And Natty won't go to oblivion quicker
Than Adams the parson or Primrose the vicar.

"There is one thing in Cooper I like, too, and
that is
That on manners he lectures his countrymen gratis
Not precisely so either, because, for a rarity,
He is paid for his tickets in unpopularity.
Now he may overcharge his American pictures,
But you'll grant there's a good deal of truth in his
strictures;
And I honor the man who is willing to sink
Half his present repute for the freedom to think,
And, when he has thought, be his cause strong or
weak,

Will risk t'other half for the freedom to speak,
Caring naught for what vengeance the mob has in store,
Let that mob be the upper ten thousand or lower.

"There are truths you Americans need to be told,
And it never'll refute them to swagger and scold;
John Bull, looking o'er the Atlantic, in choler
At your aptness for trade, says you worship the dollar;
But to scorn such i-dollar-try's what very few do,
And John goes to that church as often as you do.
No matter what John says, don't try to outcrow him,
'Tis enough to go quietly on and outgrow him;
Like most fathers, Bull hates to see Number One
Displacing himself in the mind of his son,
And detests the same faults in himself he'd neglected
When he sees them again in his child's glass reflected;
To love one another you're too like by half,
If he is a bull, you're a pretty stout calf,
And tear your own pasture for naught but to show
What a nice pair of horns you're beginning to grow.

"There are one or two things I should just like to hint,
For you don't often get the truth told you in print;
The most of you (this is what strikes all beholders)
Have a mental and physical stoop in the shoulders;
Though you ought to be free as the winds and the waves,
You've the gait and the manners of runaway slaves;

Tho' you brag of your New World, you don't half
believe in it,
And as much of the Old as is possible weave in it;
Your goddess of freedom, a tight, buxom girl,
With lips like a cherry and teeth like a pearl,
With eyes bold as Herè's, and hair floating free,
And full of the sun as the spray of the sea,
Who can sing at a husking or romp at a shearing,
Who can trip through the forests alone without
fearing,
Who can drive home the cows with a song through
the grass,
Keeps glancing aside into Europe's cracked glass,
Hides her red hands in gloves, pinches up her lithe
waist,
And makes herself wretched with transmarine
taste;
She loses her fresh country charm when she takes
Any mirror except her own rivers and lakes.

"You steal Englishmen's books and think Englishmen's thought,
With their salt on her tail your wild eagle is
caught;
Your literature suits its each whisper and motion
To what will be thought of it over the ocean;
The cast clothes of Europe your statesmanship
tries
And mumbles again the old blarneys and lies;—
Forget Europe wholly, your veins throb with blood,
To which the dull current in hers is but mud;
Let her sneer, let her say your experiment fails,
In her voice there's a tremble e'en now while she
rails,
And your shore will soon be in the nature of things
Covered thick with gilt driftwood of runaway kings,
Where alone, as it were in a Longfellow's Waif,

Her fugitive pieces will find themselves safe.
O, my friends, thank your God, if you have one, that he
'Twixt the Old World and you set the gulf of a sea
Be strong-backed, brown-handed, upright as your pines,
By the scale of a hemisphere shape your designs,
Be true to yourselves and this new nineteenth age,
As a statue by Powers, or a picture by Page,
Plough, sail, forge, build, carve, paint, all things make new,
To your own New-World instincts contrive to be true,
Keep your ears open wide to the Future's first call,
Be whatever you will, but yourselves first of all,
Stand fronting the dawn on Toil's heaven-scaling peaks,
And become my new race of more practical Greeks.—
Hem! your likeness at present, I shudder to tell o't,
Is that you have your slaves, and the Greek had his helot."

Here a gentleman present, who had in his attic
More pepper than brains, shrieked—"The man's a fanatic,
I'm a capital tailor with warm tar and feathers,
And will make him a suit that'll serve in all weathers;
But we'll argue the point first, I'm willing to rea-son 't,
Palaver before condemnation's but decent,
So, through my humble person, Humanity begs
Of the friends of true freedom a loan of bad eggs."
But Apollo let one such a look of his show forth
As when ἤϊε νύκτι ἐοικώς, and so forth,

And the gentleman somehow slunk out of the way,
But, as he was going, gained courage to say,—
"At slavery in the abstract my whole soul rebels,
I am as strongly opposed to't as any one else."
"Ay, no doubt, but whenever I've happened to meet
With a wrong or a crime, it is always concrete,"
Answered Phœbus severely; then turning to us,
"The mistake of such fellows as just made the fuss
Is only in taking a great busy nation
For a part of their pitiful cotton-plantation.—
But there comes Miranda, Zeus! where shall I flee to?
She has such a penchant for bothering me too!
She always keeps asking if I don't observe a
Particular likeness 'twixt her and Minerva;
She tells me my efforts in verse are quite clever;—
She's been travelling now, and will be worse than ever;
One would think, though, a sharp-sighted noter she'd be
Of all that's worth mentioning over the sea,
For a woman must surely see well, if she try,
The whole of whose being's a capital I:
She will take an old notion, and make it her own,
By saying it o'er in her Sibylline tone,
Or persuade you 'tis something tremendously deep,
By repeating it so as to put you to sleep;
And she well may defy any mortal to see through it,
When once she has mixed up her infinite *me* through it.
There is one thing she owns in her own single right,
It is native and genuine—namely, her spite:
Though, when acting as censor, she privately blows
A censer of vanity 'neath her own nose."

Here Miranda came up, and said, "Phœbus you know
That the infinite Soul has its infinite woe,
As I ought to know, having lived cheek by jowl
Since the day I was born, with the Infinite Soul;
I myself introduced, I myself, I alone,
To my Land's better life authors solely my own,
Who the sad heart of earth on their shoulders have taken,
Whose works sound a depth by Life's quiet unshaken,
Such as Shakspeare, for instance, the Bible, and Bacon,
Not to mention my own works; Time's nadir is fleet,
And, as for myself, I'm quite out of conceit,"—

"Quite out of conceit! I'm enchanted to hear it,"
Cried Apollo aside, "Who'd have thought she was near it?
To be sure one is apt to exhaust those commodities
He uses too fast, yet in this case as odd it is
As if Neptune should say to his turbots and whitings,
'I'm as much out of salt as Miranda's own writings,'
(Which, as she in her own happy manner has said,
Sound a depth, for 'tis one of the functions of lead.)
She often has asked me if I could not find
A place somewhere near me that suited her mind;
I know but a single one vacant, which she,
With her rare talent that way, would fit to a T.
And it would not imply any pause or cessation
In the work she esteems her peculiar vocation,—
She may enter on duty to-day, if she chooses,
And remain Tiring-woman for life to the Muses."

(Miranda meanwhile has succeeded in driving
Up into a corner, in spite of their striving,
A small flock of terrified victims, and there,
With an I-turn-the-crank-of-the-Universe air
And a tone which, at least to *my* fancy, appears
Not so much to be entering as boxing your ears,
Is unfolding a tale (of herself, I surmise,)
For 'tis dotted as thick as a peacock's with I's.)
Apropos of Miranda, I'll rest on my oars
And drift through a trifling digression on bores,
For, though not wearing ear-rings *in more majorum*,
Our ears are kept bored just as if we still wore 'em.
There was one feudal custom worth keeping, at least,
Roasted bores made a part of each well-ordered feast,
And of all quiet pleasures the very *ne plus*
Was in hunting wild bores as the tame ones hunt us.
Archæologians, I know, who have personal fears
Of this wise application of hounds and of spears,
Have tried to make out, with a zeal more than wonted,
'Twas a kind of wild swine that our ancestors hunted;
But I'll never believe that the age which has strewn
Europe o'er with cathedrals, and otherwise shown
That it knew what was what, could by chance not have known,
(Spending, too, its chief time with its buff on, no doubt,)
Which beast 'twould improve the world most to thin out.
I divide bores myself, in the manner of rifles,
Into two great divisions, regardless of trifles;—
There's your smooth-bore and screw-bore, who do not much vary
In the weight of cold lead they respectively carry.

The smooth-bore is one in whose essence the mind
Not a corner nor cranny to cling by can find;
You feel as in nightmares sometimes, when you slip
Down a steep slated roof where there's nothing to grip,
You slide and you slide, the blank horror increases,
You had rather by far be at once smashed to pieces,
You fancy a whirlpool below white and frothing,
And finally drop off and light upon—nothing.
The screw-bore has twists in him, faint predilections
For going just wrong in the tritest directions;
When he's wrong he is flat, when he's right he can't show it,
He'll tell you what Snooks said about the new poet,*
Or how Fogrum was outraged by Tennyson's Princess;
He has spent all his spare time and intellect since his
Birth in perusing, on each art and science,
Just the books in which no one puts any reliance,
And though *nemo*, we're told, *horis omnibus sapit*,
The rule will not fit him, however you shape it,
For he has a perennial foison of sappiness;
He has just enough force to spoil half your day's happiness,
And to make him a sort of mosquito to be with,
But just not enough to dispute or agree with.

These sketches I made (not to be too explicit)

* (If you call Snooks an owl, he will show by his looks
That he's morally certain you're jealous of Snooks.)

From two honest fellows who made me a visit,
And broke, like the tale of the Bear and the Fid-
dle,
My reflections on Halleck short off by the middle;
I shall not now go into the subject more deeply,
For I notice that some of my readers look sleep'ly,
I will barely remark that, 'mongst civilized nations,
There's none that displays more exemplary pa-
tience
Under all sorts of boring, at all sorts of hours,
From all sorts of desperate persons, than ours.
Not to speak of our papers, our State legislatures,
And other such trials for sensitive natures,
Just look for a moment at Congress,—appalled,
My fancy shrinks back from the phantom it called;
Why, there's scarcely a member unworthy to
frown
'Neath what Fourier nicknames the Boreal crown;
Only think what that infinite bore-pow'r could do
If applied with a utilitarian view;
Suppose, for example, we shipped it with care
To Sahara's great desert and let it bore there,
If they held one short session and did nothing
else,
They'd fill the whole waste with Artesian wells.
But 'tis time now with pen phonographic to follow
Through some more of his sketches our laughing
Apollo:—

"There comes Harry Franco, and, as he draws
near,
You find that's a smile which you took for a sneer;
One half of him contradicts t'other, his wont
Is to say very sharp things and do very blunt;
His manner 's as hard as his feelings are tender,
And a *sortie* he'll make when he means to sur-
render;

He's in joke half the time when he seems to be
sternest,
When he seems to be joking, be sure he's in earn-
est;
He has common sense in a way that's uncommon,
Hates humbug and cant, loves his friends like a
woman,
Builds his dislikes of cards and his friendships of
oak,
Loves a prejudice better than aught but a joke,
Is half upright Quaker, half downright Come-
outer,
Loves Freedom too well to go stark mad about her,
Quite artless himself is a lover of Art,
Shuts you out of his secrets and into his heart,
And though not a poet, yet all must admire
In his letters of Pinto his skill on the liar.

"There comes Poe, with his raven, like Barnaby
Rudge,
Three-fifths of him genius and two-fifths sheer
fudge,
Who talks like a book of iambs and pentameters,
In a way to make people of common-sense damn
metres,
Who has written some things quite the best of their
kind,
But the heart somehow seems all squeezed out by
the mind,
Who—but hey-day! What's this? Messieurs Math-
ews and Poe,
You mustn't fling mud-balls at Longfellow so,
Does it make a man worse that his character's such
As to make his friends love him (as you think) too
much?
Why, there is not a bard at this moment alive
More willing than he that his fellows should thrive

While you are abusing him thus, even now
He would help either one of you out of a slough;
You may say that he's smooth and all that till
you're hoarse,
But remember that elegance also is force;
After polishing granite as much as you will,
The heart keeps its tough old persistency still;
Deduct all you can that still keeps you at bay,—
Why, he'll live till men weary of Collins and Gray
I'm not over-fond of Greek metres in English,
To me rhyme 's a gain, so it be not too jinglish,
And your modern hexameter verses are no more
Like Greek ones than sleek Mr. Pope is like
Homer;
As the roar of the sea to the coo of a pigeon is,
So, compared to your moderns, sounds old Mele-
sigenes;
I may be too partial, the reason, perhaps, o't is
That I've heard the old blind man recite his own
rhapsodies,
And my ear with that music impregnate may be,
Like the poor exiled shell with the soul of the sea,
Or as one can't bear Strauss when his nature is
cloven
To its deeps within deeps by the stroke of Bee-
thoven;
But, set that aside, and 'tis truth that I speak,
Had Theocritus written in English, not Greek,
I believe that his exquisite sense would scarce
change a line
In that rare, tender, virgin-like pastoral Evange-
line.
That's not ancient nor modern, its place is apart
Where time has no sway, in the realm of pure Art,
'Tis a shrine of retreat from Earth's hubbub and
strife
As quiet and chaste as the author's own life.

"There comes Philothea, her face all a-glow,
She has just been dividing some poor creature's woe
And can't tell which pleases her most, to relieve
His want, or his story to hear and believe;
No doubt against many deep griefs she prevails,
For her ear is the refuge of destitute tales;
She knows well that silence is sorrow's best food,
And that talking draws off from the heart its black blood,
So she'll listen with patience and let you unfold
Your bundle of rags as 'twere pure cloth of gold,
Which, indeed, it all turns to as soon as she's touched it,
And, (to borrow a phrase from the nursery,) *muched* it,
She has such a musical taste, she will go
Any distance to hear one who draws a long bow;
She will swallow a wonder by mere might and main
And thinks it geometry's fault if she's fain
To consider things flat, inasmuch as they're plain;
Facts with her are accomplished, as Frenchmen would say,
They will prove all she wishes them to—either way,
And, as fact lies on this side or that, we must try,
If we're seeking the truth, to find where it don't lie;
I was telling her once of a marvellous aloe
That for thousands of years had looked spindling and sallow,
And, though nursed by the fruitfullest powers of mud,
Had never vouchsafed e'en so much as a bud,
Till its owner remarked, (as a sailor, you know,
Often will in a calm,) that it never would blow,

For he wished to exhibit the plant, and designed
That its blowing should help him in raising the wind;
At last it was told him that if he should water
Its roots with the blood of his unmarried daughter,
(Who was born, as her mother, a Calvinist said,
With a Baxter's effectual caul on her head,)
It would blow as the obstinate breeze did when by a
Like decree of her father died Iphigenia;
At first he declared he himself would be blowed
Ere his conscience with such a foul crime he would load,
But the thought, coming oft, grew less dark than before,
And he mused, as each creditor knocked at his door,
If *this* were but done they would dun me no more;
I told Philothea his struggles and doubts,
And how he considered the ins and the outs
Of the visions he had, and the dreadful dyspepsy,
How he went to the seer that lives at Po'keepsie,
How the seer advised him to sleep on it first
And to read his big volume in case of the worst,
And further advised he should pay him five dollars
For writing **Hum, Hum,** on his wristbands and collars;
Three years and ten days these dark words he had studied
When the daughter was missed, and the aloe had budded;
I told how he watched it grow large and more large,
And wondered how much for the show he should charge,—

She had listened with utter indifference to this, till
I told how it bloomed, and discharging its pistil
With an aim the Eumenides dictated, shot
The botanical filicide dead on the spot;
It had blown, but he reaped not his horrible gains,
For it blew with such force as to blow out his brains,
And the crime was blown also, because on the wad,
Which was paper, was writ 'Visitation of God,'
As well as a thrilling account of the deed
Which the coroner kindly allowed me to read.

"Well, my friend took this story up just, to be sure,
As one might a poor foundling that's laid at one's door;
She combed it and washed it and clothed it and fed it,
And as if 'twere her own child most tenderly bred it,
Laid the scene (of the legend, I mean,) far away a-
-mong the green vales underneath Himalaya.
And by artist-like touches, laid on here and there,
Made the whole thing so touching, I frankly de-clare
I have read it all thrice, and, perhaps I am weak,
But I found every time there were tears on my cheek.

"The pole, science tells us, the magnet controls,
But she is a magnet to emigrant Poles,
And folks with a mission that nobody knows,
Throng thickly about her as bees round a rose;
She can fill up the *carets* in such, make their scope
Converge to some focus of rational hope,

And, with sympathies fresh as the morning, their gall
Can transmute into honey,—but this is not all;
Not only for those she has solace, oh, say,
Vice's desperate nursling adrift in Broadway,
Who clingest, with all that is left of thee human,
To the last slender spar from the wreck of the woman,
Hast thou not found one shore where those tired drooping feet
Could reach firm mother-earth, one full heart on whose beat
The soothed head in silence reposing could hear
The chimes of far childhood throb back on the ear?
Ah, there's many a beam from the fountain of day
That to reach us unclouded, must pass, on its way,
Through the soul of a woman, and hers is wide ope
To the influence of Heaven as the blue eyes of Hope;
Yes, a great soul is hers, one that dares to go in
To the prison, the slave-hut, the alleys of sin,
And to bring into each, or to find there some line
Of the never completely out-trampled divine;
If her heart at high floods swamps her brain now and then,
'Tis but richer for that when the tide ebbs agen,
As, after old Nile has subsided, his plain
Overflows with a second broad deluge of grain;
What a wealth would it bring to the narrow and sour
Could they be as a Child but for one little hour!

"What! Irving? thrice welcome, warm heart and fine brain,
You bring back the happiest spirit from Spain,

And the gravest sweet humor, that ever were there
Since Cervantes met death in his gentle despair;
Nay, don't be embarrassed, nor look so beseech
ing,—
I shan't run directly against my own preaching,
And, having just laughed at their Raphaels and
Dantes,
Go to setting you up beside matchless Cervantes;
But allow me to speak what I honestly feel,—
To a true poet-heart add the fun of Dick Steele,
Throw in all of Addison, *minus* the chill,
With the whole of that partnership's stock and
good will,
Mix well, and while stirring, hum o'er, as a spell,
The fine *old* English Gentleman, simmer it well,
Sweeten just to your own private liking, then
strain,
That only the finest and clearest remain,
Let it stand out of doors till a soul it receives
From the warm lazy sun loitering down through
green leaves,
And you'll find a choice nature, not wholly de-
serving
A name either English or Yankee,—just Irving.

"There goes,—but *stet nominis umbra*,—his
name
You'll be glad enough, some day or other, to claim,
And will all crowd about him and swear that you
knew him
If some English hack-critic should chance to re-
view him
The old *porcos ante ne projiciatis*
MARGARITAS, for him you have verified gratis;
What matters his name? Why, it may be Syl-
vester,
Judd, Junior, or Junius, Ulysses, or Nestor,

For aught *I* know or care; 'tis enough that I look
On the author of 'Margaret,' the first Yankee book
With the *soul* of Down East in't, and things farther
East,
As far as the threshold of morning, at least,
Where awaits the fair dawn of the simple and true,
Of the day that comes slowly to make all things
new.
'T has a smack of pine woods, of bare field and
bleak hill
Such as only the breed of the Mayflower could till;
The Puritan's shown in it, tough to the core,
Such as prayed, smiting Agag on red Marston
Moor;
With an unwilling humor, half-choked by the drouth
In brown hollows about the inhospitable mouth;
With a soul full of poetry, though it has qualms
About finding a happiness out of the Psalms;
Full of tenderness, too, though it shrinks in the
dark,
Hamadryad-like, under the coarse, shaggy bark;
That sees visions, knows wrestlings of God with
the Will,
And has its own Sinais and thunderings still."

Here,—"Forgive me, Apollo," I cried, "while I
pour
My heart out to my birthplace: O, loved more
and more
Dear Baystate, from whose rocky bosom thy sons
Should suck milk, strong-will-giving, brave, such as
runs
In the veins of old Graylock,—who is it that dares
Call thee peddler, a soul wrapt in bank-books and
shares?
It is false! She's a Poet! I see, as I write,
Along the far railroad the steam-snake glide white,

The cataract-throb of her mill-hearts I hear,
The swift strokes of trip-hammers weary my ear,
Sledges ring upon anvils, through logs the saw screams,
Blocks swing to their place, beetles drive home the beams:—
It is songs such as these that she croons to the din
Of her fast-flying shuttles, year out and year in,
While from earth's farthest corner there comes not a breeze
But wafts her the buzz of her gold-gleaning bees:
What though those horn hands have as yet found small time
For painting and sculpture and music and rhyme?
These will come in due order, the need that pressed sorest
Was to vanquish the seasons, the ocean, the forest,
To bridle and harness the rivers, the steam,
Making that whirl her mill-wheels, this tug in her team,
To vassalize old tyrant Winter, and make
Him delve surlily for her on river and lake;—
When this New World was parted, she strove not to shirk
Her lot in the heirdom, the tough, silent Work,
The hero-share ever, from Herakles down
To Odin, the Earth's iron sceptre and crown;
Yes, thou dear, noble Mother! if ever men's praise
Could be claimed for creating heroical lays,
Thou hast won it; if ever the laurel divine
Crowned the Maker and Builder, that glory is thine!
Thy songs are right epic, they tell how this rude
Rock-rib of our earth here was tamed and subdued;
Thou hast written them plain on the face of the planet

In brave, deathless letters of iron and granite;
Thou hast printed them deep for all time; they
are set
From the same runic type-fount and alphabet
With thy stout Berkshire hills and the arms of thy
Bay,—
They are staves from the burly old Mayflower lay
If the drones of the Old World, in querulous ease,
Ask thy Art and thy Letters, point proudly to
these,
Or, if they deny these are Letters and Art,
Toil on with the same old invincible heart;
Thou art rearing the pedestal broad-based and
grand
Whereon the fair shapes of the Artist shall stand,
And creating, through labors undaunted and long,
The theme for all Sculpture and Painting and
Song!

"But my good mother Baystate wants no praise
of mine,
She learned from *her* mother a precept divine
About something that butters no parsnips, her *forte*
In another direction lies, work is her sport,
(Though she'll curtsey and set her cap straight,
that she will,
If you talk about Plymouth and one Bunker's
hill.)
Dear, notable goodwife! by this time of night,
Her hearth is swept clean, and her fire burning
bright,
And she sits in a chair (of home plan and make)
rocking,
Musing much, all the while, as she darns on a
stocking,
Whether turkeys will come pretty high next
Thanksgiving,

Whether flour 'll be so dear, for, as sure as she's
living,
She will use rye-and-injun then, whether the pig
By this time ain't got pretty tolerable big,
And whether to sell it outright will be best,
Or to smoke hams and shoulders and salt down the
rest,—
At this minute, she'd swop all my verses, ah,
cruel!
For the last patent stove that is saving of fuel;
So I'll just let Apollo go on, for his phiz
Shows I've kept him awaiting too long as it is."

"If our friend, there, who seems a reporter, is
done
With his burst of emotion, why, *I* will go on,"
Said Apollo; some smiled, and, indeed, I must own
There was something sarcastic, perhaps, in his
tone;—

"There's Holmes, who is matchless among you
for wit;
A Leyden-jar always full-charged, from which flit
The electrical tingles of hit after hit;
In long poems 'tis painful sometimes and invites
A thought of the way the new Telegraph writes,
Which pricks down its little sharp sentences spite-
fully
As if you got more than you'd title to rightfully,
And you find yourself hoping its wild father Light-
ning
Would flame in for a second and give you a
fright'ning.
He has perfect sway of what *I* call a sham metre,
But many admire it, the English pentameter,
And Campbell, I think, wrote most commonly
worse,

With less nerve, swing, and fire in the same kind of verse,
Nor e'er achieved aught in't so worthy of praise
As the tribute of Holmes to the grand *Marseillaise.*
You went crazy last year over Bulwer's New Timon;—
Why, if B., to the day of his dying, should rhyme on,
Heaping verses on verses and tomes upon tomes,
He could ne'er reach the best point and vigor of Holmes.
His are just the fine hands, too, to weave you a lyric
Full of fancy, fun, feeling, or spiced with satyric
In a measure so kindly, you doubt if the toes
That are trodden upon are your own or your foes'.

"There is Lowell, who's striving Parnassus to climb
With a whole bale of *isms* tied together with rhyme,
He might get on alone, spite of brambles and boulders,
But he can't with that bundle he has on his shoulders,
The top of the hill he will ne'er come nigh reaching
Till he learns the distinction 'twixt singing and preaching;
His lyre has some chords that would ring pretty well,
But he'd rather by half make a drum of the shell,
And rattle away till he's old as Methusalem,
At the head of a march to the last new Jerusalem.

"There goes Halleck, whose Fanny's a pseudo
Don Juan,
With the wickedness out that gave salt to the true
one,
He's a wit, though, I hear, of the very first order,
And once made a pun on the words soft Recorder;
More than this, he's a very great poet, I'm told,
And has had his works published in crimson and
gold,
With something they call 'Illustrations,' to wit,
Like those with which Chapman obscured Holy
Writ,*
Which are said to illustrate, because, as I view it,
Like *lucus a non*, they precisely don't do it;
Let a man who can write what himself under-
stands
Keep clear, if he can, of designing men's hands,
Who bury the sense, if there's any worth having,
And then very honestly call it engraving.
But, to quit *badinage*, which there isn't much wit
in,
Halleck's better, I doubt not, than all he has writ-
ten;
In his verse a clear glimpse you will frequently
find,
If not of a great, of a fortunate mind,
Which contrives to be true to its natural loves
In a world of back-offices, ledgers, and stoves.
When his heart breaks away from the brokers and
banks,
And kneels in its own private shrine to give
thanks,
There's a genial manliness in him that earns
Our sincerest respect, (read, for instance, his
"Burns,")

* (Cuts rightly called wooden, as all must admit.

And we can't but regret (seek excuse where we may)
That so much of a man has been peddled away.

"But what's that? a mass-meeting? No, there come in lots
The American Disraelis, Bulwers, and Scotts,
And in short the American everything-elses,
Each charging the others with envies and jealousies;—
By the way, 'tis a fact that displays what profusions
Of all kinds of greatness bless free institutions,
That while the Old World has produced barely eight
Of such poets as all men agree to call great,
And of other great characters hardly a score,
(One might safely say less than that rather than more,)
With you every year a whole crop is begotten,
They're as much of a staple as corn is, or cotton;
Why, there's scarcely a huddle of log-huts and shanties
That has not brought forth its own Miltons and Dantes;
I myself know ten Byrons, one Coleridge, three Shelleys,
Two Raphaels, six Titians, (I think) one Apelles,
Leonardos and Rubenses plenty as lichens,
One (but that one is plenty) American Dickens,
A whole flock of Lambs, any number of Tennysons,—
In short, if a man has the luck to have any sons,
He may feel pretty certain that one out of twain
Will be some very great person over again.
There is one inconvenience in all this which lies

In the fact that by contrast we estimate size,*
And, where there are none except Titans, great stature
Is only a simple proceeding of nature.
What puff the strained sails of your praise shall you furl at, if
The calmest degree that you know is superlative?
At Rome, all whom Charon took into his wherry must,
As a matter of course, be well *issimus*ed and *errimus*ed,
A Greek, too, could feel, while in that famous boat he tost,
That his friends would take care he was ιστοςed and ωτατοςed,
And formerly we, as through graveyards we past,
Thought the world went from bad to worse fearfully fast;
Let us glance for a moment, 'tis well worth the pains,
And note what an average graveyard contains;
There lie levellers levelled, duns done up themselves,
There are booksellers finally laid on their shelves,
Horizontally there lie upright politicians,
Dose-a-dose with their patients sleep faultless physicians,
There are slave-drivers quietly whipt underground,
There bookbinders, done up in boards, are fast bound,
There card-players wait till the last trump be played,

* That is in most cases we do, but not all,
Past a doubt, there are men who are innately small,
Such as Blank, who, without being 'minished a tittle,
Might stand for a type of the Absolute Little.

There all the choice spirits get finally laid,
There the babe that's unborn is supplied with a
berth,
There men without legs get their six feet of earth,
There lawyers repose, each wrapt up in his case,
There seekers of office are sure of a place,
There defendant and plaintiff get equally cast,
There shoemakers quietly stick to the last,
There brokers at length become silent as stocks,
There stage-drivers sleep without quitting their
box,
And so forth and so forth and so forth and so on,
With this kind of stuff one might endlessly go on;
To come to the point, I may safely assert you
Will find in each yard every cardinal virtue;*
Each has six truest patriots: four discoverers of
ether,
Who never had thought on't nor mentioned it
either:
Ten poets, the greatest who ever wrote rhyme:
Two hundred and forty first men of their time:
One person whose portrait just gave the least hint
Its original had a most horrible squint:
One critic, most (what do they call it?) reflective,
Who never had used the phrase ob- or subjective:
Forty fathers of Freedom, of whom twenty bred
Their sons for the rice-swamps, at so much a head,
And their daughters for—faugh! thirty mothers of
Gracchi:
Non-resistants who gave many a spiritual black-
eye:
Eight true friends of their kind, one of whom was
a jailer:
Four captains almost as astounding as Taylor:

* (And at this just conclusion will surely arrive,
That the goodness of earth is more dead than alive.)

Two dozen of Italy's exiles who shoot us his
Kaisership daily, stern pen-and-ink Brutuses,
Who, in Yankee back-parlors, with crucified smile,*
Mount serenely their country's funereal pile:
Ninety-nine Irish heroes, ferocious rebellers
'Gainst the Saxon in cis-marine garrets and cellars,
Who shake their dread fists o'er the sea and all
 that,—
As long as a copper drops into the hat:
Nine hundred Teutonic republicans stark
From Vaterland's battles just won—in the Park,
Who the happy profession of martyrdom take
Whenever it gives them a chance at a steak:
Sixty-two second Washingtons: two or three Jack-
 sons:
And so many everythings else that it racks one's
Poor memory too much to continue the list,
Especially now they no longer exist;—
I would merely observe that you've taken to giv-
 ing
The puffs that belong to the dead to the living,
And that somehow your trump-of-contemporary-
 doom's tones
Is tuned after old dedications and tombstones."—

Here the critic came in and a thistle pre-
 sented†—
From a frown to a smile the god's features relented,
As he stared at his envoy, who, swelling with pride,
To the god's asking look, nothing daunted, replied,
"You're surprised, I suppose, I was absent so long,
But your godship respecting the lilies was wrong;
I hunted the garden from one end to t'other,
And got no reward but vexation and bother,

* Not forgetting their tea and their toast, though, the while
† Turn back now to page—goodness only knows what,
And take a fresh hold on the thread of my plot.

Till, tossed out with weeds in a corner to wither,
This one lily I found and made haste to bring
hither."

"Did he think I had given him a book to re-
view?
I ought to have known what the fellow would do,"
Muttered Phœbus aside, "for a thistle will pass
Beyond doubt for the queen of all flowers with an
ass;
He has chosen in just the same way as he'd choose
His specimens out of the books he reviews;
And now, as this offers an excellent text,
I'll give 'em some brief hints on criticism next."
So, musing a moment, he turned to the crowd,
And, clearing his voice, spoke as follows aloud,—

"My friends, in the happier days of the muse,
We were luckily free from such things as reviews;
Then naught came between with its fog to make
clearer
The heart of the poet to that of his hearer;
Then the poet brought heaven to the people, and
they
Felt that they, too, were poets in hearing his lay;
Then the poet was prophet, the past in his soul
Pre-created the future, both parts of one whole;
Then for him there was nothing too great or too
small,
For one natural deity sanctified all;
Then the bard owned no clipper and meter of
moods
Save the spirit of silence that hovers and broods
O'er the seas and the mountains, the rivers and
woods;
He asked not earth's verdict, forgetting the clods,
His soul soared and sang to an audience of gods;

'Twas for them that he measured the thought and
the line,
And shaped for their vision the perfect design,
With as glorious a foresight, a balance as true,
As swung out the worlds in the infinite blue;
Then a glory and greatness invested man's heart,
The universal, which now stands estranged and
apart,
In the free individual moulded, was Art;
Then the forms of the Artist seemed thrilled with
desire
For something as yet unattained, fuller, higher,
As once with her lips, lifted hands, and eyes listen-
ing,
And her whole upward soul in her countenance
glistening,
Eurydice stood—like a beacon unfired,
Which, once touch'd with flame, will leap heav'n-
ward inspired—
And waited with answering kindle to mark
The first gleam of Orpheus that pained the red
Dark.
Then painting, song, sculpture, did more than re-
lieve
The need that men feel to create and believe,
And as, in all beauty, who listens with love,
Hears these words oft repeated—'beyond and
above,'
So these seemed to be but the visible sign
Of the grasp of the soul after things more di-
vine;
They were ladders the Artist erected to climb
O'er the narrow horizon of space and of time,
And we see there the footsteps by which men had
gained
To the one rapturous glimpse of the never-at-
tained,

As shepherds could erst sometimes trace in the sod
The last spurning print of a sky-cleaving god.

"But now, on the poet's dis-privacied moods
With *do this* and *do that* the pert critic intrudes;
While he thinks he's been barely fulfilling his duty
To interpret 'twixt men and their own sense of beauty,
And has striven, while others sought honor or pelf,
To make his kind happy as he was himself,
He finds he's been guilty of horrid offences
In all kinds of moods, numbers, genders, and tenses;
He's been *ob* and *sub*jective, what Kettle calls Pot,
Precisely, at all events, what he ought not,
You have done this, says one judge; *done that*, says another;
You should have done this, grumbles one; *that*, says t'other;
Never mind what he touches, one shrieks out *Taboo!*
And while he is wondering what he shall do,
Since each suggests opposite topics for song,
They all shout together *you're right!* and *you're wrong!*

"Nature fits all her children with something to do,
He who would write and can't write, can surely review,
Can set up a small booth as critic and sell us his
Petty conceit and his pettier jealousies;
Thus a lawyer's apprentice, just out of his teens,
Will do for the Jeffrey of six magazines;
Having read Johnson's lives of the poet's half through,

There's nothing on earth he's not competent to;
He reviews with as much nonchalance as he whistles,—
He goes through a book and just picks out the thistles,
It matters not whether he blame or commend,
If he's bad as a foe, he's far worse as a friend;
Let an author but write what's above his poor scope,
And he'll go to work gravely and twist up a rope,
And, inviting the world to see punishment done,
Hang himself up to bleach in the wind and the sun;
'Tis delightful to see, when a man comes along
Who has any thing in him peculiar and strong,
Every cockboat that swims clear its fierce (pop) gundeck at him
And make as he passes its ludicrous Peck at him,"—

Here Miranda came up and began, "As to that,"—
Apollo at once seized his gloves, cane, and hat,
And, seeing the place getting rapidly cleared,
I, too, snatched my notes and forthwith disappeared.

THE BIGLOW PAPERS.

NOTICES OF AN INDEPENDENT PRESS.

[I **HAVE** observed, reader, (bene- or male-volent, as it may happen,) that it is customary to append to the second editions of books, and to the second works of authors, short sentences commendatory of the first, under the title of *Notices of the Press*. These, I have been given to understand, are procurable at certain established rates, payment being made either in money or advertising patronage by the publisher, or by an adequate outlay of servility on the part of the author. Considering these things with myself, and also that such notices are neither intended, nor generally believed, to convey any real opinions, being a purely ceremonial accompaniment of literature, and resembling certificates to the virtues of various morbiferal panaceas, I conceived that it would be not only more economical to prepare a sufficient number of such myself, but also more immediately subservient to the end in view to prefix them to this our primary edition rather than await the contingency of a second, when they would seem to be of small utility. To delay attaching the *bobs* until the second attempt at flying the kite, would indicate but a slender experience in that useful art. Neither has it escaped my notice, nor failed to afford me matter of reflection, that, when a circus or a caravan is about to visit Jaalam, the initial step is to send forward large and highly ornamented bills of performance to be hung in the bar-room and the post-office. These having been sufficiently gazed at, and beginning to lose their attractiveness except for the flies, and, truly, the boys also, (in whom I find it impossible to repress, even during school-hours, certain oral and telegraphic communications concerning the expected show,) upon some fine morning the band enters in a gayly-painted wagon, or triumphal chariot, and with noisy advertisement, by means of brass, wood, and sheepskin, makes the circuit of our startled village-streets. Then, as the exciting sounds draw nearer and nearer, do I desiderate those eyes of Aristarchus, "whose looks were as a breeching to a boy." Then do I perceive, with vain regret of wasted opportunities, the advantage of a pancratic or pantechnic education, since he is most reverenced by my little subjects who can throw the cleanest summerset or walk most securely upon the revolving cask. The story of the Pied Piper becomes for the first time credible to me, (albeit confirmed by the Hameliners dating their legal instruments from the period of his exit,) as I behold how those strains, without pretence of magical potency, bewitch the pupillary legs, nor leave to the pedagogic an entire self-control. For these reasons, lest my kingly prerogative should suffer diminution, I prorogue my restless commons, whom I also follow into the street, chiefly lest some mischief may chance befall them. After the manner of such a band, I send forward the following notices of domestic manufacture, to make brazen proclamation, not unconscious of the advantage which will accrue, if our little craft, *cymbula sutilis*, shall seem to leave port with a clipping breeze, and to carry, in nautical phrase, a bone in her mouth. Nevertheless, I have chosen, as being more equitable, to prepare some also sufficiently objurgatory, that readers of every taste may find a dish to their palate. I have modelled them upon actually existing specimens, preserved in my own cabinet of natural curiosities. One, in particular, I had copied with tolerable exactness from a notice of one of my own discourses, which, from its superior tone and appearance of vast experience, I concluded to have been written by a man at least three hundred years of age, though I recollected no existing instance of such antediluvian longevity. Nevertheless, I afterwards discovered the author to be a young gentleman preparing for the ministry under the direction of one of my brethren in a neighbouring town, and whom I had once instinctively corrected in a Latin quantity. But this I have been forced to omit, from its too great length.—H. W.]

From the Universal Littery Universe.

Full of passages which rivet the attention of the reader..... Under a rustic garb, sentiments are conveyed which should be committed to the memory and engraven on the heart of every moral and social being......We consider this a *unique* performance.....We hope to see it soon introduced into our common schools......Mr. Wilbur has performed his duties as editor with excellent taste and judgment......This is a vein which we hope to see successfully prosecuted......We hail the appearance of this work as a long stride toward the formation of a purely aboriginal, indigenous, native, and American literature. We rejoice to meet with an author national enough to break away from the slavish deference, too common among us, to English grammar and orthography......Where all is so good, we are at a loss how to make extracts......On the whole, we may call it a volume which no library, pretending to entire completeness, should fail to place upon its shelves.

From the Higginbottomopolis Snapping-turtle.

A collection of the merest balderdash and doggerel that it was ever our bad fortune to lay eyes on. The author is a vulgar buffoon, and the editor a talkative, tedious old fool. We use strong language, but should any of our readers peruse the book, (from which calamity Heaven preserve them!) they will find reasons for it thick as the leaves of Vallumbrozer, or, to use a still more expressive comparison, as the combined heads of author and editor. The work is wretchedly got up......We should like to know how much *British gold* was pocketed by this libeller of our country and her purest patriots.

From the Oldfogrumville Mentor.

We have not had time to do more than glance through this handsomely printed volume, but the name of its respectable editor, the Rev. Mr. Wilbur, of Jaalam, will afford a sufficient guaranty for the worth of its contents......The paper is white, the type clear, and the volume of a convenient and attractive size. ......In reading this elegantly executed work, it has seemed to us that a passage or two might have been retrenched with advantage, and that the general style of diction was susceptible of a higher polish......On the whole, we may safely leave the ungrateful task of criticism to the reader. We will barely suggest, that in volumes intended, as this is, for the illustration of a provincial dialect and turns of expression, a dash of humor or satire might be thrown in with advantage......The work is admirably got up......This work will form an appropriate ornament to the centre-table. It is beautifully printed, on paper of an excellent quality.

From the Dekay Bulwark.

We should be wanting in our duty as the conductor of that tremendous engine, a public press, as an American, and as a man, did we allow such an opportunity as is presented to us by "The Biglow Papers" to pass by without entering our earnest protest against such attempts (now, alas! too common) at demoralizing the public sentiment. Under a wretched mask of stupid drollery, slavery, war, the social glass, and, in short, all the valuable and time-honored institutions justly dear to our common humanity and especially to republicans, are made the butt of coarse and senseless ribaldry by this low-minded scribbler. It is time that the respectable and religious portion of our community should be aroused to the alarming inroads of foreign Jacobinism, sansculottism, and infidelity. It is a fearful proof of the wide-spread nature of this contagion, that these secret stabs at religion and virtue are given from under the cloak (*credite, posteri!*) of a clergyman. It is a mournful spectacle indeed to the patriot and Christian to see liberality and new ideas (falsely so called,—they are as old as Eden) invading the sacred precincts of the pulpit. . . . . .On the whole, we consider this volume as one of the first shocking results which we predicted would spring out of the late French "Revolution" (!).

From the Bungtown Copper and Comprehensive Tocsin (a try-weakly family journal).

Altogether an admirable work. . . . . .Full of humor, boisterous, but delicate,—of wit withering and scorching, yet combined with a pathos cool as morning dew,—of satire ponderous as the mace of Richard, yet keen as the scymitar of Saladin. . . . . .A work full of "mountain-mirth," mischievous as Puck and lightsome as Ariel. . . . . . .We know not whether to admire most the genial, fresh, and discursive concinnity of the author, or his playful fancy, weird imagination, and compass of style, at once both objective and subjective. . . . . .We might indulge in some criticisms, but were the author other than he is, he would be a different being. As it is, he has a wonderful *pose*, which flits from flower to flower, and bears the reader irresistibly along on its eagle pinions (like Ganymede) to the "highest heaven of invention.". . . . . .We love a book so purely objective. . . . . .Many of his pictures of natural scenery have an extraordinary subjective clearness and fidelity. . . . . .In fine, we consider this as one of the most extraordinary volumes of this or any age. We know of no English author who could have written it. It is a work to which the proud genius of our country, standing with one foot on the Aroostook and the other on the Rio Grande, and holding up the star-spangled banner amid the wreck of matter and the crush of worlds, may point with bewildering scorn of the punier efforts of enslaved Europe. . . . . .We hope soon to encounter our author among those higher walks of literature in which he is evidently capable of achieving enduring fame Already we should be inclined to assign him a high position in the bright galaxy of our American bards.

From the Saltriver Pilot and Flag of Freedom.

A volume in bad grammar and worse taste. . . . . .While the pieces here collected were confined to their appropriate sphere in the corners of obscure newspapers, we considered them wholly beneath contempt, but, as the author has chosen to come forward in this public manner, he must expect the lash he so richly merits. . . . . .Contemptible slanders. . . . . .Vilest Billingsgate. . . . . . .Has raked all the gutters of our language. . . . . .The most pure, upright, and consistent politicians not safe from his malignant venom. . . . . .General Cushing comes in for a share of his vile calumnies. . . . . .The *Reverend* Homer Wilbur is a disgrace to his cloth. . . . . .

From the World-Harmonic-Æolian-Attachment.

Speech is silver: silence is golden. No utterance more Orphic than this. While, therefore, as highest author, we reverence him whose works continue heroically unwritten, we have also our hopeful word for those who with pen (from wing of goose loud-cackling, or seraph God-commissioned) record the thing that is revealed. . . . . .Under mask of quaintest irony, we detect here the deep, storm-tost (nigh shipwracked) soul, thunder-scarred, semiarticulate, but ever climbing hopefully toward the peaceful summits of an Infinite Sorrow. . . . . .Yes, thou poor, forlorn Hosea, with Hebrew fire-flaming soul in thee, for thee also this life of ours has not been without its aspects of heavenliest pity and laughingest mirth. Conceivable enough! Through coarse Thersites-cloak, we have revelation of the heart, wild-glowing, world-clasping, that is in him. Bravely he grapples with the life-problem as it presents itself to him, uncombed, shaggy, careless of the "nicer proprieties," inexpert of "elegant diction," yet with voice audible enough to whoso hath ears, up there on the gravelly side-hills, or down on the splashy, Indiarubber-like salt-marshes of native Jaalam. To this soul also the *Necessity of Creating* somewhat has unveiled its awful front. If not Œdipuses and Electras and Alcestises, then in God's name Birdofredum Sawins! These also shall get born into the world, and filch (if so need) a Zingali subsistence therein, these lank, omnivorous Yankees of his. He shall paint the Seen, since the Unseen will not sit to him. Yet in him also are Nibelungen-lays, and Iliads, and Ulysses-wanderings, and Divine Comedies,—if only once he could come at them! Therein lies much, nay all; for what truly is this which we name *All*, but that which we do *not* possess? . . . . . .Glimpses also are given us of an old father Ezekiel, not without paternal pride, as is the wont of such. A brown, parchment-hided old man of the geoponic or bucolic species, gray-eyed, we fancy, *queued* perhaps, with much weather-cunning and plentiful September-gale memories, bidding fair in good time to become the Oldest Inhabitant. After such hasty apparition, he vanishes and is seen no more. . . . . .Of "Rev. Homer Wilbur, A. M., Pastor of the First Church in Jaalam," we have small care to speak here. Spare touch in him of his Melesigenes namesake, save, haply, the—blindness! A tolerably caliginose, nephelegeretous elderly gentleman, with infinite faculty of sermonizing, muscularized by long practice, and excellent digestive apparatus, and, for the rest, well-meaning enough, and with small private illuminations (somewhat tallowy, it is to be feared) of his own. To him, there, "Pastor of the First Church in Jaalam," our Hosea presents himself as a quite inexplicable Sphinx-riddle. A rich poverty of Latin and Greek,—so far is clear enough, even to eyes peering myopic through horn-lensed editorial spectacles,—but naught farther? O purblind, well-meaning, altogether fuscous Melesigenes-Wilbur, there are things in him incommunicable by stroke of birch! Did it ever enter that old bewildered head of thine that there was the *Possibility of the Infinite* in him? To thee, quite wingless (and even featherless) biped, has not so much even as a dream of wings ever come? "Talented young parishioner"? Among the Arts whereof thou art *Magister*, does that of *seeing* happen to be one? Unhappy *Artium Magister!* Somehow a Nemean lion, fulvous, torrid-eyed, dry-nursed in broad-howling sand-wildernesses of a sufficiently rare spirit-Libya (it may be supposed) has got whelped among the sheep. Already he stands wild-glaring, with feet clutching the ground as with oak-roots, gathering for a Remus-spring over the walls of thy little fold. In Heaven's name, go not near him with that flybite crook of thine! In good time, thou painful preacher, thou wilt go to the appointed place of departed Artillery-Election Sermons, Right-Hands of Fellowship, and Results of Councils, gathered to thy spiritual fathers with much Latin of the Epitaphial sort; thou, too, shalt have thy reward; but on him the Eumenides have looked, not Xantippes of the pit, snake-tressed, finger-threatening, but radiantly calm as on antique gems; for him paws impatient the winged courser of the gods, champing unwelcome bit; him the starry deeps, the empyrean glooms, and far-flashing splendors await.

From the Onion Grove Phœnix.

A talented young townsman of ours, recently returned from a Continental tour, and who is already favorably known to our readers by his sprightly letters from abroad which have graced our columns, called at our office yesterday. We learn from him, that, having enjoyed the distinguished privilege, while in Germany, of an introduction to the celebrated Von Humbug, he took the opportunity to present that eminent man with a copy of the "Biglow Papers." The next morning he received the following note, which he has kindly furnished us for publication. We prefer to print it *verbatim*, knowing that our readers will readily forgive the few errors into which the illustrious writer has fallen, through ignorance of our language.

"High-Worthy Mister!

"I shall also now especially happy starve, because I have more or less a work of one those aboriginal Red-Men seen in which have I so deaf an interest ever taken fullworthy on the self shelf with our Gottsched to be upset.

"Pardon my in the English-speech unpractice!

"Von Humbug."

He also sent with the above note a copy of his famous work on "Cosmetics," to be presented to Mr. Biglow; but this was taken from our friend by the English custom-house officers, probably through a petty national spite. No doubt, it has by this time found its way into the British Museum. We trust this outrage will be exposed in all our American papers. We shall do our best to bring it to the notice of the State Department. Our numerous readers will share in the pleasure we experience at seeing our young and vigorous national literature thus encouragingly patted on the head by this venerable and world-renowned German. We love to see these reciprocations of good-feeling between the different branches of the great Anglo-Saxon race.

[The following genuine "notice" having met my eye

I gladly insert a portion of it here, the more especially as it contains one of Mr. Biglow's poems not elsewhere printed.—H. W.]

From the Jaalam Independent Blunderbuss.

.... But, while we lament to see our young townsman thus mingling in the heated contests of party politics, we think we detect in him the presence of talents which, if properly directed, might give an innocent pleasure to many. As a proof that he is competent to the production of other kinds of poetry, we copy for our readers a short fragment of a pastoral by him, the manuscript of which was loaned us by a friend. The title of it is "The Courtin'."

Zekle crep' up, quite unbeknown,
  An' peeked in thru the winder,
An' there sot Huldy all alone,
  'ith no one nigh to hender.

Agin' the chimbly crooknecks hung,
  An' in amongst 'em rusted
The ole queen's arm thet gran'ther Young
  Fetched back frum Concord busted.

The wannut logs shot sparkles out
  Towards the pootiest, bless her!
An' leetle fires danced all about
  The chiny on the dresser.

The very room, coz she wuz in,
  Looked warm frum floor to ceilin',
An' she looked full ez rosy agin
  Ez th' apples she wuz peelin'.

She heerd a foot an' knowed it, tu,
  Araspin' on the scraper,—

All ways to once her feelins flew
  Like sparks in burnt-up paper.

He kin' o' l'itered on the mat,
  Some doubtfle o' the seekle;
His heart kep' goin' pitypat,
  But hern went pity Zekle.

An' yet she gin her cheer a jerk
  Ez though she wished him furder,
An' on her apples kep' to work
  Ez ef a wager spurred her.

"You want to see my Pa, I spose?"
  "Wal, no; I come designin'—"
"To see my Ma? She's sprinklin' clo'es
  Agin tomorrow's i'nin'."

He stood a spell on one foot fust
  Then stood a spell on tother,
An' on which one he felt the wust
  He couldn't ha' told ye, nuther.

Sez he, "I'd better call agin;"
  Sez she, "think likely, *Mister;*"
The last word pricked him like a pin,
  An'—wal, he up and kist her.

When Ma bimeby upon 'em slips,
  Huldy sot pale ez ashes,
All kind o' smily round the lips
  An' teary round the lashes.

Her blood riz quick, though, like the tide
  Down to the Bay o' Fundy,
An' all I know is they wuz cried
  In meetin', come nex Sunday.

SATIS multis sese emptores futuros libri professis, Georgius Nichols, Cantabrigiensis, opus emittet de parte gravi sed adhuc neglecta historiæ naturalis, cum titulo sequenti, videlicet:

Conatus ad Delineationem naturalem nonnihil perfectiorem Scarabæi Bombilatoris, vulgo dicti HUMBUG, ab HOMERO WILBUR, Artium Magistro, Societatis historico-naturalis Jaalamensis Præside, (Secretario, Socioque (eheu!) singulo,) multarumque aliarum Societatum eruditarum (sive ineruditarum) tam domesticarum quam transmarinarum Socio—forsitan futuro.

PROEMIUM.

LECTORI BENEVOLO S.

Toga scholastica nondum deposita, quum systemata varia entomologica, a viris ejus scientiæ cultoribus studiosissimis summa diligentia ædificata, penitus indagâssem, non fuit quin luctuose omnibus in iis, quamvis aliter laude dignissimis, hiatum magni momenti perciperem. Tunc, nescio quo motu superiore impulsus, aut qua captus dulcedine operis, ad eum implendum (Curtius alter) me solemniter devovi. Nec ab isto labore, *δαιμονίως* imposito, abstinui antequam tractatulum sufficienter inconcinnum lingua vernacula perfeceram. Inde, juveniliter tumefactus, et barathro ineptiæ *τῶν βιβλιοπωλῶν* (necnon "Publici Legentis") nusquam explorato, me composuisse quod quasi placentas præfervidas (ut sic dicam) homines ingurgitarent credidi. Sed, quum huic et alio bibliopolæ MSS. mea submisissem et nihil solidius responsione valde negativa in Musæum meum retulissem, horror ingens atque misericordia, ob crassitudinem Lambertianam in cerebris homunculorum istius muneris cœlesti quadam ira infixam, me invasere. Extemplo mei solius impensis librum edere decrevi, nihil omnino dubitans quin "Mundus Scientificus" (ut aiunt) crumenam meam ampliter repleret. Nullam, attamen, ex agro illo meo parvulo segetem demessui, præter gaudium vacuum bene de Republica merendi. Iste panis meus pretiosus super aquas literarias fæculentas præfidenter jactus, quasi Harpyiarum quarundam (scilicet bibliopolarum istorum facinorosorum supradictorum) tactu rancidus, intra perpaucos dies mihi domum rediit. Et, quum ipse tali victu ali non tolerarem, primum in mentem venit pistori (typographo nempe) nihilominus solvendum esse. Animum non idcirco demisi, imo æque ac pueri naviculas suas penes se lino retinent (eo ut e recto cursu delapsas ad ripam retrahant), sic ego Argô meam chartaceam fluctibus laborantem a quæsitu velleris aurei, ipse potius tonsus pelleque exutus, mente solida revocavi. Metaphoram ut mutem, *boomarangam* meam a scopo aberrantem retraxi, dum majore vi, occasione ministrante, adversus Fortunam intorquerem. Ast mihi, talia volventi, et, sicut Saturnus ille παιδοβόρος, liberos intellectus mei depascere fidenti, casus miserandus, nec antea inauditus, supervenit. Nam, ut ferunt Scythas pietatis causa et parsimoniæ, parentes suos mortuos devorâsse, sic filius hic meus primogenitus, Scythis ipsis minus mansuetus, patrem vivum totum et calcitrantem exsorbere enixus est. Nec tamen hac de causa sobolem meam esurientem exheredavi. Sed famem istam pro valido testimonio virilitatis roborisque potius habui, cibumque ad eam satiandam, salva paterna mea carne, petii. Et quia bilem illam scaturientem ad æs etiam concoquendum idoneam esse estimabam, unde æs alienum, ut minoris pretii, haberem, circumspexi. Rebus ita se habentibus, ab avunculo meo Johanne Doolittle, Armigero, impetravi ut pecunias necessarias suppeditaret, ne opus esset mihi universitatem relinquendi antequam ad gradum primum in artibus pervenissem. Tunc ego, salvum facere patronum meum munificum maxime cupiens, omnes libros primæ editionis operis mei non venditos una cum privilegio in omne ævum ejusdem imprimendi et edendi avunculo meo dicto pigneravi. Ex illo die, atro lapide notando, curae vociferantes familiæ singulis annis crescentis eo usque insultabant ut nunquam tam carum pignus e vinculis istis aheneis solvere possem.

Avunculo vero nuper mortuo, quum inter alios consanguineos testamenti ejus lectionem audiendi causa advenissem, erectis auribus verba talia sequentia accepi: —" Quoniam persuasum habeo meum dilectum nepotem Homerum, longa et intima rerum angustarum domi experientia, aptissimum esse qui divitias tueatur, beneficenterque ac prudenter iis divinis creditis utatur,—ergo, motus hisce cogitationibus, exque amore meo in illum magno, do, legoque nepoti caro meo supranominato omnes singularesque istas possessiones nec ponderabiles nec computabiles meas quæ sequuntur, scilicet: quingentos libros quos mihi pigneravit dictus Homerus, anno lucis 1792, cum privilegio edendi et repetendi opus istud 'scientificum' (quod dicunt) suum, si sic elegerit. Tamen D. O. M. precor oculos Homeri nepotis mei ita aperiat eumque moveat, ut libros istos in bibliotheca unius e plurimis castellis suis Hispaniensibus tuto abscondat."

His verbis (vix credibilibus) auditis, cor meum in pectore exsultavit. Deinde, quoniam tractatus Anglice scriptus spem auctoris fefellerat, quippe quum studium Historiæ Naturalis in Republica nostra inter factionis strepitum languescat, Latine versum edere statui, et eo potius quia nescio quomodo disciplina academica et duo diplomata proficiant, nisi quod peritos linguarum omnino mortuarum (et damnandarum, ut dicebat iste *πανοῦργος* Gulielmus Cobbett) nos faciant.

Et mihi adhuc superstes est tota illa editio prima, quam quasi crepitaculum per quod dentes caninos dentibam retineo.

OPERIS SPECIMEN.

(*Ad exemplum Johannis Physiophili speciminis Monachologiæ.*)

12. S. B. *Militaris*, Wilbur. *Carnifex*, Jablonsk. *Profanus*, Desfont.

[Male hancce speciem *Cyclopem* Fabricius vocat, ut qui singulo oculo ad quod sui interest distinguitur. Melius vero Isaacus Outis nullum inter S. milit. S.que Belzebul (Fabric. 152) discrimen esse defendit.]

Habitat civitat. Americ. austral.

Aureis lineis splendidus; plerumque tamen sordidus, utpote lanienas valde frequentans, fœtore sanguinis allectus. Amat quoque insuper septa apricari, neque inde, nisi maxima conatione, detruditur. *Candidatus* ergo populariter vocatus. Caput cristam quasi pennarum ostendit. Pro cibo vaccam publicam callide mulget; abdomen enorme; facultas suctus haud facile estimanda. Otiosus, fatuus; ferox nihilominus, semperque dimicare paratus Tortuose repit.

Capite sæpe maxima cum cura dissecto, ne illud rudimentum etiam cerebri commune omnibus prope insectis detegere poteram.

Unam de hoc S. milit. rem singularem notavi; nam S. Guineens. (Fabric. 143) servos facit, et idcirco a multis summa in reverentia habitus, quasi scintillas rationis pæne humanæ demonstrans.

24. S. B. *Criticus*, Wilbur. *Zoilus*, Fabric. *Pygmæus*, Carlsen.

[Stultissime Johannes Stryx cum S. punctato (Fabric. 64-109) confundit. Specimina quamplurima scrutationi microscopicæ subjeci, nunquam tamen unum ulla indicia puncti cujusvis prorsus ostendentem inveni.]

Præcipue formidolosus, insectatusque, in proxima rima anonyma sese abscondit, *we*, *we*, creberrime stridens. Ineptus, segnipes.

Habitat ubique gentium; in sicco; nidum suum terebratione indefessa ædificans. Cibus. Libros depascit; siccos præcipue

MELIBŒUS-HIPPONAX.

THE

Biglow Papers,

EDITED,

WITH AN INTRODUCTION, NOTES, GLOSSARY, AND COPIOUS INDEX.

BY

HOMER WILBUR, A. M.,

PASTOR OF THE FIRST CHURCH IN JAALAM, AND (PROSPECTIVE) MEMBER OF MANY LITERARY, LEARNED AND SCIENTIFIC SOCIETIES,

(*for which see page* 116.)

The ploughman's whistle, or the trivial flute,
Finds more respect than great Apollo's lute.
Quarles's Emblems, B. ii. E 8.

Margaritas, munde porcine, calcâsti: en, siliquas accipe.
Jac. Car. Fil. ad Pub. Leg. § 1.

NOTE TO TITLE-PAGE.

It will not have escaped the attentive eye, that I have, on the title-page, omitted those honorary appendages to the editorial name which not only add greatly to the value of every book, but whet and exacerbate the appetite of the reader. For not only does he surmise that an honorary membership of literary and scientific societies implies a certain amount of necessary distinction on the part of the recipient of such decorations, but he is willing to trust himself more entirely to an author who writes under the fearful responsibility of involving the reputation of such bodies as the *S. Archæol. Dahom.*, or the *Acad. Lit. et Scient. Kamtschat.* I cannot but think that the early editions of Shakspeare and Milton would have met with more rapid and general acceptance, but for the barrenness of their respective title-pages; and I believe, that, even now, a publisher of the works of either of those justly distinguished men would find his account in procuring their admission to the membership of learned bodies on the Continent,—a proceeding no whit more incongruous than the reversal of the judgment against Socrates, when he was already more than twenty centuries beyond the reach of antidotes, and when his memory had acquired a deserved respectability. I conceive that it was a feeling of the importance of this precaution which induced Mr. Locke to style himself "Gent." on the title-page of his Essay, as who should say to his readers that they could receive his metaphysics on the honor of a gentleman.

Nevertheless, finding that, without descending to a smaller size of type than would have been compatible with the dignity of the several societies to be named, I could not compress my intended list within the limits of a single page, and thinking, moreover, that the act would carry with it an air of decorous modesty, I have chosen to take the reader aside, as it were, into my private closet, and there not only exhibit to him the diplomas which I already possess, but also to furnish him with a prophetic vision of those which I may, without undue presumption, hope for, as not beyond the reach of human ambition and attainment. And I am the rather induced to this from the fact, that my name has been unaccountably dropped from the last triennial catalogue of our beloved *Alma Mater*. Whether this is to be attributed to the difficulty of Latinizing any of those honorary adjuncts (with a complete list of which I took care to furnish the proper persons nearly a year beforehand), or whether it had its origin in any more culpable motives, I forbear to consider in this place, the matter being in course of painful investigation. But, however this may be, I felt the omission the more keenly, as I had, in expectation of the new catalogue, enriched the library of the Jaalam Athenæum with the old one then in my possession, by which means it has come about that my children will be deprived of a never-wearying winter-evening's amusement in looking out the name of their parent in that distinguished roll. Those harmless innocents had at least committed no —— but I forbear, having intrusted my reflections and animadversions on this painful topic to the safe-keeping of my private diary, intended for posthumous publication. I state this fact here, in order that certain nameless individuals, who are, perhaps, overmuch congratulating themselves upon my silence, may know that a rod is in pickle which the vigorous hand of a justly incensed posterity will apply to their memories.

The careful reader will note, that, in the list which I have prepared, I have included the names of several Cisatlantic societies to which a place is not commonly assigned in processions of this nature. I have ventured to do this, not only to encourage native ambition and genius, but also because I have never been able to perceive in what way distance (unless we suppose them at the end of a lever) could increase the weight of learned bodies. As far as I have been able to extend my researches among such stuffed specimens as occasionally reach America, I have discovered no generic difference between the antipodal *Fogrum Japonicum* and the *F. Americanum* sufficiently common in our own immediate neighbourhood. Yet, with a becoming deference to the popular belief that distinctions of this sort are enhanced in value by every additional mile they travel, I have intermixed the names of some tolerably distant literary and other associations with the rest.

I add here, also, an advertisement, which, that it may be the more readily understood by those persons especially interested therein, I have written in that curtailed and otherwise maltreated canine Latin, to the writing and reading of which they are accustomed.

OMNIB. PER TOT. ORB. TERRAR. CATALOG. ACADEM. EDD.

Minim. gent. diplom. ab inclytiss. acad. vest. orans

vir. honorand. operosiss., at sol. ut sciat. quant. glor. nom. meum (dipl. fort. concess.) catal. vest. temp. futur. affer., ill. subjec., addit. omnib. titul. honorar. qu. adh. non tant. opt. quam probab. put.

*** *Litt. Uncial. distinx. ut Præs. S. Hist. Nat. Jaal.*

HOMERUS WILBUR, Mr., Episc. Jaalam, S. T. D. 1850, et Yal. 1849, et Neo-Cæs. et Brun. et Gulielm. 1852, et Gul. et Mar. et Bowd. et Georgiop. et Viridimont. et Columb. Nov. Ebor. 1853, et Amherst. et Watervill. et S. Jarlath. Hib. et S. Mar. et S. Joseph. et S. And. Scot. 1854, et Nashvill. et Dart. et Dickins. et Concord. et Wash. et Columbian. et Charlest. et Jeff. et Dubl. et Oxon. et Cantab. et cæt. 1855, P. U. N. C. H. et J. U. D. Gott et Osnab. et Heidelb. 1860, et Acad. BORE US. Berolin. Soc., et SS. RR. Lugd. Bat. et Patav. et Lond. et Edinb. et Ins. Feejee. et Null. Terr. et Pekin. Soc. Hon. et S. H. S. et S. P. A. et A. A. S. et S. Humb. Univ. et S. Omn. Rer. Quarund. q. Aliar. Promov. Passamaquod. et H. P. C. et I. O. H. et A. Δ. Φ. et Π. K. P. et Φ. B. K. et Peucin. et Erosoph. et Philadelph. et Frat. in Unit. et Σ. T. et S. Archæolog. Athen. et Acad. Scient. et Lit. Panorm. et SS. R. H. Matrit. et Beeloochist. et Caffrar. et Caribb. et M. S. Reg. Paris. et S. Am. Antiserv. Soc. Hon. et P. D. Gott. et LL. D. 1852, et D. C. L. et Mus. Doc. Oxon. 1860, et M. M. S. S. et M. D. 1854, et Med. Fac. Univ. Harv. Soc. et S. pro Convers. Pollywog. Soc. Hon. et Higgl. Piggl. et LL. B. 1853, et S. pro Christianiz. Moschet. Soc., et SS. Ante-Diluv. ubiq. Gent. Soc. Hon. et Civit. Cleric. Jaalam. et S. pro Diffus. General. Tenebr. Secret. Corr.

INTRODUCTION.

WHEN, more than three years ago, my talented young parishioner, Mr. Biglow, came to me and submitted to my animadversions the first of his poems which he intended to commit to the more hazardous trial of a city newspaper, it never so much as entered my imagination to conceive that his productions would ever be gathered into a fair volume, and ushered into the august presence of the reading public by myself. So little are we short-sighted mortals able to predict the event! I confess that there is to me a quite new satisfaction in being associated (though only as sleeping partner) in a book which can stand by itself in an independent unity on the shelves of libraries. For there is always this drawback from the pleasure of printing a sermon, that, whereas the queasy stomach of this generation will not bear a discourse long enough to make a separate volume, those religious and godly-minded children (those Samuels, if I may call them so) of the brain must at first lie buried in an undistinguished heap, and then get such resurrection as is vouchsafed to them, mummy-wrapt with a score of others in a cheap binding, with no other mark of distinction than the word "*Miscellaneous*" printed upon the back. Far be it from me to claim any credit for the quite unexpected popularity which I am pleased to find these bucolic strains have attained unto. If I know myself, I am measurably free from the itch of vanity; yet I may be allowed to say that I was not backward to recognize in them a certain wild, puckery, acidulous (sometimes even verging toward that point which, in our rustic phrase, is termed *shut-eye*) flavor, not wholly unpleasing, nor unwholesome, to palates cloyed with the sugariness of tamed and cultivated fruit. It may be, also, that some touches of my own, here and there, may have led to their wider acceptance, albeit solely from my larger experience of literature and authorship.*

I was, at first, inclined to discourage Mr. Biglow's attempts, as knowing that the desire to poetize is one of the diseases naturally incident to adolescence, which, if the fitting remedies be not at once and with a bold hand applied, may become chronic,

* The reader curious in such matters may refer (if he can find them) to "A Sermon preached on the Anniversary of the Dark Day," "An Artillery Election Sermon," "A Discourse on the Late Eclipse," "Dorcas, a Funeral Sermon on the Death of Madam Submit Tidd, Relict of the late Experience Tidd, Esq.," &c., &c.

and render one, who might else have become in due time an ornament of the social circle, a painful object even to nearest friends and relatives. But thinking, on a further experience, that there was a germ of promise in him which required only culture and the pulling up of weeds from around it, I thought it best to set before him the acknowledged examples of English composition in verse, and leave the rest to natural emulation. With this view, I accordingly lent him some volumes of Pope and Goldsmith, to the assiduous study of which he promised to devote his evenings. Not long afterward, he brought me some verses written upon that model, a specimen of which I subjoin, having changed some phrases of less elegancy, and a few rhymes objectionable to the cultivated ear. The poem consisted of childish reminiscences, and the sketches which follow will not seem destitute of truth to those whose fortunate education began in a country village. And, first, let us hang up his charcoal portrait of the school-dame.

"Propt on the marsh, a dwelling now, I see
The humble school-house of my A, B, C,
Where well-drilled urchins, each behind his tire,
Waited in ranks the wished command to fire,
Then all together, when the signal came,
Discharged their *a-b abs* against the dame.
Daughter of Danaus, who could daily pour
In treacherous pipkins her Pierian store,
She, 'mid the volleyed learning firm and calm,
Patted the furloughed ferule on her palm,

And, to our wonder, could divine at once
Who flashed the pan, and who was downright dunce.

There young Devotion learned to climb with ease
The gnarly limbs of Scripture family-trees,
And he was most commended and admired
Who soonest to the topmost twig perspired;
Each name was called as many various ways
As pleased the reader's ear on different days,
So that the weather, or the ferule's stings,
Colds in the head, or fifty other things,
Transformed the helpless Hebrew thrice a week
To guttural Pequot or resounding Greek,
The vibrant accent skipping here and there,
Just as it pleased invention or despair;
No controversial Hebraist was the Dame;
With or without the points pleased her the same;
If any tyro found a name too tough,
And looked at her, pride furnished skill enough;
She nerved her larynx for the desperate thing,
And cleared the five-barred syllables at a spring.

Ah, dear old times! there once it was my hap,
Perched on a stool, to wear the long-eared cap;
From books degraded, there I sat at ease,
A drone, the envy of compulsory bees;
Rewards of merit, too, full many a time,
Each with its woodcut and its moral rhyme,
And pierced half-dollars hung on ribbons gay
About my neck—to be restored next day,
I carried home, rewards as shining then
As those which deck the lifelong pains of men,
More solid than the redemanded praise
With which the world beribbons later days.

Ah, dear old times! how brightly ye return!
How, rubbed afresh, your phosphor traces burn!
The ramble schoolward through dewsparkling meads;
The willow-wands turned Cinderella steeds;
The impromptu pinbent hook, the deep remorse
O'er the chance-captured minnow's inchlong corse;
The pockets, plethoric with marbles round,
That still a space for ball and pegtop found,
Nor satiate yet, could manage to confine
Horsechestnuts, flagroot, and the kite's wound twine,
And, like the prophet's carpet could take in,
Enlarging still, the popgun's magazine;
The dinner carried in the small tin pail,
Shared with the dog, whose most beseeching tail
And dripping tongue and eager ears belied
The assumed indifference of canine pride;
The caper homeward, shortened if the cart
Of neighbor Pomeroy, trundling from the mart,
O'ertook me,—then, translated to the seat
I praised the steed, how staunch he was and fleet,
While the bluff farmer, with superior grin,
Explained where horses should be thick, where thin,
And warned me (joke he always had in store)
To shun a beast that four white stockings wore.
What a fine natural courtesy was his!
His nod was pleasure, and his full bow bliss;
How did his well-thumbed hat, with ardor rapt,
Its decorous curve to every rank adapt!
How did it graduate with a courtly ease
The whole long scale of social differences,
Yet so gave each his measure running o'er,
None thought his own was less, his neighbor's more
The squire was flattered, and the pauper knew
Old times acknowledged 'neath the threadbare blue!
Dropped at the corner of the embowered lane,

Whistling I wade the knee-deep leaves again,
While eager Argus, who has missed all day
The sharer of his condescending play,
Comes leaping onward with a bark elate
And boisterous tail to greet me at the gate;
That I was true in absence to our love
Let the thick dog's-ears in my primer prove."

I add only one further extract, which will possess a melancholy interest to all such as have endeavored to glean the materials of revolutionary history from the lips of aged persons, who took a part in the actual making of it, and, finding the manufacture profitable, continued the supply in an adequate proportion to the demand.

" Old Joe is gone, who saw hot Percy goad
His slow artillery up the Concord road,
A tale which grew in wonder, year by year,
As, every time he told it, Joe drew near
To the main fight, till, faded and grown gray,
The original scene to bolder tints gave way;
Then Joe had heard the foe's scared double-quick
Beat on stove drum with one uncaptured stick,
And, ere death came the lengthening tale to lop,
Himself had fired, and seen a red-coat drop;
Had Joe lived long enough, that scrambling fight
Had squared more nearly with his sense of right,
And vanquished Percy, to complete the tale,
Had hammered stone for life in Concord jail."

I do not know that the foregoing extracts ought not to be called my own rather than Mr. Biglow's, as, indeed, he maintained stoutly that my file had left nothing of his in them. I should not, perhaps, have felt entitled to take so great liberties with them, had I not more than suspected an hereditary vein of poetry in myself, a very near ancestor having written a Latin poem in the Harvard *Gratulatio* on the accession of George the Third. Suffice it to say, that, whether not satisfied with such limited approbation as I could conscientiously bestow, or from a sense of natural inaptitude, certain it is that my young friend could never be induced to any further essays in this kind. He affirmed that it was to him like writing in a foreign tongue,—that Mr. Pope's versification was like the regular ticking of one of Willard's clocks, in which one could fancy, after long listening, a certain kind of rhythm or tune, but which yet was only a poverty-stricken *tick, tick*, after all,—and that he had never seen a sweet-water on a trellis growing so fairly, or in forms so pleasing to his eye, as a fox-grape over a scrub-oak in a swamp. He added I know not what, to the effect that the sweet-water would only be the more disfigured by having its leaves starched and ironed out, and that Pegāsus (so he called him) hardly looked right with his mane and tail in curl-papers. These and other such opinions I did not long strive to eradicate, attributing them rather to a defective education and senses untuned by too long familiarity with purely natural objects, than to a perverted moral sense. I was the more inclined to this leniency since sufficient evidence was not to seek, that his verses, as wanting as they certainly were in classic polish and point, had somehow taken hold of the public ear in a surprising manner. So, only setting him right as to the quantity of the proper name Pegasus, I left him to follow the bent of his natural genius.

Yet could I not surrender him wholly to the tutelage of the pagan (which, literally interpreted, signifies village) muse without yet a farther effort for his conversion, and to this end I resolved that whatever of poetic fire yet burned in myself, aided by the assiduous bellows of correct models, should be put in requisition. Accordingly, when my ingenious young parishioner brought to my study a copy of verses which he had written touching the acquisition of territory resulting from the Mexican war, and the folly of leaving the question of slavery or freedom to the adjudication of chance, I did myself indite a short fable or apologue after the manner of Gay and Prior, to the end that he might see how easily even such subjects as he treated of were capable of a more refined style and more elegant expression. Mr. Biglow's production was as follows:

THE TWO GUNNERS,

A FABLE.

Two fellers, Isrel named and Joe,
One Sundy mornin' 'greed to go
Agunnin' soon's the bells wuz done
And meetin' finally begun,
So'st no one wouldn't be about
Ther Sabbath-breakin' to spy out.

Joe didn't want to go a mite;
He felt ez though 'twarnt skeercely right,
But, when his doubts he went to speak on,
Isrel he up and called him Deacon,
An' kep' apokin' fun like sin
An' then arubbin' on it in,
Till Joe, less skeered o' doin' wrong
Than bein' laughed at, went along.

Past noontime they went trampin' round
An' nary thing to pop at found,
Till, fairly tired o' their spree,
They leaned their guns agin a tree,
An' jest ez they wuz settin' down
To take their noonin', Joe looked roun'
And see (across lots in a pond
That warn't more'n twenty rod beyond,)
A goose that on the water sot
Ez ef awaitin' to be shot.

Isrel he ups and grabs his gun;
Sez he, "By ginger, here's some fun!"

"Don't fire," sez Joe, it aint no use,
Thet's Deacon Peleg's tame wild-goose;"
Sez Isrel, "I don't care a cent,
I've sighted an' I'll let her went;"
Bang! went queen's-arm, ole gander flopped
His wings a spell, an' quorked, an' dropped.

Sez Joe, "I wouldn't ha' been hired
At that poor critter to ha' fired,
But, sence it's clean gin up the ghost,
We'll hev the tallest kind o' roast;
I guess our waistbands 'll be tight
'Fore it comes ten o'clock ternight."

"I won't agree to no such bender,"
Sez Isrel, "keep it tell it's tender;
'Taint wuth a snap afore it's ripe."
Sez Joe, "I'd jest ez lives eat tripe;
You *air* a buster ter suppose
I'd eat what makes me hole my nose!"

So they disputed to an' fro
Till cunnin' Isrel sez to Joe
"Don't less stay here an' play the fool,
Less wait till both on us git cool,
Jest for a day or two less hide it
An' then toss up an' so decide it."
"Agreed!" sez Joe, an' so they did,
An' the ole goose wuz safely hid.

Now 'twuz the hottest kind o' weather,
An' when at last they come together,
It didn't signify which won,
Fer all the mischief hed ben done:
The goose wuz there, but, fer his soul,

Joe wouldn't ha' tetched it with a pole;
But Isrel kind o' liked the smell on't
An' made *his* dinner very well on't.

My own humble attempt was in manner and form following, and I print it here, I sincerely trust, out of no vain-glory, but solely with the hope of doing good.

LEAVING THE MATTER OPEN.

A TALE.

BY HOMER WILBUR, A. M.

Two brothers once, an ill-matched pair,
Together dwelt (no matter where,)
To whom an Uncle Sam, or some one,
Had left a house and farm in common:
The two in principles and habits
Were different as rats from rabbits;
Stout farmer North, with frugal care,
Laid up provision for his heir,
Not scorning with hard sun-browned hands
To scrape acquaintance with his lands;
Whatever thing he had to do
He did, and made it pay him, too;
He sold his waste stone by the pound,
His drains made water-wheels spin round,
His ice in summer-time he sold,
His wood brought profit when 'twas cold,
He dug and delved from morn till night,

Strove to make profit square with right,
Lived on his means, cut no great dash,
And paid his debts in honest cash.

On tother hand, his brother South
Lived very much from hand to mouth,
Played gentleman, nursed dainty hands,
Borrowed North's money on his lands,
And culled his morals and his graces
From cock-pits, bar-rooms, fights, and races;
His sole work in the farming line
Was keeping droves of long-legged swine,
Which brought great bothers and expenses
To North in looking after fences,
And, when they happened to break through,
Cost him both time and temper too,
For South insisted it was plain
He ought to drive them home again,
And North consented to the work
Because he loved to buy cheap pork.

Meanwhile, South's swine increasing fast,
His farm became too small at last,
So, having thought the matter over,
And feeling bound to live in clover
And never pay the clover's worth,
He said one day to brother North:—

"Our families are both increasing,
And, though we labor without ceasing,
Our produce soon will be too scant
To keep our children out of want;
They who wish fortune to be lasting
Must be both prudent and forecasting;
We soon shall need more land; a lot

I know, that cheaply can be bo't;
You lend the cash, I'll buy the acres,
And we'll be equally partakers."

Poor North, whose Anglo-Saxon blood
Gave him a hankering after mud,
Wavered a moment, then consented,
And, when the cash was paid, repented;
To make the new land worth a pin,
Thought he, it must be all fenced in,
For, if South's swine once get the run on't
No kind of farming can be done on't;
If that don't suit the other side,
'Tis best we instantly divide.

But somehow South could ne'er incline
This way or that to run the line,
And always found some new pretence
'Gainst setting the division fence;
At last he said:—

"For peace's sake,
Liberal concessions I will make;
Though I believe, upon my soul,
I've a just title to the whole,
I'll make an offer which I call
Gen'rous,—we'll have no fence at all;
Then both of us, whene'er we choose,
Can take what part we want to use;
If you should chance to need it first,
Pick you the best, I'll take the worst."

"Agreed!" cried North; thought he, this fall
With wheat and rye I'll sow it all,
In that way I shall get the start,

And South may whistle for his part;
So thought, so done, the field was sown,
And, winter having come and gone,
Sly North walked blithely forth to spy,
The progress of his wheat and rye;
Heavens, what a sight! his brother's swine
Had asked themselves all out to dine,
Such grunting, munching, rooting, shoving,
The soil seemed all alive and moving,
As for his grain, such work they'd made on't,
He couldn't spy a single blade on't.

Off in a rage he rushed to South,
"My wheat and rye"—grief choked his mouth;
"Pray don't mind me," said South, "but plant
All of the new land that you want;"
"Yes, but your hogs," cried North;

"The grain
Won't hurt them," answered South again;
"But they destroy my grain;"

"No doubt;
'Tis fortunate you've found it out;
Misfortunes teach, and only they,
You must not sow it in their way;"
"Nay, you," says North, "must keep them out;"
"Did I create them with a snout?"
Asked South demurely; "as agreed,
"The land is open to your seed,
And would you fain prevent my pigs
From running there their harmless rigs?
God knows I view this compromise
With not the most approving eyes;
I gave up my unquestioned rights

For sake of quiet days and nights,
I offered then, you know 'tis true,
To cut the piece of land in two."
"Then cut it now," growls North;

"Abate
Your heat," says South, "'tis now too late;
I offered you the rocky corner,
But you, of your own good the scorner,
Refused to take it; I am sorry;
No doubt you might have found a quarry,
Perhaps a gold-mine, for aught I know,
Containing heaps of native rhino;
You can't expect me to resign
My right"—

"But where," quoth North, "are mine?"
"*Your* rights," says tother, "well, that's funny,
I bought the land"—

"*I* paid the money;"
"That," answered South, "is from the point,
The ownership, you'll grant, is joint;
I'm sure my only hope and trust is
Not law so much as abstract justice,
Though, you remember, 'twas agreed
That so and so—consult the deed;
Objections now are out of date,
They might have answered once, but Fate
Quashes them at the point we've got to;
Obsta principiis, that's my motto."
So saying, South began to whistle
And looked as obstinate as gristle,
While North went homeward, each brown paw
Clenched like a knot of natural law,

And all the while, in either ear,
Heard something clicking wondrous clear.

To turn now to other matters, there are two things upon which it would seem fitting to dilate somewhat more largely in this place,—the Yankee character and the Yankee dialect. And, first, of the Yankee character, which has wanted neither open maligners, nor even more dangerous enemies in the persons of those unskilful painters who have given to it that hardness, angularity, and want of proper perspective, which, in truth, belonged, not to their subject, but to their own niggard and unskilful pencil.

New England was not so much the colony of a mother country, as a Hagar driven forth into the wilderness. The little self-exiled band which came hither in 1620 came, not to seek gold, but to found a democracy. They came that they might have the privilege to work and pray, to sit upon hard benches and listen to painful preachers as long as they would, yea, even unto thirty-seventhly, if the spirit so willed it. And surely, if the Greek might boast his Thermopylæ, where three hundred men fell in resisting the Persian, we may well be proud of our Plymouth Rock, where a handful of men, women, and children not merely faced, but vanquished, winter, famine, the wilderness, and the yet more invincible *storge* that drew them back to the green island far away. These four d no lotus growing upon the surly shore, the taste of which could make them forget their little native Ithaca nor were they so wanting to themselves in faith as to burn their ship, but could see the fair west wind belly the homeward sail, and then turn unrepining to grapple with the terrible Unknown.

As Want was the prime foe these hardy exodists had to fortress themselves against, so it is little wonder if that traditional feud is long in wearing out of the stock. The wounds of the old warfare were long ahealing, and an east wind of hard times puts a new ache in every one of them. Thrift was the first lesson in their hornbook, pointed out, letter after letter, by the lean finger of the hard schoolmaster, Necessity. Neither were those plump, rosy-gilled Englishmen that came hither, but a hard-faced, atrabilious, earnest-eyed race, stiff from long wrestling with the Lord in prayer, and who had taught Satan to dread the new Puritan hug. Add two hundred years' influence of soil, climate, and exposure, with its necessary result of idiosyncrasies, and we have the present Yankee, full of expedients, half-master of all trades, inventive in all but the beautiful, full of shifts, not yet capable of comfort, armed at all points against the old enemy Hunger, longanimous, good at patching, not so careful for what is best as for what will *do*, with a clasp to his purse and a button to his pocket, not skilled to build against Time, as in old countries, but against sore-pressing Need, accustomed to move the world with no ποῦ στῶ but his own two feet, and no lever but his own long forecast. A strange hybrid, indeed, did circumstance beget, here in the New World, upon the old Puritan stock, and the earth never before saw such mystic-practicalism, such niggard-geniality, such calculating-fanaticism, such cast-iron-enthusiasm, such sourfaced-humor, such close-fisted-generosity. This new *Græculus esuriens* will make a living out of any thing. He will invent new trades as well as tools. His brain is his capital, and he will get education at all risks. Put him on Juan Fernandez, and he would make a spelling-book first, and a salt-pan afterward. *In cœlum, jusseris, ibit,*—or the other way either,—it is all one, so any thing is to be got by it. Yet, after all, thin, speculative Jonathan is more like the Englishman of two centuries ago than John Bull himself is. He has lost somewhat in solidity, has become fluent and adaptable, but more of the original groundwork of character remains. He feels more at home with Fulke Greville, Herbert of Cherbury, Quarles, George Herbert, and Browne, than with his modern English cousins. He is nearer than John, by at least a hundred years, to Naseby, Marston Moor, Worcester, and the time when, if ever, there were true Englishmen. John Bull has suffered the idea of the Invisible to be very much fattened out of him. Jonathan is conscious still that he lives in the world of the Unseen as well as of the Seen. To move John, you must make your fulcrum of solid beef and pudding; an abstract idea will do for Jonathan.

*** TO THE INDULGENT READER.

My friend, the Reverend Mr. Wilbur, having been seized with a dangerous fit of illness, before this Introduction had passed through the press, and being incapacitated for all literary exertion, sent to me his notes, memoranda, &c., and requested me to fashion them into some shape more fitting for the general eye. This, owing to the fragmentary and disjointed state of his manuscripts, I have felt wholly unable to do; yet, being unwilling that the reader should be deprived of such parts of his lucubrations as seemed more finished, and not well discerning how to segregate these from the rest, I have concluded to send them all to the press precisely as they are.

Columbus Nye,
Pastor of a Church in Bungtown Corner.

It remains to speak of the Yankee dialect. And, first, it may be premised, in a general way, that any one much read in the writings of the early colonists need not be told that the far greater share of the words and phrases now esteemed peculiar to New England, and local there, were brought from the mother country. A person familiar with the dialect of certain portions of Massachusetts will not fail to recognize, in ordinary discourse, many words now noted in English vocabularies as archaic, the greater part of which were in common use about the time of the King James translation of the Bible. Shakspeare stands less in need of a glossary to most New Englanders than to many a native of the Old Country. The peculiarities of our speech, however, are rapidly wearing out. As there is no country where reading is so universal and newspapers are so multitudinous, so no phrase remains long local, but is transplanted in the mail-bags to every remotest corner of the land. Consequently our dialect approaches nearer to uniformity than that of any other nation.

The English have complained of us for coining new words. Many of those so stigmatized were old ones by them forgotten, and all make now an unquestioned part of the currency, wherever English is spoken. Undoubtedly, we have a right to make new words, as they are needed by the fresh aspects under which life presents itself here in the New World; and, indeed, wherever a language is alive, it grows. It might be questioned whether we could not establish a stronger title to the ownership of the English tongue than the mother-islanders themselves. Here, past all question, is to be its great home and centre. And not only is it already spoken here by greater numbers, but with a far higher popular average of correctness, than in Britain. The great writers of it, too, we might claim as ours, were ownership to be settled by the number of readers and lovers.

As regards the provincialisms to be met with in this volume, I may say that the reader will not find one which is not (as I believe) either native or imported with the early settlers, nor one which I have not, with my own ears, heard in familiar use. In the metrical portion of the book, I have endeavoured to adapt the spelling as nearly as possible to the ordinary mode of pronunciation Let the reader who deems me over-particular remember this caution of Martial:—

> "*Quem recitas, meus est, O Fidentine, libellus;*
> *Sed male cum recitas, incipit esse tuus.*"

A few further explanatory remarks will not be impertinent.

I shall barely lay down a few general rules for the reader's guidance.

1. The genuine Yankee never gives the rough sound to the *r* when he can help it, and often displays considerable ingenuity in avoiding it even before a vowel.

2. He seldom sounds the final *g*, a piece of self-denial, if we consider his partiality for nasals. The same of the final *d*, as *han'* and *stan'* for *hand* and *stand*.

3. The *h* in such words as *while*, *when*, *where*, he omits altogether.

4. In regard to *a*, he shows some inconsistency, sometimes giving a close and obscure sound, as *hev*

for *have*, *hendy* for *handy*, *ez* for *as*, *thet* for *that*, and again giving it the broad sound it has in *father*, as *hânsome* for *handsome*.

5. To the sound *ou* he prefixes an *e* (hard to exemplify otherwise than orally.)

The following passage in Shakspeare he would recite thus:—

"Neow is the winta uv eour discontent
Med glorious summa by this sun o' Yock,
An' all the cleouds thet leowered upun eour heouse
In the deep buzzum o' the oshin buried;
Neow air eour breows beound 'ith victorious wreaths;
Eour breused arms hung up fer monimunce;
Eour starn alarums chănged to merry meetins,
Eour dreffle marches to delightful measures.
Grim-visaged war heth smeuthed his wrinkled front,
An' neow, instid o' mountin' barebid steeds
To fright the souls o' ferfle edverseries,
He capers nimly in a lady's chămber,
To the lascivious pleasin' uv a loot."

6. *Au*, in such words as *daughter* and *slaughter*, he pronounces *ah*.

7. To the dish thus seasoned add a drawl *ad libitum*.

[Mr. Wilbur's notes here become entirely fragmentary. —C. N.]

a. Unable to procure a likeness of Mr. Biglow, I thought the curious reader might be gratified with a sight of the editorial effigies. And here a choice between two was offered,—the one a profile (entirely black) cut by Doyle, the other a portrait painted by a native artist of much promise. The first of these seemed wanting in expression, and in the second a slight obliquity of the visual organs has been heightened (perhaps from an over-desire of force on the part of the artist) into too close an approach to actual *strabismus.* This slight divergence in my optical apparatus from the ordinary model—however I may have been taught to regard it in the light of a mercy rather than a cross, since it enabled me to give as much of directness and personal application to my discourses as met the wants of my congregation, without risk of offending any by being supposed to have him or her in my eye (as the saying is)—seemed yet to Mrs. Wilbur a sufficient objection to the engraving of the aforesaid painting. We read of many who either absolutely refused to allow the copying of their features, as especially did Plotinus and Agesilaus among the ancients, not to mention the more modern instances of Scioppius, Palæottus, Pinellus, Velserus, Gataker, and others, or were indifferent thereto, as Cromwell.

β. Yet was Cæsar desirous of concealing his baldness. *Per contra,* my Lord Protector's carefulness in the matter of his wart might be cited.

Men generally more desirous of being *improved* in their portraits than characters. Shall probably find very unflattered likenesses of ourselves in Recording Angel's gallery.

γ. Whether any of our national peculiarities may be traced to our use of stoves, as a certain closeness of the lips in pronunciation, and a smothered smoulderingness of disposition, seldom roused to open flame? An unrestrained intercourse with fire probably conducive to generosity and hospitality of soul. Ancient Mexicans used stoves, as the friar Augustin Ruiz reports, Hakluyt, III., 468,—but Popish priests not always reliable authority.

To-day picked my Isabella grapes. Crop injured by attacks of rose-bug in the spring. Whether Noah was justifiable in preserving this class of insects?

δ. Concerning Mr. Biglow's pedigree. Tolerably certain that there was never a poet among his ancestors. An ordination hymn attributed to a maternal uncle, but perhaps a sort of production not demanding the creative faculty.

His grandfather a painter of the grandiose or Michael Angelo school. Seldom painted objects smaller than houses or barns, and these with uncommon expression.

ε. Of the Wilburs no complete pedigree. The crest said to be a *wild boar*, whence, perhaps, the name.(?) A connection with the Earls of Wilbraham (*quasi* wild boar ham) might be made out. This suggestion worth following up. In 1677, John W. m. Expect——, had issue, 1. John, 2. Haggai, 3. Expect, 4. Ruhamah, 5. Desire.

> "Hear lyes ye bodye of Mrs Expect Wilber,
> Y^e^ crewell salvages they kil'd her
> Together wth other Christian soles eleaven,
> October ye ix daye, 1707.
> Y^e^ stream of Jordan sh' as crost ore
> And now expeacts me on ye other shore:
> I live in hope her soon to join;
> Her earthlye yeeres were forty and nine."
>
> *From Gravestone in Pekussett, North Parish.*

This is unquestionably the same John who afterward (1711) married Tabitha Hagg or Ragg.

But if this were the case, she seems to have died early; for only three years after, namely, 1714, we have evidence that he married Winifred, daughter of Lieutenant Tipping.

He seems to have been a man of substance, for we find him in 1696 conveying "one undivided eightieth part of a salt-meadow" in Yabbok, and he commanded a sloop in 1702.

Those who doubt the importance of genealogical studies *fuste potius quam argumento erudiendi.*

I trace him as far as 1723, and there lose him. In that year he was chosen selectman.

No gravestone. Perhaps overthrown when new hearse-house was built, 1802.

He was probably the son of John, who came from Bilham Comit. Salop. circa 1642.

This first John was a man of considerable importance, being twice mentioned with the honorable prefix of *Mr.* in the town records. Name spelt with two *l*-s.

> "Hear lyeth ye bod [*stone unhappily broken.*]
> Mr. Ihon Willber [Esq.] [*I inclose this in brackets as doubtful. To me it seems clear.*]
> Ob't die [*illegible; looks like xviii.*] . . . . . iii [*prob.* 1693.]
> . . . . . . paynt
> . . . . . deseased seinte:
> A friend and [fath]er untoe all ye opreast,
> Hee gave ye wicked familists noe reast,
> When Sat[an bl]ewe his Antinomian blaste,
> Wee clong to [Willber as a steadf]ast maste.
> [A]gaynst ye horrid Qua[kers] . . . . .

It is greatly to be lamented that this curious epitaph is mutilated. It is said that the sacrilegious British soldiers made a target of this stone during the war of Independence. How odious an animosity which pauses not at the grave! How brutal that which spares not the monuments of authentic history! This is not improbably from the pen of Rev. Moody Pyram, who is mentioned by Hubbard as having been noted for a silver vein of poetry. If his papers be still extant, a copy might possibly be recovered.

CONTENTS.

THE BIGLOW PAPERS.

No. I.

A LETTER

FROM MR. EZEKIEL BIGLOW OF JAALAM TO THE HON. JOSEPH T. BUCKINGHAM, EDITOR OF THE BOSTON COURIER, INCLOSING A POEM OF HIS SON, MR. HOSEA BIGLOW.

JAYLEM, june 1846.

MISTER EDDYTER:—Our Hosea wuz down to Boston last week, and he see a cruetin Sarjunt a struttin round as popler as a hen with 1 chicking, with 2 fellers a drummin and fifin arter him like all nater. the sarjunt he thout Hosea hedn't gut his i teeth cut cos he looked a kindo's though he'd jest com down, so he cal'lated to hook him in, but Hosy woodn't take none o' his sarse for all he hed much as 20 Rooster's tales stuck onto his hat and eenamost enuf brass a bobbin up and down on his shoulders and figureed onto his coat and trousis, let alone wut nater hed sot in his featers, to make a 6 pounder out on.

wal, Hosea he com home considerabal riled, and arter I'd gone to bed I heern Him a thrashin round like a short-tailed Bull in fli-time. The old Woman ses she to me ses she, Zekle, ses she, our Hosee's gut the chollery or suthin anuther ses she, don't you Bee skeered, ses I, he's oney amakin pottery * ses i, he's ollers on hand at that ere busynes like Da & martin, and shure enuf, cum mornin, Hosy he cum down stares full chizzle, hare on eend and cote tales flyin, and sot rite of to go reed his varses to Parson Wilbur bein he haint aney grate shows o' book larnin himself, bimeby he cum back and sed the parson wuz dreffle tickled with 'em as i hoop you will Be, and said they wuz True grit.

Hosea ses taint hardly fair to call 'em hisn now, cos the parson kind o' slicked off sum o' the last varses, but he told Hosee he didnt want to put his ore in to tetch to the Rest on 'em, bein they wuz verry well As thay wuz, and then Hosy ses he sed suthin a nuther about Simplex Mundishes or sum sech feller, but I guess Hosea kind o' didn't hear him, for I never hearn o' nobody o' that name in this villadge, and I've lived here man and boy 76 year cum next tater diggin, and thair aint no wheres a kitting spryer 'n I be.

* *Aut insanit, aut versos facit.*—H. W.

If you print 'em I wish you'd jest let folks know who hosy's father is, cos my ant Keziah used to say it's nater to be curus ses she, she aint livin though and he's a likely kind o' lad.

EZEKIEL BIGLOW

THRASH away, you'll *hev* to rattle
  On them kittle-drums o' yourn,—
'Taint a knowin' kind o' cattle
  Thet is ketched with mouldy corn;
Put in stiff, you fifer feller,
  Let folks see how spry you be,—
Guess you'll toot till you are yeller
  'Fore you git ahold o' me!

Thet air flag's a leetle rotten,
  Hope it aint your Sunday's best;—
Fact! it takes a sight o' cotton
  To stuff out a soger's chest:
Sence we farmers hev to pay fer't,
  Ef you must wear humps like these,
Sposin' you should try salt hay fer't,
  It would du ez slick ez grease.

'Twouldn't suit them Southun fellers,
  They're a dreffle graspin' set,
We must ollers blow the bellers
  Wen they want their irons het;
May be it's all right ez preachin',
  But *my* narves it kind o' grates,
Wen I see the overreachin'
  O' them nigger-drivin' States.

Them thet rule us, them slave-traders,
  Haint they cut a thunderin' swarth,
(Helped by Yankee renegaders,)
  Thru the vartu o' the North!
We begin to think it's nater
  To take sarse an' not be riled;—
Who'd expect to see a tater
  All on eend at bein' biled?

Ez fer war, I call it murder,—
  There you hev it plain an' flat;
I don't want to go no furder
  Than my Testyment fer that;
God hez sed so plump an' fairly,
  It's ez long ez it is broad,
An' you've gut to git up airly
  Ef you want to take in God.

'Taint your eppyletts an' feathers
  Make the thing a grain more right;
'Taint afollerin' your bell-wethers
  Will excuse ye in His sight;
Ef you take a sword an' dror it,
  An' go stick a feller thru,
Guv'ment aint to answer for it,
  God'll send the bill to you.

Wut's the use o' meetin'-goin'
  Every Sabbath, wet or dry,
Ef it's right to go amowin'
  Feller-men like oats an' rye?
I dunno but wut it's pooty
  Trainin' round in bobtail coats,—
But it's curus Christian dooty
  This 'ere cuttin' folks's throats.

They may talk o' Freedom's airy
  Tell they're pupple in the face,—

It's a grand gret cemetary
  Fer the barthrights of our race;
They jest want this Californy
  So's to lug new slave-states in
To abuse ye, an' to scorn ye,
  An' to plunder ye like sin.

Aint it cute to see a Yankee
  Take sech everlastin' pains,
All to git the Devil's thankee,
  Helpin' on 'em weld their chains?
Wy, it's jest ez clear ez figgers,
  Clear ez one an' one make two,
Chaps thet make black slaves o' niggers
  Want to make wite slaves o' you.

Tell ye jest the eend I've come to
  Arter cipherin' plaguy smart,
An' it makes a handy sum, tu,
  Any gump could larn by heart;
Laborin' man an' laborin' woman
  Hev one glory an' one shame,
Ev'y thin' thet's done inhuman
  Injers all on 'em the same.

'Taint by turnin' out to hack folks
  You're agoin' to git your right,
Nor by lookin' down on black folks
  Coz you're put upon by wite;
Slavery aint o' nary color,
  'Taint the hide thet makes it wus,
All it keers fer in a feller
  'S jest to make him fill its pus.

Want to tackle *me* in, du ye?
  I expect you'll hev to wait;

Wen cold lead puts daylight thru ye
  You'll begin to kal'late;
'Spose the crows wun't fall to pickin'
  All the carkiss from your bones,
Coz you helped to give a lickin'
  To them poor half-Spanish drones?

Jest go home an' ask our Nancy
  Wether I'd be sech a goose
Ez to jine ye,—guess you'd fancy
  The etarnal bung wuz loose!
She wants me fer home consumption,
  Let alone the hay's to mow,—
Ef you're arter folks o' gumption,
  You've a darned long row to hoe.

Take them editors thet's crowin'
  Like a cockerel three months old,—
Don't ketch any on 'em goin',
  Though they *be* so blasted bold;
Aint they a prime lot o' fellers?
  'Fore they think on't they will sprout,
(Like a peach thet's got the yellers,)
  With the meanness bustin' out.

Wal, go 'long to help 'em stealin'
  Bigger pens to cram with slaves,
Help the men thet's ollers dealin'
  Insults on your fathers' graves;
Help the strong to grind the feeble,
  Help the many agin the few,
Help the men thet call your people
  Witewashed slaves an' peddlin' crew!

Massachusetts, God forgive her,
  She's akneelin' with the rest,

She, thet ough' to ha' clung fer ever
  In her grand old eagle-nest;
She thet ough' to stand so fearless
  Wile the wracks are round her hurled,
Holdin' up a beacon peerless
  To the oppressed of all the world!

Haint they sold your colored seamen?
  Haint they made your env'ys wiz?
Wut'll make ye act like freemen?
  Wut'll git your dander riz?
Come, I'll tell ye wut I'm thinkin'
  Is our dooty in this fix,
They'd ha' done 't ez quick ez winkin'
  In the days o' seventy-six.

Clang the bells in every steeple,
  Call all true men to disown
The tradoocers of our people,
  The enslavers o' their own;
Let our dear old Bay State proudly
  Put the trumpet to her mouth,
Let her ring this messidge loudly
  In the ears of all the South:—

"I'll return ye good fer evil
  Much ez we frail mortils can,
But I wun't go help the Devil
  Makin' man the cus o' man;
Call me coward, call me traiter,
  Jest ez suits your mean idees,—
Here I stand a tyrant-hater,
  An' the friend o' God an' Peace!"

Ef I'd *my* way I hed ruther
  We should go to work an' part,—

They take one way, we take t'other,—
  Guess it wouldn't break my heart;
Man hed ough' to put asunder
  Them thet God has noways jined;
An' I shouldn't gretly wonder
  Ef there's thousands o' my mind.

[The first recruiting sergeant on record I conceive to have been that individual who is mentioned in the Book of Job as *going to and fro in the earth, and walking up and down in it*. Bishop Latimer will have him to have been a bishop, but to me that other calling would appear more congenial. The sect of Cainites is not yet extinct, who esteemed the first-born of Adam to be the most worthy, not only because of that privilege of primogeniture, but inasmuch as he was able to overcome and slay his younger brother. That was a wise saying of the famous Marquis Pescara to the Papal Legate, that *it was impossible for men to serve Mars and Christ at the same time*. Yet in time past the profession of arms was judged to be κατ' ἐξοχήν that of a gentleman, nor does this opinion want for strenuous upholders even in our day. Must we suppose, then, that the profession of Christianity was only intended for losels, or, at best, to afford an opening for plebeian ambition? Or shall we hold with that nicely metaphysical Pomeranian, Captain Vratz, who was Count Königsmark's chief instrument in the murder of Mr. Thynne, that the Scheme of Salvation has been arranged with an especial eye to the necessities of the upper classes, and that "God would consider *a gentleman* and deal with him suitably to the condition and profession he had placed him in"? It may be said of us all, *Exemplo plus quam ratione vivimus.* —H. W.]

No. II.

A LETTER

FROM MR. HOSEA BIGLOW TO THE HON. J. T. BUCKINGHAM, EDITOR OF THE BOSTON COURIER, COVERING A LETTER FROM MR. B. SAWIN, PRIVATE IN THE MASSACHUSETTS REGIMENT.

[This letter of Mr. Sawin's was not originally written in verse. Mr. Biglow, thinking it peculiarly susceptible of metrical adornment, translated it, so to speak, into his own vernacular tongue. This is not the time to consider the question, whether rhyme be a mode of expression natural to the human race. If leisure from other and more important avocations be granted, I will handle the matter more at large in an appendix to the present volume. In this place I will barely remark, that I have sometimes noticed in the unlanguaged prattlings of infants a fondness for alliteration, assonance, and even rhyme, in which natural predisposition we may trace the three degrees through which our Anglo-Saxon verse rose to its culmination in the poetry of Pope. I would not be understood as questioning in these remarks that pious theory which supposes that children, if left entirely to themselves, would naturally discourse in Hebrew. For this the authority of one experiment is claimed, and I could, with Sir Thomas Browne, desire its establishment, inasmuch as the acquirement of that sacred tongue would thereby be facilitated. I am aware that Herodotus states the conclusion of Psammeticus to have been in favor of a dialect of the Phrygian. But, beside the chance that a trial of this importance would hardly be blessed to a Pagan monarch whose only motive was curiosity, we have on the Hebrew side the comparatively recent investigation of James the Fourth of Scotland. I will add to this prefatory remark, that Mr. Sawin, though a native of Jaalam, has never been a stated attendant on the religious exercises of my congregation. I consider my humble efforts prospered in that not one of my sheep hath ever indued the wolf's clothing of war, save for the comparatively innocent diversion of a militia training. Not that my flock are backward to undergo the hardships of *defensive* warfare. They serve cheerfully in the great army which fights even unto death *pro aris et focis*, accoutred with the spade, the axe, the plane, the sledge, the spelling-book, and other such effectual weapons against want and ignorance and unthrift. I have taught them (under God) to esteem our human institutions as but tents of a night, to be stricken whenever Truth puts the bugle to her lips and sounds a march to the heights of wider-viewed intelligence and more perfect organization.—H. W.]

Mister Buckinum, the follerin Billet was writ hum by a Yung feller of our town that wuz cussed fool enuff to goe atrottin inter Miss Chiff arter a Drum and fife. it ain't Nater for a feller to let on that he's sick o' any bizness that He went intu off his own free will and a Cord, but I rather cal'late he's middlin tired o' voluntearin By this Time. I bleeve u may put dependunts on his statemence. For I never heered nothin bad on him let Alone his havin what Parson Wilbur cals a *pongshong* for cocktales, and he ses it wuz a soshiashun of idees sot him agoin arter the Crootin Sargient cos he wore a cocktale onto his hat.

his Folks gin the letter to me and i shew it to parson Wilbur and he ses it oughter Bee printed. send It to mister Buckinum, ses he, i don't ollers agree with him, ses he, but by Time,* ses he, I *du* like a feller that ain't a Feared.

I have intusspussed a Few reflecksbuns hear and thair. We're kind o' prest with Hayin.

Ewers respecfly

HOSEA BIGLOW.

THIS kind o' sogerin' aint a mite like our October
trainin',
A chap could clear right out from there ef 't only
looked like rainin',
An' th' Cunnles, tu, could kiver up their shappoes
with bandanners,

* In relation to this expression, I cannot but think that Mr. Biglow has been too hasty in attributing it to me. Though Time be a comparatively innocent personage to swear by, and though Longinus in his discourse Περὶ Ὕψους has commended timely oaths as not only a useful but sublime figure of speech, yet I have always kept my lips free from that abomination. *Odi profanum vulgus*, I hate your swearing and hectoring fellows.—H. W.

An' send the insines skootin' to the bar-room with their banners,
(Fear o' gittin' on 'em spotted,) an' a feller could cry quarter
Ef he fired away his ramrod arter tu much rum an' water.
Recollect wut fun we hed, you'n' I an' Ezry Hollis,
Up there to Waltham plain last fall, along o' the Cornwallis? *
This sort o' thing aint *jest* like thet,—I wish thet I wuz furder,—†
Nimepunce a day fer killin' folks comes kind o' low fer murder,
(Wy I've worked out to slarterin' some fer Deacon Cephas Billins,
An' in the hardest times there wuz I ollers tetched ten shillins,)
There's sutthin' gits into my throat thet makes it hard to swaller,
It comes so nateral to think about a hempen collar;
It's glory,—but, in spite o' all my tryin' to git callous,
I feel a kind o' in a cart, aridin' to the gallus.
But wen it comes to *bein'* killed,—I tell ye I felt streaked
The fust time 'tever I found out wy baggonets wuz peaked;
Here's how it wuz: I started out to go to a fandango,
The sentinul he ups an' sez, "Thet's furder 'an you can go."

* i hait the Site of a feller with a muskit as I du pizn But their is fun to a cornwallis I aint agoin' to deny it.—H. B.

† he means Not quite so fur I guess.—H. B.

"None o' your sarse," sez I; sez he, "Stan' back!"
"Aint you a buster?"
Sez I, "I'm up to all thet air, I guess I've ben to muster;
I know wy sentinuls air sot; you aint agoin' to eat us;
Caleb haint no monopoly to court the seenoreetas;
My folks to hum air full ez good ez hisn be, by golly!"
An' so ez I wuz goin' by, not thinkin' wut would folly,
The everlastin' cus he stuck his one-pronged pitchfork in me
An' made a hole right thru my close ez ef I wuz an in'my.

Wal, it beats all how big I felt hoorawin' in ole Funnel
Wen Mister Bolles he gin the sword to our Leftenant Cunnle,
(It's Mister Secondary Bolles,* thet writ the prize peace essay;
Thet's why he didn't list himself along o' us, I dessay,)
An' Rantoul, tu, talked pooty loud, but don't put *his* foot in it,
Coz human life's so sacred thet he's principled agin it,—
Though I myself can't rightly see it's any wus achokin' on 'em,
Than puttin' bullets thru their lights, or with a bagnet pokin' on 'em;
How dreffle slick he reeled it off, (like Blitz at our lyceum

* the ignerant creeter means Sekketary; but he ollers stuck to his books like cobbler's wax to an ile-stone.—H. B.

Ahaulin' ribbins from his chops so quick you skeercely see 'em,)
About the Anglo-Saxon race (an' saxons would be handy
To du the buryin' down here upon the Rio Grandy),
About our patriotic pas an' our star-spangled banner,
Our country's bird alookin' on an' singin' out hosanner,
An' how he (Mister B. himself) wuz happy fer Ameriky,—
I felt, ez sister Patience sez, a leetle mite histericky.
I felt, I swon, ez though it wuz a dreffle kind o' privilege
Atrampin' round thru Boston streets among the gutter's drivelage;
I act'lly thought it wuz a treat to hear a little drummin',
An' it did bonyfidy seem millanyum wuz acomin'
Wen all on us got suits (darned like them wore in the state prison)
An' every feller felt ez though all Mexico wuz hisn.*

This 'ere's about the meanest place a skunk could wal diskiver

* it must be aloud that thare's a streak o' nater in lovin' sho, but it sartinly is 1 of the curusest things in nater to see a rispecktable dri goods dealer (deekon off a chutch mayby) a riggin' himself out in the Weigh they du and struttin' round in the Reign aspilin' his trowsis and makin' wet goods of himself. Ef any thin's foolisher and moor dicklus than militerry gloary it is milishy gloary.—H. B.

(Saltillo 's Mexican, I b'lieve, fer wut we call Salt-river);
The sort o' trash a feller gits to eat doos beat all nater,
I'd give a year's pay fer a smell o' one good blue-nose tater;
The country here thet Mister Bolles declared to be so charmin'
Throughout is swarmin' with the most alarmin' kind o' varmin'.

He talked about delishis froots, but then it wuz a wopper all,
The holl on't 's mud an' prickly pears, with here an' there a chapparal;
You see a feller peekin' out, an', fust you know, a lariat
Is round your throat an' you a copse, 'fore you can say, "Wut air ye at?"*
You never see sech darned gret bugs (it may not be irrelevant
To say I've seen a *scarabœus pilularius*† big ez a year old elephant,)
The rigiment come up one day in time to stop a red bug
From runnin' off with Cunnle Wright,—'t wuz jest a common *cimex lectularius*.

One night I started up on eend an' thought I wuz to hum agin,

* these fellers are verry proppilly called Rank Heroes, and the more tha kill the ranker and more Herowick tha bekum.—H. B.

† it wuz "tumblebug" as he Writ it, but the parson put the Latten instid. i sed tother maid better meeter, but he said tha was eddykated peepl to Boston and tha wouldn't stan' it no how. idnow as tha *wood* and idnow *as* tha wood.—H. B.

I heern a horn, thinks I it's Sol the fisherman hez
    come agin,
His bellowses is sound enough,—ez I'm a livin'
    creeter,
I felt a thing go thru my leg,—'twuz nothin' more
    'n a skeeter!
Then there's the yaller fever, tu, they call it here
    el vomito,—
(Come, thet wun't du, you landcrab there, I tell ye
    to le' *go* my toe!
My gracious! it's a scorpion thet's took a shine to
    play with't,
I darsn't skeer the tarnal thing fer fear he'd run
    away with't.)
Afore I come away from hum I hed a strong per-
    suasion
Thet Mexicans worn't human beans,*—an ourang
    outang nation,
A sort o' folks a chap could kill an' never dream
    on't arter,
No more'n a feller'd dream o' pigs thet he hed
    hed to slarter;
I'd an idee thet they were built arter the darkie
    fashion all,
An' kickin' colored folks about, you know, 's a
    kind o' national;
But wen I jined I wornt so wise ez thet air queen
    o' Sheby,
Fer, come to look at 'em, they aint much diff'rent
    from wut we be,
An' here we air ascrougin' 'em out o' thir own
    dominions,

* he means human beins, that's wut he means. i spose he kinder thought tha wuz human beans ware the Xisle Poles comes from.—H. B.

Ashelterin' 'em, ez Caleb sez, under our eagle's
pinions,
Wich means to take a feller up jest by the slack o'
's trowsis
An' walk him Spanish clean right out o' all his
homes an' houses;
Wal, it doos seem a curus way, but then hooraw
fer Jackson!
It must be right, fer Caleb sez it's reg'lar Anglo-
saxon.
The Mex'cans don't fight fair, they say, they piz'n
all the water,
An' du amazin' lots o' things thet isn't wut they
ough' to;
Bein' they haint no lead, they make their bullets
out o' copper
An' shoot the darned things at us, tu, wich Caleb
sez aint proper;
He sez they'd ough' to stan' right up an' let us pop
'em fairly,
(Guess wen he ketches 'em at thet he'll hev to git
up airly,)
Thet our nation's bigger'n theirn an' so its rights
air bigger,
An' thet it's all to make 'em free thet we air pullin'
trigger,
Thet Anglo Saxondom's idee's abreakin' 'em to
pieces,
An' thet idee's thet every man doos jest wut he
damn pleases;
Ef I don't make his meanin' clear, perhaps in some
respex I can,
I know thet "every man" don't mean a nigger or
a Mexican;
An' there's another thing I know, an' thet is, et
these creeturs,
Thet stick an Anglosaxon mask onto State-prison
feeturs.

Should come to Jaalam Centre fer to argify an
spout on't,
The gals 'ould count the silver spoons the minnit
they cleared out on't.

This goin' ware glory waits ye haint one agreeable
feetur,
An' ef it worn't fer wakin' snakes, I'd home agin
short meter;
O, wouldn't I be off, quick time, ef't worn't thet
I wuz sartin
They'd let the daylight into me to pay me fer
desartin!
I don't approve o' tellin' tales, but jest to you I
may state
Our ossifers aint wut they wuz afore they left the
Bay-state;
Then it wuz "Mister Sawin, sir, you're middlin'
well now, be ye?
Step up an' take a nipper, sir; I'm dreffle glad to
see ye";
But now it's "Ware's my eppylet? here, Sawin,
step an' fetch it!
An' mind your eye, be thund'rin' spry, or, damn
ye, you shall ketch it!"
Wal, ez the Doctor sez, some pork will bile so, but
by mighty,
Ef I hed some on 'em to hum, I'd give 'em linkum
vity,
I'd play the rogue's march on their hides an' other
music follerin'——
But I must close my letter here, fer one on' em's
ahollerin',
These Anglosaxon ossifers,—wal, taint no use
ajawin',
I'm safe enlisted fer the war,

Yourn,

BIRDOFREDOM SAWIN.

[Those have not been wanting (as, indeed, when hath Satan been to seek for attorneys?) who have maintained that our late inroad upon Mexico was undertaken, not so much for the avenging of any national quarrel, as for the spreading of free institutions and of Protestantism. *Capita vix duabus Anticyris medenda!* Verily I admire that no pious sergeant among these new Crusaders beheld Martin Luther riding at the front of the host upon a tamed pontifical bull, as, in that former invasion of Mexico, the zealous Gomara (spawn though he were of the Scarlet Woman) was favored with a vision of St. James of Compostella, skewering the infidels upon his apostolical lance. We read, also, that Richard of the lion heart, having gone to Palestine on a similar errand of mercy, was divinely encouraged to cut the throats of such Paynims as refused to swallow the bread of life (doubtless that they might be thereafter incapacitated for swallowing the filthy gobbets of Mahound) by angels of heaven, who cried to the king and his knights,—*Seigneurs, tuez! tuez!* providentially using the French tongue, as being the only one understood by their auditors. This would argue for the pantoglottism of these celestial intelligences, while, on the other hand, the Devil, *teste* Cotton Mather, is unversed in certain of the Indian dialects. Yet must he be a semeiologist the most expert, making himself intelligible to every people and kindred by signs; no other discourse, indeed, being needful, than such as the mackerel-fisher holds with his finned quarry, who, if other bait be wanting, can by a bare bit of white rag at the end of a string captivate those foolish fishes. Such piscatorial oratory is Satan cunning in. Before one he trails a hat and feather, or a bare feather without a hat; before another, a Presidential chair, or a tidewaiter's stool, or a pulpit in the city, no matter what. To us, dangling there over our heads, they seem junkets dropped out of the seventh heaven, sops dipped in nectar, but, once in our mouths, they are all one, bits of fuzzy cotton.

This, however, by the way. It is time now *revocare gradum.* While so many miracles of this sort, vouched by eyewitnesses, have encouraged the arms of Papists not to speak of Echetlæus at Marathon and those *Dioscuri* (whom we must conclude imps of the pit) who sundry times captained the pagan Roman soldiery, it is strange that our first American crusade was not in some such wise also signalized. Yet it is said that the Lord hath manifestly prospered our armies. This opens the question, whether, when our hands are strengthened to make great slaughter of our enemies, it be absolutely and demonstratively certain that this might is added to us from above, or whether some Potentate from an opposite quarter may not have a finger in it, as there are few pies into which his meddling digits are not thrust. Would the Sanctifier and Setter-apart of the seventh day have assisted in a victory gained on the Sabbath, as was one in the late war? Or has that day become less an object of his especial care since the year 1697, when so manifest a providence occurred to Mr. William Trowbridge, in answer to whose prayers, when he and all on shipboard with him were starving, a dolphin was sent daily, "which was enough to serve 'em; only on *Saturdays* they still catched a couple, and on the *Lord's Days* they could catch none at all"? Haply they might have been permitted, by way of mortification, to take some few sculpins (those banes of the salt-water angler), which unseemly fish would, moreover, have conveyed to them a symbolical reproof for their breach of the day, being known in the rude dialect of our mariners as *Cape Cod Clergymen.*

It has been a refreshment to many nice consciences to know that our Chief Magistrate would not regard with eyes of approval the (by many esteemed) sinful pastime of dancing, and I own myself to be so far of that mind, that I could not but set my face against this Mexican Polka, though danced to the Presidential piping with a Gubernatorial second. If ever the country should be seized with another such mania *de propagandâ fide*, I think it would be wise to fill our bombshells with alternate copies of the Cambridge Platform and the Thirty-nine Articles, which would produce a mixture of the highest explosive power, and to wrap every one of our cannon-balls in a leaf of the New Testament, the reading of which is denied to those who sit in the darkness of Popery. Those iron evangelists would thus be able to disseminate vital religion and Gospel truth in quarters inaccessible to the ordinary missionary. I have seen lads, unimpregnate with the more sublimated punctiliousness of Walton, secure pickerel, taking their unwary *siesta* beneath the lily-pads too nigh the surface, with a gun and small shot. Why not, then, since gunpowder was unknown in the time of the Apostles (not to enter here upon the question whether it were discovered before that period by the Chinese), suit our metaphor to the age in which we live, and say *shooters* as well as *fishers* of men?

I do much fear that we shall be seized now and then with a Protestant fervor, as long as we have neighbor Naboths whose wallowings in Papistical mire excite our horror in exact proportion to the size and desirableness of their vineyards. Yet I rejoice that some earnest Protestants have been made by this war,—I mean those who protested against it. Fewer they were than I could wish, for one might imagine America to have been colonized by a tribe of those nondescript African animals the Aye-Ayes, so difficult a word is *No* to us all. There is some malformation or defect of the vocal organs, which either prevents our uttering it at all, or gives it so thick a pronunciation as to be unintelligible. A mouth filled with the national pudding, or watering in expectation thereof, is wholly incompetent to this refractory monosyllable. An abject and herpetic Public Opinion is the Pope, the Anti-Christ, for us to protest against *e corde cordium*. And by what College of Cardinals is this our God's-vicar, our binder and looser, elected? Very like, by the sacred conclave of Tag, Rag, and Bobtail, in the gracious atmosphere of the grog-shop. Yet it is of this that we must all be puppets. This thumps the pulpit-cushion, this guides the editor's pen, this wags the senator's tongue. This decides what Scriptures are canonical, and shuffles Christ away into the Apocrypha. According to that sentence fathered upon Solon, *Οὕτω δημόσιον κακὸν ἔρχεται οἴκαδ' ἑκάστῳ.* This unclean spirit is skilful to assume various shapes. I have known it to enter my own study and nudge my elbow of a Saturday, under the semblance of a wealthy member of my congregation. It were a great blessing, if every particular of what in the sum we call popular sentiment could carry about the name of its manufacturer stamped legibly upon it. I gave a stab under the fifth rib to that pestilent fallacy,—"Our country, right or wrong,"—by tracing its original to a speech of Ensign Cilley at a dinner of the Bungtown Fencibles.—H. W.]

No. III.

WHAT MR. ROBINSON THINKS.

[A FEW remarks on the following verses will not be out of place. The satire in them was not meant to have any personal, but only a general, application. Of the gentleman upon whose letter they were intended as a commentary Mr. Biglow had never heard, till he saw the letter itself. The position of the satirist is oftentimes one which he would not have chosen, had the election been left to himself. In attacking bad principles, he is obliged to select some individual who has made himself their exponent, and in whom they are impersonate, to the end that what he says may not, through ambiguity, be dissipated *tenues in auras.* For what says Seneca? *Longum iter per præcepta, breve et efficace per exempla.* A bad principle is comparatively harmless while it continues to be an abstraction, nor can the general mind comprehend it fully till it is printed in that large type which all men can read at sight, namely, the life and character, the sayings and doings, of particular persons. It is one of the cunningest fetches of Satan, that he never exposes himself directly to our arrows, but, still dodging behind this neighbor or that acquaintance, compels us to wound him through them, if at all. He holds our affections as hostages, the while he patches up a truce with our conscience.

Meanwhile, let us not forget that the aim of the true satirist is not to be severe upon persons, but only upon falsehood, and, as Truth and Falsehood start from the same point, and sometimes even go along together for a little way, his business is to follow the path of the latter after it diverges, and to show her floundering in the bog at the end of it. Truth is quite beyond the reach of satire. There is so brave a simplicity in her, that she can no more be made ridiculous than an oak or a pine. The danger of the satirist is, that continual use may deaden his sensibility to the force of language. He becomes more and more liable to strike harder than he knows or intends. He may be careful to put on his boxing-gloves, and yet forget, that, the older they grow, the more plainly may the knuckles inside be felt. Moreover, in the heat of contest, the eye is insensibly drawn to the crown of victory, whose tawdry tinsel glitters through that dust of the ring which obscures Truth's wreath of simple leaves. I have sometimes thought that my young friend, Mr. Biglow, needed a monitory hand laid on his arm,—*aliquid sufflaminandus erat*. I have never thought it good husbandry to water the tender plants of reform with *aqua fortis*, yet, where so much is to do in the beds, he were a sorry gardener who should wage a whole day's war with an iron scuffle on those ill weeds that make the garden-walks of life unsightly, when a sprinkle of Attic salt will wither them up. *Est ars etiam maledicendi*, says Scaliger, and truly it is a hard thing to say where the graceful gentleness of the lamb merges in downright sheepishness. We may conclude with worthy and wise Dr. Fuller, that "one may be a lamb in private wrongs, but in hearing general affronts to goodness they are asses which are not lions."—H. W.]

GUVENER B. is a sensible man;
He stays to his home an' looks arter his folks;
He draws his furrer ez straight ez he can,
An' into nobody's tater-patch pokes;—
But John P.
Robinson he
Sez he wunt vote fer Guvener B.

My! aint it terrible? Wut shall we du?
We can't never choose him, o' course,—thet's flat;
Guess we shall hev to come round, (don't you?)
An' go in fer thunder an' guns, an' all that;
Fer John P.
Robinson he
Sez he wunt vote fer Guvener B.

Gineral C. is a dreffle smart man:
He's ben on all sides thet give places or pelf;
But consistency still wuz a part of his plan,—
He's ben true to *one* party,—an' thet is himself;—
So John P.
Robinson he
Sez he shall vote fer Gineral C.

Gineral C. he goes in fer the war;
He don't vally principle more'n an old cud;
Wut did God make us raytional creeturs fer,
But glory an' gunpowder, plunder an' blood?
So John P.
Robinson he
Sez he shall vote fer Gineral C.

We were gittin' on nicely up here to our village,
With good old idees o' wut's right an' wut aint
We kind o' thought Christ went agin war an' pillage,

An' thet eppyletts worn't the best mark of a saint
But John P.
Robinson he
Sez this kind o' thing's an exploded idee.

The side of our country must ollers be took,
An' Presidunt Polk, you know, *he* is our country
An' the angel thet writes all our sins in a book
Puts the *debit* to him, an' to us the *per contry;*
An' John P.
Robinson he
Sez this is his view o' the thing to a T.

Parson Wilbur he calls all these argimunts lies;
Sez they're nothin' on airth but jest *fee, faw fum:*
An' thet all this big talk of our destinies
Is half on it ignorance, an' t'other half rum;
But John P.
Robinson he
Sez it aint no sech thing; an', of course, so must we.

Parson Wilbur sez *he* never heerd in his life
Thet th' Apostles rigged out in their swaller-tail coats,
An' marched round in front of a drum an' a fife,
To git some on 'em office, an' some on 'em votes;
But John P.
Robinson he
Sez they didn't know everythin' down in Judee.

Wal, it's a marcy we've gut folks to tell us
The rights an' the wrongs o' these matters, I vow,—
God sends country lawyers, an' other wise fellers,

To start the world's team wen it gits in a slough;
Fer John P.
Robinson he
Sez the world'll go right, ef he hollers out Gee!

[The attentive reader will doubtless have perceived in the foregoing poem an allusion to that pernicious sentiment,—"Our country, right or wrong." It is an abuse of language to call a certain portion of land, much more, certain personages, elevated for the time being to high station, our country. I would not sever nor loosen a single one of those ties by which we are united to the spot of our birth, nor minish by a tittle the respect due to the Magistrate. I love our own Bay State too well to do the one, and as for the other, I have myself for nigh forty years exercised, however unworthily, the function of Justice of the Peace, having been called thereto by the unsolicited kindness of that most excellent man and upright patriot, Caleb Strong. *Patriæ fumus igne alieno luculentior* is best qualified with this,—*Ubi libertas, ibi patria.* We are inhabitants of two worlds, and owe a double but not a divided, allegiance. In virtue of our clay, this little ball of earth exacts a certain loyalty of us, while, in our capacity as spirits, we are admitted citizens of an invisible and holier fatherland. There is a patriotism of the soul whose claim absolves us from our other and terrene fealty. Our true country is that ideal realm which we represent to ourselves under the names of religion, duty, and the like. Our terrestrial organizations are but far-off approaches to so fair a model, and all they are verily traitors who resist not any attempt to divert them from this their original intendment. When, therefore, one would have us to fling up our caps and shout with the multitude,—"*Our country, however bounded!*" he demands of us that we sacrifice the larger to the less, the higher to the lower, and that we yield to the imaginary claims of a few acres of soil our duty and privilege as liegemen of Truth. Our true country is bounded on the north and the south, on the east and the west, by Justice, and when she oversteps that invisible boundary-line by so much as a hair's-breadth, she ceases to be our mother, and chooses rather to be looked upon *quasi noverca*. That is a hard choice, when our earthly love of country calls upon us to tread one path and our duty points us to another. We must make as noble and becoming an election as did Penelope between Icarius and Ulysses. Veiling our faces, we must take silently the hand of Duty to follow her.

Shortly after the publication of the foregoing poem, there appeared some comments upon it in one of the public prints which seemed to call for animadversion. I accordingly addressed to Mr. Buckingham, of the Boston Courier, the following letter.

JAALAM, November 4, 1847.

"*To the Editor of the Courier:*

"RESPECTED SIR,—Calling at the post-office this morning, our worthy and efficient postmaster offered for my perusal a paragraph in the Boston Morning Post of the 3d instant, wherein certain effusions of the pastoral muse are attributed to the pen of Mr. James Russell Lowell. For aught I know or can affirm to the contrary, this Mr. Lowell may be a very deserving person and a youth of parts (though I have seen verses of his which I could never rightly understand); and if he be such, he, I am certain, as well as I, would be free from any proclivity to appropriate to himself whatever of credit (or discredit) may honestly belong to another. I am confident, that, in penning these few lines, I am only forestalling a disclaimer from that young gentleman, whose silence hitherto, when rumor pointed to himward, has excited in my bosom mingled emotions of sorrow and surprise. Well may my young parishioner, Mr. Biglow, exclaim with the poet,

'Sic vos non vobis' &c.;

though, in saying this, I would not convey the impression that he is a proficient in the Latin tongue,—the tongue, I might add, of a Horace and a Tully.

"Mr. B. does not employ his pen, I can safely say, for any lucre of worldly gain, or to be exalted by the carnal plaudits of men *digito monstrari*, &c. He does not wait upon Providence for mercies, and in his heart mean *merces*. But I should esteem myself as verily deficient in my duty (who am his friend and in some unworthy sort his spiritual *fidus Achates*, &c.), if I did not step forward to claim for him whatever measure of applause might be assigned to him by the judicious.

"If this were a fitting occasion, I might venture here a brief dissertation touching the manner and kind of my young friend's poetry. But I dubitate whether this abstruser sort of speculation (though enlivened by some apposite instances from Aristophanes) would sufficiently interest your oppidan readers. As regards their satirical tone, and their plainness of speech, I will only say, that, in my pastoral experience, I have found that the Arch-Enemy loves nothing better than to be treated as a religious, moral, and intellectual being, and that there is no *apage Sathanas!* so potent as ridicule. But it is a kind of weapon that must have a button of good-nature on the point of it.

"The productions of Mr. B. have been stigmatized in some quarters as unpatriotic; but I can vouch that he loves his native soil with that hearty, though discriminating, attachment which springs from an intimate social intercourse of many years' standing. In the ploughing season, no one has a deeper share in the well-being of the country than he. If Dean Swift were right in saying that he who makes two blades of grass grow where one grew before confers a greater benefit on the state than he who taketh a city, Mr. B. might exhibit a fairer claim to the Presidency than General Scott himself. I think that some of those disinterested lovers of the hard-handed democracy, whose fingers have never touched any thing rougher than the dollars of our common country, would hesitate to compare palms with him. It would do your heart good, respected Sir, to see that young man mow. He cuts a cleaner and wider swarth than any in this town.

"But it is time for me to be at my Post. It is very clear that my young friend's shot has struck the lintel, for the Post is shaken (Amos ix. 1). The editor of that paper is a strenuous advocate of the Mexican war, and a colonel, as I am given to understand. I presume, that, being necessarily absent in Mexico, he has left his journal in some less judicious hands. At any rate, the Post has been too swift on this occasion. It could hardly have cited a more incontrovertible line from any poem than that which it has selected for animadversion, namely,—

'We kind o' thought Christ went agin war an' pillage.'

"If the Post maintains the converse of this proposition, it can hardly be considered as a safe guide-post for the moral and religious portions of its party, however many other excellent qualities of a post it may be blessed with. There is a sign in London on which is painted,—'The Green Man.' It would do very well as a portrait of any individual who would support so unscriptural a thesis. As regards the language of the line in question, I am bold to say that He who readeth the hearts of men will not account any dialect unseemly which conveys a sound and pious sentiment. I could wish that such sentiments were more common, however uncouthly expressed. Saint Ambrose affirms, that *veritas a quocunque* (why not, then, *quomodocunque?*) *dicatur, a spiritu sancto est.* Digest also this of Baxter:—'The plainest words are the most profitable oratory in the weightiest matters.'

"When the paragraph in question was shown to Mr. Biglow, the only part of it which seemed to give him any dissatisfaction was that which classed him with the Whig party. He says, that, if resolutions are a nourishing kind of diet, that party must be in a very hearty and flourishing condition; for that they have quietly eaten more good ones of their own baking than he could have conceived to be possible without repletion. He has been for some years past (I regret to say) an ardent opponent of those sound doctrines of protective policy which form so prominent a portion of the creed of that party. I confess, that, in some discussions which I have had with him on this point in my study, he has displayed a vein of obstinacy which I had not hitherto detected in his composition. He is also (*horresco referens*) infected in no small measure with the peculiar notions of a print called the Liberator, whose heresies I take every proper opportunity of combating, and of which, I thank God, I have never read a single line.

"I did not see Mr. B.'s verses until they appeared in print, and there *is* certainly one thing in them which I consider highly improper. I allude to the personal references to myself by name. To confer notoriety on an humble individual who is laboring quietly in his vocation, and who keeps his cloth as free as he can from the dust of the political arena (though *væ mihi si non evangelizavero*), is no doubt an indecorum. The sentiments which he attributes to me I will not deny to be mine. They were embodied, though in a different form, in a discourse preached upon the last day of public fasting, and were acceptable to my entire people (of whatever political views), except the postmaster, who dissented *ex officio.* I observe that you sometimes devote a portion of your paper to a religious summary. I should be well pleased to furnish a copy of my discourse for insertion in this department of your instructive journal. By omitting the advertisements, it might easily be got within the limits of a single number, and I venture to insure you the sale of some scores of copies in this town. I will cheerfully render myself responsible for ten. It might possibly be advantageous to issue it as an *extra.* But perhaps you will not esteem it an object, and I will not press it. My offer does not spring from any weak desire of seeing my name in print; for I can enjoy this satisfaction at any time by turning to the Triennial Catalogue of the University, where it also possesses that added emphasis of Italics with which those of my calling are distinguished.

"I would simply add, that I continue to fit ingenuous youth for college, and that I have two spacious and airy sleeping apartments at this moment unoccupied. *Ingenuas didicisse*, &c. Terms, which vary according to the circumstances of the parents, may be known on application to me by letter, post paid. In all cases the lad will be expected to fetch his own towels. This rule, Mrs. W. desires me to add, has no exceptions.

"Respectfully, your obedient servant,

"HOMER WILBUR, A. M.

"P. S. Perhaps the last paragraph may look like an attempt to obtain the insertion of my circular gratuitously. If it should appear to you in that light, I desire that you would erase it, or charge for it at the usual rates, and deduct the amount from the proceeds in your hands from the sale of my discourse, when it shall be printed. My circular is much longer and more explicit, and will be forwarded without charge to any who may desire it. It has been very neatly executed on a letter sheet, by a very deserving printer, who attends upon my ministry, and is a creditable specimen of the typographic art. I have one hung over my mantelpiece in a neat frame, where it makes a beautiful and appropriate ornament, and balances the profile of Mrs. W., cut with her toes by the young lady born without arms. H. W."

I have in the foregoing letter mentioned General Scott in connection with the Presidency, because I have been given to understand that he has blown to pieces and otherwise caused to be destroyed more Mexicans than any other commander. His claim would therefore be deservedly considered the strongest. Until accurate returns of the Mexicans killed, wounded, and maimed be obtained, it will be difficult to settle these nice points of precedence. Should it prove that any other officer has been more meritorious and destructive than General S., and has thereby rendered himself more worthy of the confidence and support of the conservative portion of our community, I shall cheerfully insert his name, instead of that of General S., in a future edition. It may be thought, likewise, that General S. has invalidated his claims by too much attention to the decencies of apparel, and the habits belonging to a gentleman. These abstruser points of statesmanship are beyond my scope. I wonder not that successful military achievement should attract the admiration of the multitude. Rather do I rejoice with wonder to behold how rapidly this sentiment is losing its hold upon the popular mind. It is related of Thomas Warton, the second of that honored name who held the office of Poetry Professor at Oxford, that, when one wished to find him, being absconded, as was his wont, in some obscure alehouse, he was counselled to traverse the city with a drum and fife, the sound of which inspiring music would be sure to draw the Doctor from his retirement into the street. We are all more or less bitten with this martial insanity. *Nescio quâ dulcedine .....cunctos ducit.* I confess to some infection of that itch myself. When I see a Brigadier-General maintaining his insecure elevation in the saddle under the severe fire of the training-field, and when I remember that some military enthusiasts, through haste, inexperience, or an over-desire to lend reality to those fictitious combats, will sometimes discharge their ramrods, I cannot but admire, while I deplore, the mistaken devotion of those heroic officers. *Semel insanivimus omnes.* I was myself, during the late war with Great Britain, chaplain of a regiment, which was fortunately never called to active military duty. I mention this circumstance with regret rather than pride. Had I been summoned to actual warfare, I trust that I might have been strengthened to bear myself after the manner of that reverend father in our New England Israel, Dr. Benjamin Colman, who, as we are told in Turell's life of him, when the vessel in which he had taken passage for England was attacked by a French privateer, "fought like a philosopher and a Christian,.....and prayed all the while he charged and fired." As this note is already long, I shall not here enter upon a discussion of the question, whether Christians may lawfully be soldiers. I think it sufficiently evident, that during the first two centuries of the Christian era, at least, the two professions were esteemed incompatible. Consult Jortin on this head.—H. W.]

No. IV.

REMARKS OF INCREASE D. O'PHACE, ESQUIRE, AT AN EXTRUMPERY CAUCUS IN STATE STREET, REPORTED BY MR. H. BIGLOW.

[THE ingenious reader will at once understand that no such speech as the following was ever *totidem verbis* pronounced. But there are simpler and less guarded wits, for the satisfying of which such an explanation may be needful. For there are certain invisible lines, which as Truth successively overpasses, she becomes Untruth to one and another of us, as a large river, flowing from one kingdom into another, sometimes takes a new name, albeit the waters undergo no change, how small soever. There is, moreover, a truth of fiction more veracious than the truth of fact, as that of the Poet, which represents to us things and events as they ought to be, rather than servilely copies them as they are imperfectly imaged in the crooked and smoky glass of our mundane affairs. It is this which makes the speech of Antonius, though originally spoken in no wider a forum than the brain of Shakspeare, more historically valuable than that other which Appian has reported, by as much as the understanding of the Englishman was more comprehensive than that of the Alexandrian. Mr. Biglow, in the present instance, has only made use of a license assumed by all the historians of antiquity, who put into the mouths of various characters such words as seem to them most fitting to the occasion and to the speaker. If it be objected that no such oration could ever have been delivered, I answer, that there are few assemblages for speech-making which do not better deserve the title of *Parliamentum Indoctorum* than did the sixth Parliament of Henry the Fourth, and that men still continue to have as much faith in the Oracle of Fools as ever Pantagruel had. Howell, in his letters, recounts a merry tale of a certain ambassador of Queen Elizabeth, who, having written two letters, one to her Majesty and the other to his wife, directed them at cross-purposes, so that the Queen was beducked and bedeared and requested to send a change of hose, and the wife was beprincessed and otherwise unwontedly besuperlatived, till the one feared for the wits of her ambassador, and the other for those of her husband. In like manner it may be presumed that our speaker has misdirected some of his thoughts, and given to the whole theatre what he would have wished to confide only to a select auditory at the back of the curtain. For it is seldom that we can get any frank utterance from men, who address, for the most part, a Buncombe either in this world or the next. As for their audiences, it may be truly said of our people, that they enjoy one political institution in common with the ancient Athenians: I mean a certain profitless kind of *ostracism*, wherewith, nevertheless, they seem hitherto well enough content. For in Presidential elections, and other affairs of the sort, whereas I observe that the *oysters* fall to the lot of comparatively few, the *shells* (such as the privileges of voting as they are told to do by the *ostrivori* aforesaid, and of huzzaing at public meetings) are very liberally distributed among the people, as being their prescriptive and quite sufficient portion.

The occasion of the speech is supposed to be Mr. Palfrey's refusal to vote for the Whig candidate for the Speakership.—H. W.]

No? Hez he? He haint, though? Wut? Voted agin him?
Ef the bird of our country could ketch him, she'd skin him;
I seem's though I see her, with wrath in each quill,
Like a chancery lawyer, afilin' her bill,
An' grindin' her talents ez sharp ez all nater,
To pounce like a writ on the back o' the traitor.
Forgive me, my friends, ef I seem to be het,
But a crisis like this must with vigor be met;
Wen an Arnold the star-spangled banner bestains,
Holl Fourth o' Julys seem to bile in my veins.

Who ever'd ha' thought sech a pisonous rig
Would be run by a chap thet wuz chose fer a Wig?
"We knowed wut his principles wuz 'fore we sent him"?
Wut wuz ther in them from this vote to prevent him?
A marciful Providunce fashioned us holler
O' purpose thet we might our principles swaller;
It can hold any quantity on 'em, the belly can,
An' bring 'em up ready fer use like the pelican,
Or more like the kangaroo, who (wich is stranger)
Puts her family into her pouch wen there's danger.
Aint principle precious? then, who 's goin' to use it
Wen there 's resk o' some chap's gittin' up to abuse it?
I can't tell the wy on't, but nothin' is *so* sure

Ez thet principle kind o' gits spiled by exposure; *
A man thet lets all sorts o' folks git a sight on't
Ough' to hev it all took right away, every mite
 on't;
Ef he can't keep it all to himself wen it's wise to,
He aint one it's fit to trust nothin' so nice to.

Besides, ther's a wonderful power in latitude
To shift a man's morril relations an' attitude;
Some flossifers think thet a fakkilty's granted
The minnit it's proved to be thoroughly wanted,
Thet a change o' demand makes a change o' con-
 dition,
An' thet everythin' 's nothin' except by position,
Ez, fer instance, thet rubber-trees fust begun
 bearin'
Wen p'litikle conshunces come into wearin',—
Thet the fears of a monkey, whose holt chanced
 to fail,
Drawed the vertibry out to a prehensile tail;
So, wen one's chose to Congriss, ez soon ez he's
 in it,
A collar grows right round his neck in a minnit,
An' sartin it is thet a man cannot be strict
In bein' himself, wen he gits to the Deestrict,

* The speaker is of a different mind from Tully, who, in his recently discovered tractate *De Republicâ*, tells us,—*Nec vero habere virtutem satis est, quasi artem aliquam, nisi utare*, and from our Milton, who says,—"I cannot praise a fugitive and cloistered virtue, unexercised and unbreathed, that never sallies out and sees her adversary, but slinks out of the race where that immortal garland is to be run for, *not without dust and heat*."—*Areop.* He had taken the words out of the Roman's mouth, without knowing it, and might well exclaim with Austin (if a saint's name may stand sponsor for a curse,) *Pereant qui ante nos nostra dixerint!*—H. W.

Fer a coat thet sets wal here in ole Massachusetts,
Wen it gits on to Washinton, somehow askew sets

Resolves, do you say, o' the Springfield Convention?
Thet's percisely the pint I was goin' to mention;
Resolves air a thing we most gen'ally keep ill,
They're a cheap kind o' dust fer the eyes o' the people;
A parcel o' delligits jest get together
An' chat fer a spell o' the crops an' the weather,
Then, comin' to order, they squabble awile
An' let off the speeches they're ferful 'll spile;
Then—Resolve,—Thet we wunt hev an inch o' slave territory;
Thet President Polk's holl perceedins air very tory;
Thet the war is a damned war, an' them thet enlist in it
Should hev a cravat with a dreffle tight twist in it;
Thet the war is a war fer the spreadin' o' slavery;
Thet our army desarves our best thanks fer their bravery;
Thet we're the original friends o' the nation,
All the rest air a paltry an' base fabrication;
Thet we highly respect Messrs. A, B, an' C,
An' ez deeply despise Messrs. E, F, an' G.
In this way they go to the eend o' the chapter,
An' then they bust out in a kind of a raptur
About their own vartoo, an' folks's stone-blindness
To the men thet 'ould actilly do 'em a kindness,—
The American eagle,—the Pilgrims thet landed,—
Till on ole Plymouth Rock they git finally stranded.
Wal, the people they listen and say, "Thet's the ticket;
Ez fer Mexico, t'aint no great glory to lick it.

But 'twould be a darned shame to go pullin' o' triggers
To extend the aree of abusin' the niggers."

So they march in percessions, an' git up hooraws,
An' tramp thru the mud fer the good o' the cause,
An' think they're a kind o' fulfillin' the prophecies,
Wen they're on'y jest changin' the holders of offices;
Ware A sot afore, B is comf'tably seated,
One humbug's victor'ous, an' t'other defeated,
Each honnable doughface gits jest wut he axes,
An' the people—their annooal soft-sodder an' taxes.

Now, to keep unimpaired all these glorious feeturs
Thet characterize morril an' reasonin' creeturs,
Thet give every paytriot all he can cram,
Thet oust the untrustworthy Presidunt Flam,
And stick honest Presidunt Sham in his place,
To the manifest gain o' the holl human race,
An' to some indervidgewals on't in partickler,
Who love Public Opinion an' know how to tickle her,—
I say thet a party with great aims like these
Must stick jest ez close ez a hive full o' bees.

I'm willin' a man should go tollable strong
Agin wrong in the abstract, fer thet kind o' wrong
Is ollers unpop'lar an' never gits pitied,
Because it's a crime no one never committed;
But he mus'n't be hard on partickler sins,
Coz then he'll be kickin' the people's own shins;
On'y look at the Demmercrats, see wut they've done
Jest simply by stickin' together like fun;
They've sucked us right into a mis'able war

Thet no one on airth aint responsible for;
They've run us a hundred cool millions in debt,
(An' fer Demmercrat Horners ther's good plums left yet;)
They talk agin tayriffs, but act fer a high one,
An' so coax all parties to build up their Zion;
To the people they're ollers ez slick ez molasses,
An' butter their bread on both sides with The Masses,
Half o' whom they've persuaded, by way of a joke,
Thet Washinton's mantelpiece fell upon Polk.

Now all o' these blessin's the Wigs might enjoy,
Ef they'd gumption enough the right means to imploy; *
Fer the silver spoon born in Dermocracy's mouth
Is a kind of a scringe thet they hev to the South;
Their masters can cuss 'em an' kick 'em an' wale 'em,
An' they notice it less 'an the ass did to Balaam;
In this way they screw into second-rate offices
Wich the slaveholder thinks 'ould substract too much off his ease;
The file-leaders, I mean, du, fer they, by their wiles,
Unlike the old viper, grow fat on their files.
Wal, the Wigs hev been tryin' to grab all this prey frum 'em
An' to hook this nice spoon o' good fortin' away frum 'em,
An' they might ha' succeeded, ez likely ez not,
In lickin' the Demmercrats all round the lot,

* That was a pithy saying of Persius, and fits our politicians without a wrinkle,—*Magister artis, ingeniique largitor venter*
—H W.

Ef it warn't thet, wile all faithful Wigs were their knees on,
Some stuffy old codger would holler out,—"Treason!
You must keep a sharp eye on a dog thet hez bit you once,
An' *I* aint agoin' to cheat my constitoounts,"—
Wen every fool knows thet a man represents
Not the fellers thet sent him, but them on the fence,—
Impartially ready to jump either side
An' make the fust use of a turn o' the tide,—
The waiters on Providunce here in the city,
Who compose wut they call a State Centerl Committy.
Constitoounts air hendy to help a man in,
But arterwards don't weigh the heft of a pin.
Wy, the people can't all live on Uncle Sam's pus,
So they've nothin' to du with't fer better or wus;
It's the folks thet air kind o' brought up to depend on't
Thet hev any consarn in't, an' thet is the end on't.

Now here wuz New England ahevin' the honor
Of a chance at the Speakership showered upon her;—
Do you say,—"She don't want no more Speakers, but fewer;
She's hed plenty o' them, wut she wants is *doer*"?
Fer the matter o' thet, it's notorous in town
Thet her own representatives du her quite brown.
But thet's nothin' to du with it; wut right hed Palfrey
To mix himself up with fanatical small fry?
Warn't we gittin' on prime with our hot an' cold blowin',

Acondemnin' the war wilst we kep' it agoin'?
We'd assumed with gret skill a commandin' position,
On this side or thet, no one couldn't tell wich one,
So, wutever side wipped, we'd a chance at the plunder
An' could sue fer infringin' our paytented thunder;
We were ready to vote fer whoever wuz eligible,
Ef on all pints at issoo he'd stay unintelligible.
Wal, sposin' we hed to gulp down our perfessions,
We were ready to come out next mornin' with fresh ones;
Besides, ef we did, 'twas our business alone,
Fer couldn't we du wut we would with our own?
An' ef a man can, wen pervisions hev riz so,
Eat up his own words, it's a marcy it is so.

Wy, these chaps frum the North, with back-bones to 'em, darn 'em,
'Ould be wuth more 'an Gennle Tom Thumb is to Barnum;
Ther's enough thet to office on this very plan grow,
By exhibitin' how very small a man can grow;
But an M. C. frum here ollers hastens to state he
Belongs to the order called invertebraty,
Wence some gret filologists judge primy fashy
Thet M. C. is M. T. by paronomashy;
An' these few exceptions air *loosus naytury*
Folks 'ould put down their quarters to stare at, like fury.

It's no use to open the door o' success,
Ef a member can bolt so fer nothin' or less;
Wy, all o' them grand constitootional pillers
Our fore-fathers fetched with 'em over the billers,
Them pillers the people so soundly hev slep' on,

Wile to slav'ry, invasion, an' debt they were swep'
on,
Wile our Destiny higher an' higher kep' mountin',
(Though I guess folks'll stare wen she hends her
account in,)
Ef members in this way go kickin' agin 'em,
They wunt hev so much ez a feather left in 'em.

An', ez fer this Palfrey,* we thought wen we'd
gut him in,
He'd go kindly in wutever harness we put him in;
Supposin' we *did* know thet he wuz a peace man?
Doos he think he can be Uncle Sammle's police-
man,
An' wen Sam gits tipsy an' kicks up a riot,
Lead him off to the lockup to snooze till he's
quiet?
Wy, the war is a war thet true paytriots can bear,
ef
It leads to the fat promised land of a tayriff;
We don't go an' fight it, nor aint to be driv on,
Nor Demmercrats nuther, thet hev wut to live on;
Ef it aint jest the thing thet's well pleasin' to God,
It makes us thought highly on elsewhere abroad;
The Rooshian black eagle looks blue in his eerie
An' shakes both his heads wen he hears o' Mon-
teery;
In the Tower Victory sets, all of a fluster,
An' reads, with locked doors, how we won Cherry
Buster;
An' old Philip Lewis—thet come an' kep' school
here
Fer the mere sake o' scorin' his ryalist ruler

* There is truth yet in this of Juvenal,—

"Dat veniam corvis, vexat censura columbas."

H. W.

On the tenderest part of our kings *in futuro*—
Hides his crown underneath an old shut in his
    bureau,
Breaks off in his brags to a suckle o' merry kings,
How he often hed hided young native Amerrikins,
An, turnin' quite faint in the midst of his fooleries,
Sneaks down stairs to bolt the front door o' the
    Tooleries.*

You say,—"We'd ha' scared 'em by growin' in
    peace,
A plaguy sight more then by bobberies like these"?
Who is it dares say thet "our naytional eagle
Wun't much longer be classed with the birds thet
    air regal,
Coz theirn be hooked beaks, an' she, arter this
    slaughter,

* Jortin is willing to allow of other miracles besides those recorded in Holy Writ, and why not of other prophecies? It is granting too much to Satan to suppose him, as divers of the learned have done, the inspirer of the ancient oracles. Wiser, I esteem it, to give chance the credit of the successful ones. What is said here of Louis Philippe was verified in some of its minute particulars within a few months' time. Enough to have made the fortune of Delphi or Hammon, and no thanks to Beelzebub neither! That of Seneca in Medea will suit here:—

"Rapida fortuna ac levis
Præcepsque regno eripuit, exsilio dedit."

Let us allow, even to richly deserved misfortune, our commiseration, and be not over-hasty meanwhile in our censure of the French people, left for the first time to govern themselves, remembering that wise sentence of Æschylus,—

Ἅπας δὲ τραχὺς ὅστις ἂν νέον κρατῇ.

H. W.

'll bring back a bill ten times longer'n she ough'
to "?
Wut's your name? Come, I see ye, you up-
country feller,
You've put me out severil times with your beller;
Out with it! Wut? Biglow? I say nothin'
furder,
Thet feller would like nothin' better'n a murder;
He's a traiter, blasphemer, an' wut ruther worse
is,
He puts all his ath'ism in dreffle bad verses;
Socity aint safe till sech monsters air out on it,
Refer to the Post, ef you hev the least doubt on it;
Wy, he goes agin war, agin indirect taxes,
Agin sellin' wild lands 'cept to settlers with axes,
Agin holdin' o' slaves, though he knows it's the
corner
Our libbaty rests on, the mis'able scorner!
In short, he would wholly upset with his ravages
All thet keeps us above the brute critters an' sav-
ages,
An' pitch into all kinds o' briles an' confusions
The holl of our civilized, free institutions;
He writes fer thet ruther unsafe print, the Courier,
An' likely ez not hez a squintin' to Foorier;
I'll be ——, thet is, I mean I'll be blest,
Ef I hark to a word frum so noted a pest;
I shan't talk with *him*, my religion 's too fervent.—
Good mornin', my friends, I'm your most humble
servant.

[Into the question, whether the ability to express ourselves in articulate language has been productive of more good or evil, I shall not here enter at large. The two faculties of speech and of speech-making are wholly diverse in their natures. By the first we make ourselves intelligible, by the last unintelligible, to our fellows. It has not seldom occurred to me (noting how in our national legislature every thing runs to talk, as lettuces, if the season or the soil be unpropitious, shoot up lankly to seed, instead of forming handsome heads) that Babel was the first Congress, the earliest mill erected for the manufacture of gabble. In these days, what with Town Meetings, School Committees, Boards (lumber) of one kind and another, Congresses, Parliaments, Diets, Indian Councils, Palavers, and the like, there is scarce a village which has not its factories of this description driven by (milk-and-)water power. I cannot conceive the confusion of tongues to have been the curse of Babel, since I esteem my ignorance of other languages as a kind of Martello-tower, in which I am safe from the furious bombardments of foreign garrulity. For this reason I have ever preferred the study of the dead languages, those primitive formations being Ararats upon whose silent peaks I sit secure and watch this new deluge without fear, though it rain figures (*simulacra*, semblances) of speech forty days and nights together, as it not uncommonly happens. Thus is my coat, as it were, without buttons by which any but a vernacular wild bore can seize me. Is it not possible that the Shakers may intend to convey a quiet reproof and hint, in fastening their outer garments with hooks and eyes?

This reflection concerning Babel, which I find in no Commentary, was first thrown upon my mind when an excellent deacon of my congregation (being infected with the Second Advent delusion) assured me that he had received a first instalment of the gift of tongues as a small earnest of larger possessions in the like kind to follow. For, of a truth, I could not reconcile it with my ideas of the Divine justice and mercy that the single wall which protected people of other languages from the incursions of this otherwise well-meaning propagandist should be broken down.

In reading Congressional debates, I have fancied, that, after the subsidence of those painful buzzings in the brain which result from such exercises, I detected a slender residuum of valuable information. I made the discovery that *nothing* takes longer in the saying than any thing else, for, as *ex nihilo nihil fit*, so from one polypus *nothing* any number of similar ones may be produced. I would recommend to the attention of *vivâ voce* debaters and controversialists the admirable example of the monk Copres, who, in the fourth century, stood for half an hour in the midst of a great fire, and thereby silenced a Manichæan antagonist who had less of the salamander in him. As for those who quarrel in print, I have no concern with them here, since the eyelids are a divinely-granted shield against all such. Moreover, I have observed in many modern books that the printed portion is becoming gradually smaller, and the number of blank or fly-leaves (as they are called) greater. Should this fortunate tendency of literature continue, books will grow more valuable from year to year, and the whole Serbonian bog yield to the advances of firm arable land.

The sagacious Lacedæmonians hearing that Tesephone had bragged that he could talk all day long on any given subject, made no more ado, but forthwith banished him, whereby they supplied him a topic and at the same time took care that his experiment upon it should be tried out of ear-shot.

I have wondered, in the Representatives' Chamber of our own Commonwealth, to mark how little impression seemed to be produced by that emblematic fish suspended over the heads of the members. Our wiser ancestors, no doubt, hung it there as being the animal which the Pythagoreans reverenced for its silence, and which certainly in that particular does not so well merit the epithet *cold-blooded*, by which naturalists distinguish it, as certain bipeds, afflicted with ditch-water on the brain, who take occasion to tap themselves in Fanueil Halls, meeting-houses, and other places of public resort.—H. W.]

No. V.

THE DEBATE IN THE SENNIT.

SOT TO A NUSRY RHYME.

[THE incident which gave rise to the debate satirized in the following verses was the unsuccessful attempt of Drayton and Sayres to give freedom to seventy men and women, fellow-beings and fellow-Christians. Had Tripoli, instead of Washington, been the scene of this undertaking, the unhappy leaders in it would have been as secure of the theoretic as they now are of the practical part of martyrdom. I question whether the Dey of Tripoli is blessed with a District Attorney so benighted as ours at the seat of government. Very fitly is he named Key, who would allow himself to be made the instrument of locking the door of hope against sufferers in such a cause. Not all the waters of the ocean can cleanse the vile smutch of the jailer's fingers from off that little Key. *Ahenea clavis*, a brazen Key indeed!

Mr. Calhoun, who is made the chief speaker in this burlesque, seems to think that the light of the nineteenth century is to be put out as soon as he tinkles his little cow-bell curfew. Whenever slavery is touched, he sets up his scarecrow of dissolving the Union. This may do for the North, but I should conjecture that something more than a pumpkin-lantern is required to scare manifest and irretrievable Destiny out of her path. Mr. Calhoun cannot let go the apron-string of the Past. The Past is a good nurse, but we must be weaned from her sooner or later, even though, like Plotinus, we should run home from school to ask the breast, after we are tolerably well-grown youths. It will not do for us to hide our faces in her lap, whenever the strange Future holds out her arms and asks us to come to her.

But we are all alike. We have all heard it said, often enough, that little boys must not play with fire; and yet, if the matches be taken away from us and put out of reach upon the shelf, we must needs get into our little corner, and scowl and stamp and threaten the dire revenge of going to bed without our supper. The world shall stop till we get our dangerous plaything again. Dame Earth, meanwhile, who has more than enough household matters to mind, goes bustling hither and thither as a hiss or a sputter tells her that this or that kettle of hers is boiling over and before bedtime we are glad to eat our porridge cold, and gulp down our dignity along with it.

Mr. Calhoun has somehow acquired the name of a great statesman, and, if it be great statesmanship to put lance in rest and run a tilt at the Spirit of the Age with the certainty of being next moment hurled neck and heels into the dust amid universal laughter, he deserves the title. He is the Sir Kay of our modern chivalry. He should remember the old Scandinavian mythus. Thor was the strongest of gods, but he could not wrestle with Time, nor so much as lift up a fold of the great snake which knit the universe together; and when he smote the Earth, though with his terrible mallet, it was but as if a leaf had fallen. Yet all the while it seemed to Thor that he had only been wrestling with an old woman, striving to lift a cat, and striking a stupid giant on the head.

And in old times, doubtless, the giants *were* stupid, and

there was no better sport for the Sir Launcelots and Sir Gawains than to go about cutting off their great blundering heads with enchanted swords. But things have wonderfully changed. It is the giants, now-a-days, that have the science and the intelligence, while the chivalrous Don Quixotes of Conservatism still cumber themselves with the clumsy armor of a by-gone age. On whirls the restless globe through unsounded time, with its cities and its silences, its births and funerals, half light, half shade, but never wholly dark, and sure to swing round into the happy morning at last. With an involuntary smile, one sees Mr. Calhoun letting slip his pack-thread cable with a crooked pin at the end of it to anchor South Carolina upon the bank and shoal of the Past.—H. W.]

TO MR. BUCKENAM.

MR. EDITER, As i wuz kinder prunin round, in a little nussry sot out a year or 2 a go, the Dbait in the sennit cum inter my mine An so i took & Sot it to wut I call a nussry rime. I hev made sum onnable Gentlemun speak that dident speak in a Kind uv Poetikul lie sense the seeson is dreffle backerd up This way

ewers as ushul

HOSEA BIGLOW.

"HERE we stan' on the Constitution, by thunder!
It's a fact o' wich ther's bushils o' proofs;
Fer how could we trample on't so, I wonder,
Ef't worn't thet it's ollers under our hoofs?"
Sez John C. Calhoun, sez he;

"Human rights haint no more
Right to come on this floor,
No more'n the man in the moon," sez he.

"The North haint no kind o' bisness with nothin',
An' you've no idee how much bother it saves;
We aint none riled by their frettin' an' frothin',
We're *used* to layin' the string on our slaves,"
Sez John C. Calhoun, sez he;—
Sez Mister Foote,
"I should like to shoot
The holl gang, by the gret horn spoon!"
sez he.

"Freedom's Keystone is Slavery, thet ther's no
doubt on,
It's sutthin' thet's—wha' d' ye call it?—divine,—
An' the slaves thet we ollers *make* the most out on
Air them north o' Mason an' Dixon's line,"
Sez John C. Calhoun, sez he;—
"Fer all thet," sez Mangum,
"'T would be better to hang 'em,
An' so git red on 'em soon," sez he.

"The mass ough' to labor an' we lay on soffies,
Thet's the reason I want to spread Freedom's
aree;
It puts all the cunninest on us in office,
An' reelises our Maker's orig'nal idee,"
Sez John C. Calhoun, sez he;—
"Thet's ez plain," sez Cass,
"Ez thet some one's an ass,
It's ez clear ez the sun is at noon," sez he.

"Now don't go to say I'm the friend of oppression,
But keep all your spare breath fer coolin' your
broth,

Fer I ollers hev strove (at least thet's my impression)
To make cussed free with the rights o' the North,"
Sez John C. Calhoun, sez he;—
"Yes," sez Davis o' Miss.,
"The perfection o' bliss
Is in skinnin' thet same old coon," sez he.

"Slavery's a thing thet depends on complexion,
It's God's law thet fetters on black skins don't chafe;
Ef brains wuz to settle it (horrid reflection!)
Wich of our onnable body'd be safe?"
Sez John C. Calhoun, sez he;—
Sez Mister Hannegan,
Afore he began agin,
"Thet exception is quite oppertoon," sez he.

"Gen'nle Cass, Sir, you needn't be twitchin' your collar,
Your merit's quite clear by the dut on your knees,
At the North we don't make no distinctions o' color;
You can all take a lick at our shoes wen you please,"
Sez John C. Calhoun, sez he;—
Sez Mister Jarnagin,
"They wunt hev to larn agin,
They all on 'em know the old toon," sez he.

"The slavery question aint no ways bewilderin'.
North an' South hev one int'rest, it's plain to a glance;
No'thern men, like us patriarchs, don't sell their childrin,
But they *du* sell themselves, ef they git a good chance,"
Sez John C. Calhoun, sez he;—

Sez Atherton here,
"This is gittin' severe,
I wish I could dive like a loon," sez he.

"It'll break up the Union, this talk about freedom,
An' your fact'ry gals (soon ez we split) 'll make head,
An' gittin' some Miss chief or other to lead 'em,
'll go to work raisin' promiscoous Ned,"
Sez John C. Calhoun, sez he;—
"Yes, the North," sez Colquitt,
"Ef we Southeners all quit,
Would go down like a busted balloon," sez he.

"Jest look wut is doin', wut annyky's brewin'
In the beautiful clime o' the olive an' vine,
All the wise aristoxy is tumblin' to ruin,
An' the sankylots drorin' an' drinkin' their wine,"
Sez John C. Calhoun, sez he;—
"Yes," sez Johnson, "in France
They're beginnin' to dance
Beelzebub's own rigadoon," sez he.

"The South's safe enough, it don't feel a mite skeery,
Our slaves in their darkness an' dut air tu blest
Not to welcome with proud hallylugers the ery
Wen our eagle kicks yourn from the naytional nest,"
Sez John C. Calhoun, sez he;—
"O," sez Westcott o' Florida,
"Wut treason is horrider
Then our priv'leges tryin' to proon?" sez he.

"It's 'coz they're so happy, thet, wen crazy sarpints
Stick their nose in our bizness, we git so darned riled;

We think it's our dooty to give pooty sharp hints,
  Thet the last crumb of Edin on airth shan't be
    spiled,"
   Sez John C. Calhoun, sez he;—
     "Ah," sez Dixon H. Lewis,
     "It perfectly true is
   Thet slavery 's airth's grettest boon," sez he.

[It was said of old time, that riches have wings; and, though this be not applicable in a literal strictness to the wealth of our patriarchal brethren of the South, yet it is clear that their possessions have legs, and an unaccountable propensity for using them in a northerly direction. I marvel that the grand jury of Washington did not find a true bill against the North Star for aiding and abetting Drayton and Sayres. It would have been quite of a piece with the intelligence displayed by the South on other questions connected with slavery. I think that no ship of state was ever freighted with a more veritable Jonah than this same domestic institution of ours. Mephistopheles himself could not feign so bitterly, so satirically sad a sight as this of three millions of human beings crushed beyond help or hope by this one mighty argument,—*Our fathers knew no better!* Nevertheless, it is the unavoidable destiny of Jonahs to be cast overboard sooner or later. Or shall we try the experiment of hiding our Jonah in a safe place, that none may lay hands on him to make jetsam of him? Let us, then, with equal forethought and wisdom, lash ourselves to the anchor, and await, in pious confidence, the certain result. Perhaps our suspicious passenger is no Jonah after all, being black. For it is well known that a superintending Providence made a kind of sandwich of Ham and his descendants, to be devoured by the Caucasian race.

In God's name, let all, who hear nearer and nearer the

hungry moan of the storm and the growl of the breakers, speak out! But, alas! we have no right to interfere. If a man pluck an apple of mine, he shall be in danger of the justice; but if he steal my brother, I must be silent. Who says this? Our Constitution, consecrated by the callous consuetude of sixty years, and grasped in triumphant argument by the left hand of him whose right hand clutches the clotted slave-whip. Justice, venerable with the undethronable majesty of countless æons, says,—SPEAK! The Past, wise with the sorrows and desolations of ages, from amid her shattered fanes and wolf-housing palaces, echoes,—SPEAK! Nature, through her thousand trumpets of freedom, her stars, her sunrises, her seas, her winds, her cataracts, her mountains blue with cloudy pines, blows jubilant encouragement, and cries,—SPEAK! From the soul's trembling abysses the still, small voice not vaguely murmurs,—SPEAK! But, alas! the Constitution and the Honorable Mr. Bagowind, M. C., say,—BE DUMB!

It occurs to me to suggest, as a topic of inquiry in this connection, whether, on that momentous occasion when the goats and the sheep shall be parted, the Constitution and the Honorable Mr. Bagowind, M. C., will be expected to take their places on the left as our hircine vicars.

Quid sum miser tunc dicturus?
Quem patronum rogaturus?

There is a point where toleration sinks into sheer baseness and poltroonery. The toleration of the worst leads us to look on what is barely better as good enough, and to worship what is only moderately good. Woe to that man, or that nation, to whom mediocrity has become an ideal!

Has our experiment of self-government succeeded, if

it barely manage to *rub and go?* Here, now, is a piece of barbarism which Christ and the nineteenth century say shall cease, and which Messrs. Smith, Brown, and others say shall *not* cease. I would by no means deny the eminent respectability of these gentlemen, but I confess, that, in such a wrestling-match, I cannot help having my fears for them.

Discite justitiam, moniti, et non temnere divos.

H. W.]

No. VI.

THE PIOUS EDITOR'S CREED.

[At the special instance of Mr. Biglow, I preface the following satire with an extract from a sermon preached during the past summer, from Ezekiel xxxiv. 2:—"Son of man, prophesy against the shepherds of Israel." Since the Sabbath on which this discourse was delivered, the editor of the "Jaalam Independent Blunderbuss" has unaccountably absented himself from our house of worship.

"I know of no so responsible position as that of the public journalist. The editor of our day bears the same relation to his time that the clerk bore to the age before the invention of printing. Indeed, the position which he holds is that which the clergyman should hold even now. But the clergyman chooses to walk off to the extreme edge of the world, and to throw such seed as he has clear over into that darkness which he calls the Next Life. As if *next* did not mean *nearest*, and as if any life were nearer than that immediately present one which boils and eddies all around him at the caucus, the ratification meeting, and the polls! Who taught him to exhort men to prepare for eternity, as for some future era of which the present forms no integral part? The furrow which Time is even now turning runs through the Everlasting, and in that must he plant, or nowhere. Yet he would fain believe and teach that we are *going* to have more of eternity than we have now. This *going* of his is like that of the auctioneer, on which *gone* follows before we have made up our minds to bid,—in which manner, not three months back, I lost an excellent copy of Chappelow on Job. So it has come to pass that the preacher, instead of being a living force, has faded into an emblematic figure at christenings, weddings, and funerals. Or, if he exercise any other function, it is as keeper and feeder of certain theologic dogmas, which, when occasion offers, he unkennels with a *staboy!* "to bark and bite as 'tis their nature to," whence that reproach of *odium theologicum* has arisen.

"Meanwhile, see what a pulpit the editor mounts daily, sometimes with a congregation of fifty thousand within reach of his voice, and never so much as a nodder, even, among them! And from what a Bible can he choose his text,—a Bible which needs no translation, and which no priestcraft can shut and clasp from the laity,—the open volume of the world, upon which, with a pen of sunshine or destroying fire, the inspired Present is even now writing the annals of God! Methinks the editor who should understand his calling, and be equal thereto, would truly deserve that title of *ποιμὴν λαῶν*, which Homer bestows upon princes. He would be the Moses of our nineteenth century; and whereas the old Sinai, silent now, is but a common mountain stared at by the elegant tourist and crawled over by the hammering geologist, he must find his tables of the new law here among factories and cities in this Wilderness of Sin (Numbers xxxiii. 12) called Progress of Civilization, and be the captain of our Exodus into the Canaan of a truer social order.

"Nevertheless, our editor will not come so far within even the shadow of Sinai as Mahomet did, but chooses rather to construe Moses by Joe Smith. He takes up the crook, not that the sheep may be fed, but that he may never want a warm woollen suit and a joint of mutton.

Immemor, O, fidei, pecorumque oblite tuorum!

For which reason I would derive the name *editor* not so much from *edo*, to publish, as from *edo*, to eat, that being the peculiar profession to which he esteems himself called. He blows up the flames of political discord for no other occasion than that he may thereby handily boil his own pot. I believe there are two thousand of these mutton-loving shepherds in the United States, and of these, how many have even the dimmest perception of their immense power, and the duties consequent thereon? Here and there, haply, one. Nine hundred and ninety-nine labor to impress upon the people the great principles of *Tweedledum*, and other nine hundred and ninety-nine preach with equal earnestness the gospel according to *Tweedledee.*"—H. W.]

I DU believe in Freedom's cause,
  Ez fur away ez Payris is;
I love to see her stick her claws
  In them infarnal Phayrisees;
It's wal enough agin a king
  To dror resolves an' triggers,—
But libbaty's a kind o' thing
  Thet don't agree with niggers.

I du believe the people want
  A tax on teas an' coffees,
Thet nothin' aint extravygunt,—
  Purvidin' I'm in office;
Fer I hev loved my country sence
  My eye-teeth filled their sockets,

An' Uncle Sam I reverence,
  Partic'larly his pockets.

I du believe in *any* plan
  O' levyin' the taxes,
Ez long ez, like a lumberman,
  I git jest wut I axes:
I go free-trade thru thick an' thin,
  Because it kind o' rouses
The folks to vote,—an' keeps us in
  Our quiet custom-houses.

I du believe it's wise an' good
  To sen' out furrin missions,
Thet is, on sartin understood
  An' orthydox conditions;—
I mean nine thousan' dolls. per ann.,
  Nine thousan' more fer outfit,
An' me to recommend a man
  The place 'ould jest about fit.

I du believe in special ways
  O' prayin' an' convartin';
The bread comes back in many days,
  An' buttered, tu, fer sartin;
I mean in preyin' till one busts
  On wut the party chooses,
An' in convartin' public trusts
  To very privit uses.

I du believe hard coin the stuff
  Fer 'lectioneers to spout on;
The people's ollers soft enough
  To make hard money out on;
Dear Uncle Sam pervides fer his,
  An' gives a good-sized junk to all,—

I don't care *how* hard money is,
  Ez long ez mine's paid punctooal.

I du believe with all my soul
  In the gret Press's freedom,
To pint the people to the goal
  An' in the traces lead 'em;
Palsied the arm thet forges yokes
  At my fat contracts squintin',
An' withered be the nose thet pokes
  Inter the gov'ment printin'!

I du believe thet I should give
  Wut's his'n unto Cæsar,
Fer it's by him I move an' live,
  Frum him my bread an' cheese air;
I du believe thet all o' me
  Doth bear his superscription,—
Will, conscience, honor, honesty,
  An' things o' thet description.

I du believe in prayer an' praise
  To him that hez the grantin'
O' jobs,—in every thin' thet pays,
  But most of all in CANTIN';
This doth my cup with marcies fill,
  This lays all thought o' sin to rest,—
I *don't* believe in princerple,
  But O, I *du* in interest.

I du believe in bein' this
  Or thet, ez it may happen
One way or t'other hendiest is
  To ketch the people nappin';
It aint by princerples nor men
  My preudunt course is steadied,—

I scent wich pays the best, an' then
Go into it baldheaded.

I du believe thet holdin' slaves
Comes nat'ral tu a Presidunt,
Let 'lone the rowdedow it saves
To hev a wal-broke precedunt;
Fer any office, small or gret,
I couldn't ax with no face,
Without I'd ben, thru dry an' wet,
Th' unrizzest kind o' doughface.

I du believe wutever trash
'll keep the people in blindness,—
Thet we the Mexicuns can thrash
Right inter brotherly kindness,
Thet bombshells, grape, an' powder 'n' ball
Air good-will's strongest magnets,
Thet peace, to make it stick at all,
Must be druv in with bagnets.

In short, I firmly du believe
In Humbug generally,
Fer it's a thing thet I perceive
To hev a solid vally;
This heth my faithful shepherd ben,
In pasturs sweet heth led me,
An' this'll keep the people green
To feed ez they hev fed me.

[I subjoin here another passage from my before-mentioned discourse.

"Wonderful, to him that has eyes to see it rightly, is the newspaper. To me, for example, sitting on the critical front bench of the pit, in my study here in Jaalam, the advent of my weekly journal is as that of a strolling theatre, or rather of a puppet-show, on whose stage, narrow as it is, the tragedy, comedy, and farce of life are played in little. Behold the whole huge earth sent to me hebdomadally in a brown-paper wrapper!

"Hither, to my obscure corner, by wind or steam, on horseback or dromedary-back, in the pouch of the Indian runner, or clicking over the magnetic wires, troop all the famous performers from the four quarters of the globe. Looked at from a point of criticism, tiny puppets they seem all, as the editor sets up his booth upon my desk and officiates as showman. Now I can truly see how little and transitory is life. The earth appears almost as a drop of vinegar, on which the solar microscope of the imagination must be brought to bear in order to make out any thing distinctly. That animalcule there, in the pea-jacket, is Louis Philippe, just landed on the coast of England. That other, in the gray surtout and cocked hat, is Napoleon Bonaparte Smith, assuring France that she need apprehend no interference from him in the present alarming juncture. At that spot, where you seem to see a speck of something in motion, is an immense mass-meeting. Look sharper, and you will see a mite brandishing his mandibles in an excited manner. That is the great Mr. Soandso, defining his position amid tumultuous and irrepressible cheers. That infinitesimal creature, upon whom some score of others, as minute as he, are gazing in open-mouthed admiration, is a famous philosopher, expounding to a select audience their capacity for the Infinite. That scarce discernible pufflet of smoke and dust is a revolution. That speck there is a reformer, just arranging the lever with which he is to move the world. And lo, there creeps forward the shadow of a skeleton that blows one breath between its grinning teeth, and all our distinguished actors are whisked off the slippery stage into the dark Beyond.

"Yes, the little show-box has its solemner suggestions. Now and then we catch a glimpse of a grim old man, who lays down a scythe and hour-glass in the corner while he shifts the scenes. There, too, in the dim background, a weird shape is ever delving. Sometimes he leans upon his mattock, and gazes, as a coach whirls by, bearing the newly married on their wedding jaunt, or glances carelessly at a babe brought home from christening. Suddenly (for the scene grows larger and larger as we look) a bony hand snatches back a performer in the midst of his part, and him, whom yesterday two infinities (past and future) would not suffice, a handful of dust is enough to cover and silence forever. Nay, we see the same fleshless fingers opening to clutch the showman himself, and guess, not without a shudder, that they are lying in wait for spectator also.

"Think of it: for three dollars a year I buy a season-ticket to this great Globe Theatre, for which God would write the dramas (only that we like farces, spectacles, and the tragedies of Apollyon better), whose scene-shifter is Time, and whose curtain is rung down by Death.

"Such thoughts will occur to me sometimes as I am tearing off the wrapper of my newspaper. Then suddenly that otherwise too often vacant sheet becomes invested for me with a strange kind of awe. Look! deaths and marriages, notices of inventions, discoveries, and books, lists of promotions, of killed, wounded, and missing, news of fires, accidents, of sudden wealth and as sudden poverty;—I hold in my hand the ends of myriad invisible electric conductors, along which tremble the joys, sorrows, wrongs, triumphs, hopes, and despairs of as many men and women everywhere. So that upon that mood of mind which seems to isolate me from mankind as a spectator of their puppet-pranks, another supervenes, in which I feel that I, too, unknown and unheard of, am yet of some import to my fellows. For, through my newspaper here, do not families take pains to send me, an entire stranger, news of a death among them? Are not here two who would have me know of their marriage? And, strangest of all, is not this singular person anxious to have me informed that he has received a fresh supply of Dimitry Bruisgins? But to none of us does the Present continue miraculous (even if for a moment discerned as such). We glance carelessly at the sunrise, and get used to Orion and the Pleiades. The wonder wears off, and to-morrow this sheet, in which a vision was let down to me from Heaven, shall be the wrappage to a bar of soap or the platter for a beggar's broken victuals."—H. W.]

No. VII.

A LETTER

FROM A CANDIDATE FOR THE PRESIDENCY IN ANSWER TO SUTTIN QUESTIONS PROPOSED BY MR. HOSEA BIGLOW, INCLOSED IN A NOTE FROM MR. BIGLOW TO S. H. GAY, ESQ., EDITOR OF THE NATIONAL ANTI-SLAVERY STANDARD.

[CURIOSITY may be said to be the quality which preeminently distinguishes and segregates man from the lower animals. As we trace the scale of animated nature downward, we find this faculty (as it may truly be called) of the mind diminished in the savage, and quite extinct in the brute. The first object which civilized man proposes to himself I take to be the finding out whatsoever he can concerning his neighbors. *Nihil humanum a me alienum puto;* I am curious about even John Smith. The desire next in strength to this (an opposite pole, indeed, of the same magnet) is that of communicating the unintelligence we have carefully picked up.

Men in general may be divided into the inquisitive and the communicative. To the first class belong Peeping Toms, eaves-droppers, navel-contemplating Brahmins metaphysicians, travellers, Empedocleses, spies, the various societies for promoting Rhinothism, Columbuses, Yankees, discoverers, and men of science, who present themselves to the mind as so many marks of interrogation wandering up and down the world, or sitting in studies and laboratories. The second class I should again subdivide into four. In the first subdivision I would rank those who have an itch to tell us about themselves,—as keepers of diaries, insignificant persons generally, Montaignes, Horace Walpoles, autobiographers, poets. The second includes those who are anxious to impart information concerning other people,—as historians, barbers, and such. To the third belong those who labor to give us intelligence about nothing at all,—as novelists, political orators, the large majority of authors, preachers, lecturers, and the like. In the fourth come those who are communicative from motives of public benevolence, —as finders of mares'-nests and bringers of ill news. Each of us two-legged fowls without feathers embraces all these subdivisions in himself to a greater or less degree, for none of us so much as lays an egg, or incubates a chalk one, but straightway the whole barn-yard shall know it by our cackle or our cluck. *Omnibus hoc vitium est.* There are different grades in all these classes. One will turn his telescope toward a back-yard, another toward Uranus; one will tell you that he dined with Smith, another that he supped with Plato. In one particular, all men may be considered as belonging to the first grand division, inasmuch as they all seem equally desirous of discovering the mote in their neighbor's eye.

To one or another of these species every human being may safely be referred. I think it beyond a peradventure that Jonah prosecuted some inquiries into the digestive apparatus of whales, and that Noah sealed up a letter in an empty bottle, that news in regard to him might not be wanting in case of the worst. They had else been super or subter human. I conceive, also, that, as there are certain persons who continually peep and pry at the keyhole of that mysterious door through which, sooner or later, we all make our exits, so there are doubtless ghosts fidgetting and fretting on the other side of it, because they have no means of conveying back to this world the scraps of news they have picked up in that. For there is an answer ready somewhere to every question, the great law of *give and take* runs through all nature, and if we see a hook, we may be sure that an eye is waiting for it. I read in every face I meet a standing advertisement of information wanted in regard to A. B., or that the friends of C. D. can hear something to his disadvantage by application to such a one.

It was to gratify the two great passions of asking and answering that epistolary correspondence was first invented. Letters (for by this usurped title epistles are now commonly known) are of several kinds. First, there are those which are not letters at all,—as letters-patent, letters dimissory, letters inclosing bills, letters of administration, Pliny's letters, letters of diplomacy, of Cato, of Mentor, of Lords Lyttelton, Chesterfield, and Orrery, of Jacob Behmen, Seneca (whom St. Jerome includes in his list of sacred writers), letters from abroad, from sons in college to their fathers, letters of marque, and letters generally, which are in nowise letters of mark. Second, are real letters, such as those of Gray, Cowper, Walpole, Howel, Lamb, D. Y., the first letters from children, (printed in staggering capitals,) Letters from New York, letters of credit, and others, interesting for the sake of the writer or the thing written. I have read also letters from Europe by a gentleman named Pinto, containing some curious gossip, and which I hope to see collected for the benefit of the curious. There are. besides letters addressed to posterity,—as epitaphs, for example, written for their own monuments by monarchs, whereby we have lately become possessed of the names of several great conquerors and kings of kings, hitherto unheard of and still unpronounceable, but valuable to the student of the entirely dark ages. The letter which St. Peter sent to King Pepin in the year of grace 755, that of the Virgin to the magistrates of Messina, that of St. Gregory Thaumaturgus to the D—l, and that of this last-mentioned active police-magistrate to a nun of Girgenti, I would place in a class by themselves, as also the letters of candidates, concerning which I shall dilate more fully in a note at the end of the following poem. At present, *sat prata biberunt.* Only, concerning the shape of letters, they are all either square or oblong, to which general figures circular letters and round-robins also conform themselves.—H. W.]

DEER SIR its gut to be the fashun now to rite letters to the candid 8s and i wus chose at a publick Meetin in Jaalam to du wut wus nessary fur that town. i writ to 271 ginerals and gut ansers to 209. tha air called candid 8s but I don't see nothin candid about em. this here 1 wich I send wus thought satty's factory. I dunno as it's ushle to print Poscrips, but as all the ansers I got hed the saim, I sposed it wus best. times has gretly changed. Formaly to knock a man into a cocked hat wus to use him up, but now it ony gives him a chance fur the cheef madgustracy.—H. B.

DEAR SIR,—You wish to know my notions
  On sartin pints thet rile the land;

There's nothin' thet my natur so shuns
  Ez bein' mum or underhand;
I'm a straight-spoken kind o' creetur
  Thet blurts right out wut's in his head,
An' ef I've one pecooler feetur,
  It is a nose thet wunt be led.

So, to begin at the beginnin',
  An' come direcly to the pint,
I think the country's underpinnin'
  Is some consid'ble out o' jint;
I aint agoin' to try your patience
  By tellin' who done this or thet,
I don't make no insinooations,
  I jest let on I smell a rat.

Thet is, I mean, it seems to me so,
  But, ef the public think I'm wrong,
I wunt deny but wut I be so,—
  An', fact, it don't smell very strong;
My mind's tu fair to lose its balance
  An' say wich party hez most sense;
There may be folks o' greater talence
  Thet can't set stiddier on the fence.

I'm an eclectic; ez to choosin'
  'Twixt this an' thet, I'm plaguy lawth;
I leave a side thet looks like losin',
  But (wile there's doubt) I stick to both;
I stan' upon the Constitution,
  Ez preudunt statesmun say, who've planned
A way to git the most profusion
  O' chances ez to *ware* they'll stand.

Ez fer the war, I go agin it,—
  I mean to say I kind o' du,—

Thet is, I mean thet, bein' in it,
  The best way wuz to fight it thru;
Not but wut abstract war is horrid,
  I sign to thet with all my heart,—
But civlyzation *doos* git forrid
  Sometimes upon a powder-cart.

About thet darned Proviso matter
  I never hed a grain o' doubt,
Nor I aint one my sense to scatter
  So'st no one couldn't pick it out;
My love fer North an' South is equil,
  So I'll jest answer plump an' frank,—
No matter wut may be the sequil,—
  Yes, Sir, I *am* agin a Bank.

Ez to the answerin' o' questions,
  I'm an off ox at bein' druv,
Though I aint one thet ary test shuns
  'll give our folks a helpin' shove;
Kind o' promiscoous I go it
  Fer the holl country, an' the ground
I take, ez nigh ez I can show it,
  Is pooty gen'ally all round.

I don't appruve o' givin' pledges;
  You'd ough' to leave a feller free,
An' not go knockin' out the wedges
  To ketch his fingers in the tree;
Pledges air awfle breachy cattle
  Thet prudunt farmers don't turn out,—
Ez long 'z the people git their rattle,
  Wut is there fer'm to grout about?

Ez to the slaves, there's no confusion
  In *my* idees consarnin' them,—

I think they air an Institution,
  A sort of—yes, jest so,—ahem:
Do *I* own any? Of my merit
  On thet pint you yourself may jedge
All is, I never drink no sperit,
  Nor I haint never signed no pledge.

Ez to my princerples, I glory
  In hevin' nothin' o' the sort;
I aint a Wig, I aint a Tory,
  I'm jest a candidate, in short;
Thet's fair an' square an' parpendicler,
  But, ef the Public cares a fig
To hev me an' thin' in particler,
  Wy, I'm a kind o' peri-wig.

P. S.

Ez we're a sort o' privateerin',
  O' course, you know, it's sheer an' sheer,
An' there is sutthin' wuth your hearin'
  I'll mention in *your* privit ear;
Ef you git *me* inside the White House,
  Your head with ile I'll kin' o' 'nint
By gittin' *you* inside the Light-house
  Down to the eend o' Jaalam Pint.

An' ez the North hez took to brustlin'
  At bein' scrouged frum off the roost,
I'll tell ye wut'll save all tusslin'
  An' give our side a harnsome boost,—
Tell 'em thet on the Slavery question
  I'm RIGHT, although to speak I'm lawth;
This gives you a safe pint to rest on,
  An' leaves me frontin' South by North.

[And now of epistles candidatial, which are of two kinds,—namely, letters of acceptance, and letters definitive of position. Our republic, on the eve of an election, may safely enough be called a republic of letters. Epistolary composition becomes then an epidemic, which seizes one candidate after another, not seldom cutting short the thread of political life. It has come to such a pass, that a party dreads less the attacks of its opponents than a letter from its candidate. *Litera scripta manet*, and it will go hard if something bad cannot be made of it. General Harrison, it is well understood, was surrounded, during his candidacy, with the *cordon sanitaire* of a vigilance committee. No prisoner in Spielberg was ever more cautiously deprived of writing materials. The soot was scraped carefully from the chimney-places; outposts of expert rifle-shooters rendered it sure death for any goose (who came clad in feathers) to approach within a certain limited distance of North Bend; and all domestic fowls about the premises were reduced to the condition of Plato's original man. By these precautions the General was saved. *Parva componere magnis*, I remember, that, when party-spirit once ran high among my people, upon occasion of the choice of a new deacon, I, having my preferences, yet not caring too openly to express them, made use of an innocent fraud to bring about that result which I deemed most desirable. My stratagem was no other than the throwing a copy of the Complete Letter-Writer in the way of the candidate whom I wished to defeat. He caught the infection, and addressed a short note to his constituents, in which the opposite party detected so many and so grave improprieties, (he had modelled it upon the letter of a young lady accepting a proposal of marriage,) that he not only lost his election, but, falling under a suspicion of Sabellianism and I know not what, (the widow Endive assured me that he was a Paralipomenon, to her certain knowledge,) was forced to leave the town. Thus it is that the letter killeth.

The object which candidates propose to themselves in writing is to convey no meaning at all. And here is a quite unsuspected pitfall into which they successively plunge headlong. For it is precisely in such cryptographies that mankind are prone to seek for and find a wonderful amount and variety of significance. *Omne ignotum pro mirifico.* How do we admire at the antique world striving to crack those oracular nuts from Delphi, Hammon, and elsewhere, in only one of which can I so much as surmise that any kernel had ever lodged; that, namely, wherein Apollo confessed that he was mortal. One Didymus is, moreover, related to have written six thousand books on the single subject of grammar, a topic rendered only more tenebrific by the labors of his successors, and which seems still to possess an attraction for authors in proportion as they can make nothing of it. A singular loadstone for theologians, also, is the Beast in the Apocalypse, whereof, in the course of my studies, I have noted two hundred and three several interpretations, each lethiferal to all the rest. *Non nostrum est tantas componere lites,* yet I have myself ventured upon a two hundred and fourth, which I embodied in a discourse preached on occasion of the demise of the late usurper, Napoleon Bonaparte, and which quieted, in a large measure, the minds of my people. It is true that my views on this important point were ardently controverted by Mr. Shearjashub Holden, the then preceptor of our academy, and in other particulars a very deserving and sensible young man, though possessing a somewhat limited knowledge of the Greek tongue. But his heresy struck down no deep root, and, he having been lately removed by the hand of Providence, I had the satisfaction of reaffirming my cherished sentiments in a sermon preached upon the Lord's day immediately succeeding his funeral. This might seem like taking an unfair advantage, did I not add that he had made provision in his last will (being celibate) for the publication of a posthumous tractate in support of his own dangerous opinions.

I know of nothing in our modern times which approaches so nearly to the ancient oracle as the letter of a Presidential candidate. Now, among the Greeks, the eating of beans was strictly forbidden to all such as had it in mind to consult those expert amphibologists, and this same prohibition on the part of Pythagoras to his disciples is understood to imply an abstinence from politics, beans having been used as ballots. That other explication, *quod videlicet sensus eo cibo obtundi existimaret*, though supported *pugnis et calcibus* by many of the learned, and not wanting the countenance of Cicero, is confuted by the larger experience of New England. On the whole, I think it safer to apply here the rule of interpretation which now generally obtains in regard to antique cosmogonies, myths, fables, proverbial expressions, and knotty points generally, which is, to find a common-sense meaning, and then select whatever can be imagined the most opposite thereto. In this way we arrive at the conclusion, that the Greeks objected to the questioning of candidates. And very properly, if, as I conceive, the chief point be not to discover what a person in that position is, or what he will do, but whether he can be elected. *Vos exemplaria Græca nocturna versate manu, versate diurna.*

But, since an imitation of the Greeks in this particular (the asking of questions being one chief privilege of freemen) is hardly to be hoped for, and our candidates will answer, whether they are questioned or not, I would recommend that these ante-electionary dialogues should be carried on by symbols, as were the diplomatic correspondences of the Scythians and Macrobii, or confined to the language of signs, like the famous interview of Panurge and Goatsnose. A candidate might then convey a suitable reply to all committees of inquiry by closing one eye, or by presenting them with a phial of Egyptian darkness to be speculated upon by their respective constituencies. These answers would be susceptible of whatever retrospective construction the exigencies of the political campaign might seem to demand, and the candidate could take his position on either side of the fence with entire consistency. Or, if letters must be written, profitable use might be made of the Dighton rock hieroglyphic or the cuneiform script, every fresh decipherer of which is enabled to educe a different meaning, whereby a sculptured stone or two supplies us, and will probably continue to supply posterity, with a very vast and various body of authentic history. For even the briefest epistle in the ordinary chirography is dangerous. There is scarce any style so compressed that superfluous words may not be detected in it. A severe critic might curtail that famous brevity of Cæsar's by two thirds, drawing his pen through the supererogatory *veni* and *vidi*. Perhaps, after all, the surest footing of hope is to be found in the rapidly increasing tendency to demand less and less of qualification in candidates. Already have statesmanship, experience, and the possession (nay, the profession, even) of principles been rejected as superfluous, and may not the patriot reasonably hope that the ability to write will follow? At present, there may be death in pot-hooks as well as pots, the loop of a letter may suffice for a bow-string, and all the dreadful heresies of Anti-slavery may lurk in a flourish.—H. W.]

No. VIII.

A SECOND LETTER FROM B. SAWIN, ESQ.

[In the following epistle, we behold Mr. Sawin returning, a *miles emeritus*, to the bosom of his family. *Quantum mutatus!* The good Father of us all had doubtless intrusted to the keeping of this child of his certain faculties of a constructive kind. He had put in him a share of that vital force, the nicest economy of every minute atom of which is necessary to the perfect development of Humanity. He had given him a brain and heart, and so had equipped his soul with the two strong wings of knowledge and love, whereby it can mount to hang its nest under the eaves of heaven. And this child, so dowered, he had intrusted to the keeping of his vicar, the State. How stands the account of that stewardship? The State, or Society, (call her by what name you will,) had taken no manner of thought of him till she saw him swept out into the street, the pitiful leavings of last night's debauch, with cigar-ends, lemon-parings, tobacco-quids, slops, vile stenches, and the whole loathsome next-morning of the bar-room,—an own child of the Almighty God! I remember him as he was brought to be christened, a ruddy, rugged babe; and now there he wallows, reeking, seething,—the dead corpse, not of a man, but of a soul,—a putrefying lump, horrible for the life that is in it. Comes the wind of heaven, that good Samaritan, and parts the hair upon his forehead, nor is too nice to kiss those parched, cracked lips; the morning opens upon him her eyes full of pitying sunshine, the sky yearns down to him,—and there he lies fermenting. O sleep! let me not profane thy holy name by calling that stertorous unconsciousness a slumber! By and by comes along the State, God's vicar. Does she say,—"My poor, forlorn foster-child! Behold here a force which I will make dig and plant and build for me?" Not so, but,—"Here is a recruit ready-made to my hand, a piece of destroying energy lying unprofitably idle." So she claps an ugly gray suit on him, puts a musket in his grasp, and sends him off, with Gubernatorial and other godspeeds, to do duty as a destroyer.

I made one of the crowd at the last Mechanics' Fair, and, with the rest, stood gazing in wonder at a perfect machine, with its soul of fire, its boiler-heart that sent the hot blood pulsing along the iron arteries, and its thews of steel. And while I was admiring the adaptation of means to end, the harmonious involutions of contrivance, and the never-bewildered complexity, I saw a grimed and greasy fellow, the imperious engine's lackey and drudge, whose sole office was to let fall, at intervals, a drop or two of oil upon a certain joint. Then my soul said within me, See there a piece of mechanism to which that other you marvel at is but as the rude first effort of a child,—a force which not merely suffices to set a few wheels in motion, but which can send an impulse all through the infinite future,—a contrivance, not for turning out pins, or stitching button-holes, but for making Hamlets and Lears. And yet this thing of iron shall be housed, waited on, guarded from rust and dust, and it shall be a crime but so much as to scratch it with a pin; while the other, with its fire of God in it, shall be buffeted hither and thither, and finally sent carefully a thousand miles to be the target for a Mexican cannon-ball. Unthrifty Mother State! My heart burned within me for pity and indignation, and I renewed this covenant with my own soul,—*In aliis mansuetus ero, at, in blasphemiis contra Christum, non ita.*—H. W.]

I SPOSE you wonder ware I be; I can't tell, fer the soul o' me,
Exacly ware I be myself,—meanin' by thet the holl o' me.
Wen I left hum, I hed two legs, an' they worn't bad ones neither,
(The scaliest trick they ever played wuz bringin' on me hither,)
Now one on 'em's I dunno ware;—they thought I wuz adyin',
An' sawed it off because they said 'twuz kin' o' mortifyin';
I'm willin' to believe it wuz, an' yit I don't see, nuther,
Wy one should take to feelin' cheap a minnit sooner 'n t'other,
Sence both wuz equilly to blame; but things is ez they be;
It took on so they took it off, an' thet's enough fer me:
There's one good thing, though, to be said about my wooden new one,—
The liquor can't git into it ez't used to in the true one;
So it saves drink; an' then, besides, a feller couldn't beg
A gretter blessin' then to hev one ollers sober peg;

It's true a chap's in want o' two fer follerin' a
drum,
But all the march I'm up to now is jest to Kingdom
Come.

I've lost one eye, but thet's a loss it's easy to supply
Out o' the glory that I've gut, fer thet is all my
eye;
An' one is big enough, I guess, by diligently usin' it,
To see all I shall ever git by way o' pay fer losin' it;
Off'cers, I notice, who git paid fer all our thumps
an' kickins,
Du wal by keepin' single eyes arter the fattest
pickins;
So, ez the eye's put fairly out, I'll larn to go with-
out it,
An' not allow *myself* to be no gret put out about
it.
Now, le' me see, thet isn't all; I used, 'fore leavin'
Jaalam,
To count things on my finger-eends, but sutthin'
seems to ail 'em:
Ware's my left hand? O, darn it, yes, I recollect
wut's come on't;
I haint no left arm but my right, an' thet's gut jest
a thumb on't;
It aint so hendy ez it wuz to cal'late a sum on't.
I've hed some ribs broke,—six (I b'lieve),—I haint
kep' no account on 'em;
Wen pensions git to be the talk, I'll settle the
amount on 'em.
An' now I'm speakin' about ribs, it kin' o' brings
to mind
One thet I couldn't never break,—the one I lef'
behind;
Ef you should see her, jest clear out the spout o
your invention

An' pour the longest sweetnin' in about an annooal pension,
An' kin' o' hint (in case, you know, the critter should refuse to be
Consoled) I aint so 'xpensive now to keep ez wut I used to be;
There's one arm less, ditto one eye, an' then the leg thet's wooden
Can be took off an' sot away wenever ther's a puddin'.

I spose you think I'm comin' back ez opperlunt ez thunder,
With shiploads o' gold images an' varus sorts o' plunder;
Wal, 'fore I vullinteered, I thought this country wuz a sort o'
Canaan, a regl'ar Promised Land flowin' with rum an' water,
Ware propaty growed up like time, without no cultivation,
An' gold wuz dug ez taters be among our Yankee nation,
Ware nateral advantages were pufficly amazin',
Ware every rock there wuz about with precious stuns wuz blazin',
Ware mill-sites filled the country up ez thick ez you could cram 'em,
An' desput rivers run about abeggin' folks to dam 'em;
Then there were meetinhouses, tu, chockful o' gold an' silver
Thet you could take, an' no one couldn't hand ye in no bill fer;—
Thet's wut I thought afore I went, thet's wut them fellers told us
Thet stayed to hum an' speechified an' to the buzzards sold us;

I thought thet gold mines could be gut cheaper than
Chiny asters,
An' see myself acomin' back like sixty Jacob
Astors;
But sech idees soon melted down an' didn't leave
a grease-spot;
I vow my holl sheer o' the spiles wouldn't come
nigh a V spot;
Although, most anywares we've ben, you needn't
break no locks,
Nor run no kin' o' risks, to fill your pocket full o'
rocks.

I guess I mentioned in my last some o' the nateral
feeturs
O' this all-fiered buggy hole in th' way o' awfle
creeturs,
But I fergut to name (new things to speak on so
abounded)
How one day you'll most die o' thust, an' 'fore the
next git drownded.
The clymit seems to me jest like a teapot made o'
pewter
Our Prudence hed, thet wouldn't pour (all she
could du) to suit her;
Fust place the leaves 'ould choke the spout, so's
not a drop 'ould dreen out,
Then Prude 'ould tip an' tip an' tip, till the holl
kit bust clean out,
The kiver-hinge-pin bein' lost, tea-leaves an' tea
an' kiver
'ould all come down *kerswosh!* ez though the dam
broke in a river.
Jest so 't is here; holl months there aint a day o'
rainy weather,
An' jest ez th' officers 'ould be alayin' heads to-
gether

Ez t' how they'd mix their drink at sech a miling-
 tary deepot,—
'T 'ould pour ez though the lid wuz off the ever-
 lastin' teapot.
The cons'quence is, thet I shall take, wen I'm
 allowed to leave here,
One piece o' propaty along,—an' thet's the shakin'
 fever;
It's reggilar employment, though, an' thet aint
 thought to harm one,
Nor 't aint so tiresome ez it wuz with t'other leg
 an' arm on;
An' it's a consolation, tu, although it doosn't pay,
To hev it said you're some gret shakes in any kin'
 o' way.
'Tworn't very long, I tell ye wut, I thought o'
 fortin-makin',—
One day a reg'lar shiver-de-freeze, an' next ez
 good ez bakin',—
One day abrilin' in the sand, then smoth'rin' in the
 mashes,—
Git up all sound, be put to bed a mess o' hacks an'
 smashes.
But then, thinks I, at any rate there's glory to be
 hed,—
Thet's an investment, arter all, thet mayn't turn
 out so bad;
But somehow, wen we'd fit an' licked, I ollers
 found the thanks
Gut kin' o' lodged afore they come ez low down ez
 the ranks;
The Gin'rals gut the biggest sheer, the Cunnles
 next, an' so on,—
We never gut a blasted mite o' glory ez I know
 on;
An' spose we hed, I wonder how you're goin' to
 contrive its

Division so's to give a piece to twenty thousand
privits;
Ef you should multiply by ten the portion o' the
brav'st one,
You wouldn't git more'n half enough to speak of
on a grave-stun;
We git the licks,—we're jest the grist thet's put
into War's hoppers;
Leftenants is the lowest grade thet helps pick up
the coppers.
It may suit folks thet go agin a body with a soul
in't,
An' aint contented with a hide without a bagnet
hole in't;
But glory is a kin' o' thing *I* shan't pursue no
furder,
Coz thet's the off'cers parquisite,—yourn's on'y
jest the murder.

Wal, arter I gin glory up, thinks I at least there's
one
Thing in the bills we aint hed yit, an' thet's the
GLORIOUS FUN;
Ef once we git to Mexico, we fairly may persume
we
All day an' night shall revel in the halls o' Monte-
zumy.
I'll tell ye wut *my* revels wuz, an' see how you
would like 'em;
We never gut inside the hall: the nighest ever *I*
come
Wuz stan'in' sentry in the sun (an', fact, it *seemed*
a cent'ry)
A ketchin' smells o' biled an' roast thet come out
thru the entry,
An' hearin' ez I sweltered thru my passes an' re-
passes,

A rat-tat-too o' knives an' forks, a clinkty-clink o
glasses:
I can't tell off the bill o' fare the Gin'rals hed in-
side;
All I know is, thet out o' doors a pair o' soles wuz
fried,
An' not a hunderd miles away frum ware this child
wuz posted,
A Massachusetts citizen wuz baked an' biled an'
roasted;
The on'y thing like revellin' thet ever come to me
Wuz bein' routed out o' sleep by thet darned
revelee.

They say the quarrel's settled now; fer my part
I've some doubt on't,
'T 'll take more fish-skin than folks think to take
the rile clean out on't;
At any rate, I'm so used up I can't do no more
fightin',
The on'y chance thet's left to me is politics or
writin';
Now, ez the people's gut to hev a milingtary
man,
An' I aint nothin' else jest now, I've hit upon a
plan;
The can'idatin' line, you know, 'ould suit me to
a T,
An' ef I lose, 'twunt hurt my ears to lodge another
flea;
So I'll set up ez can'idate fer any kin' o' office,
(I mean fer any thet includes good easy-cheers an'
soffies;
Fer ez to runnin' fer a place ware work's the time
o' day,
You know thet's wut I never did,—except the
other way;)

Ef it's the Presidential cheer fer wich I'd better
run,
Wut two legs anywares about could keep up with
my one?
There aint no kin' o' quality in can'idates, it's said,
So useful ez a wooden leg,—except a wooden head;
There's nothin' aint so poppylar—(wy, it's a parfect sin
To think wut Mexico hez paid fer Santy Anny's
pin;)—
Then I haint gut no princerples, an', sence I wuz
knee-high,
I never *did* hev any gret, ez you can testify;
I'm a decided peace-man, tu, an' go agin the war,—
Fer now the holl on't's gone an' past, wut is there
to go *for?*
Ef, wile you're 'lectioneerin' round, some curus
chaps should beg
To know my views o' state affairs, jest answer
WOODEN LEG!
Ef they aint settisfied with thet, an' kin' o' pry an'
doubt
An' ax fer sutthin' deffynit, jest say ONE EYE PUT
OUT!
Thet kin' o' talk I guess you'll find'll answer to a
charm,
An' wen you're druv tu nigh the wall, hol' up my
missin' arm;
Ef they should nose round fer a pledge, put on a
vartoous look
An' tell 'em thet's percisely wut I never gin nor—
took!

Then you can call me "Timbertoes,"—thet's wut
the people likes;
Sutthin' combinin' morril truth with phrases sech
ez strikes;

Some say the people's fond o' this, or thet, or wut you please,—
I tell ye wut the people want is jest correct idees;
"Old Timbertoes," you see, 's a creed it's safe to be quite bold on,
There's nothin' in't the other side can any ways git hold on;
It's a good tangible idee, a sutthin' to embody
Thet valooable class o' men who look thru brandy-toddy;
It gives a Party Platform, tu, jest level with the mind
Of all right-thinkin', honest folks thet mean to go it blind;
Then there air other good hooraws to dror on ez you need 'em,
Sech ez the ONE-EYED SLARTERER, the BLOODY BIRDOFREDUM;
Them's wut takes hold o' folks thet think, ez well ez o' the masses,
An' makes you sartin o' the aid o' good men of all classes.

There's one thing I'm in doubt about; in order to be Presidunt,
It's absolutely ne'ssary to be a Southern residunt;
The Constitution settles thet, an' also thet a feller
Must own a nigger o' some sort, jet black, or brown, or yeller.
Now I haint no objections agin particklar climes,
Nor agin ownin' anythin' (except the truth sometimes),
But, ez I haint no capital, up there among ye, may be,
You might raise funds enough fer me to buy a low-priced baby,

An' then, to suit the No'thern folks, who feel
obleeged to say
They hate an' cuss the very thing they vote fer
every day,
Say you're assured I go full butt fer Libbaty's dif-
fusion
An' made the purchis on'y jest to spite the Insti-
tootion ;—
But, golly! there's the currier's hoss upon the
pavement pawin'!
I'll be more 'xplicit in my next.
Yourn,
BIRDOFREDUM SAWIN.

[We have now a tolerably fair chance of estimating how the balance-sheet stands between our returned volunteer and glory. Supposing the entries to be set down on both sides of the account in fractional parts of one hundred, we shall arrive at something like the following result:—

B. SAWIN, Esq., in account with (BLANK) GLORY.

Cr.		Dr	
By loss of one leg, .	20	To one 675th three cheers in Faneuil Hall, . .	30
" do. one arm, .	15	" do. do. on occasion of presentation of sword to Colonel Wright, .	25
" do. four fingers,	5	" one suit of gray clothes (ingeniously unbecoming), .	15
" do. one eye, .	10	" musical entertainments (drum and fife six months), .	5
" the breaking of six ribs, . .	6		
" having served under Colonel Cushing one month, . .	44		

Am't bro't forward,	100	Am't bro't forward,	75
		" one dinner after return, . .	1
		" chance of pension,	1
		" privilege of drawing long-bow during rest of natural life, .	23
	100		100

E. E.

It would appear that Mr. Sawin found the actual feast curiously the reverse of the bill of fare advertised in Faneuil Hall and other places. His primary object seems to have been the making of his fortune. *Quærenda pecunia primum, virtus post nummos.* He hoisted sail for Eldorado, and shipwrecked on Point Tribulation. *Quid non mortalia pectora cogis, auri sacra fames?* The speculation has sometimes crossed my mind, in that dreary interval of drought which intervenes between quarterly stipendiary showers, that Providence, by the creation of a money-tree, might have simplified wonderfully the sometimes perplexing problem of human life. We read of bread-trees, the butter for which lies ready-churned in Irish bogs. Milk-trees we are assured of in South America, and stout Sir John Hawkins testifies to water-trees in the Canaries. Boot-trees bear abundantly in Lynn and elsewhere; and I have seen, in the entries of the wealthy, hat-trees with a fair show of fruit. A family-tree I once cultivated myself, and found therefrom but a scanty yield, and that quite tasteless and innutritious. Of trees bearing men we are not without examples; as those in the park of Louis the Eleventh of France. Who has forgotten, moreover, that olive-tree, growing in the Athenian's back-garden, with its strange uxorious crop, for the general propagation of which, as of a new and precious variety, the philosopher Diogenes, hitherto uninterested in arboriculture, was so zealous? In the *sylva* of our own Southern States, the females of my family have called my attention to the china-tree. Not to multiply examples, I will barely add to my list the birch-tree, in the smaller branches of which has been implanted so miraculous a virtue for communicating the Latin and Greek languages, and which may well, therefore, be classed among the trees producing necessaries of life,—*venerabile donum fatalis virgæ.* That money-trees existed in the golden age there want not prevalent reasons for our believing. For does not the old proverb, when it asserts that money does not grow on *every* bush, imply *a fortiori* that there were certain bushes which did produce it? Again, there is another ancient saw to the effect that money is the *root* of all evil. From which two adages it may be safe to infer that the aforesaid species of tree first degenerated into a shrub, then absconded underground, and finally, in our iron age, vanished altogether. In favorable exposures it may be conjectured that a specimen or two survived to a great age, as in the garden of the Hesperides; and, indeed, what else could that tree in the Sixth Æneid have been, with a branch whereof the Trojan hero procured admission to a territory, for the entering of which money is a surer passport than to a certain other more profitable (too) foreign kingdom? Whether these speculations of mine have any force in them, or whether they will not rather, by most readers, be deemed impertinent to the matter in hand, is a question which I leave to the determination of an indulgent posterity. That there were, in more primitive and happier times, shops where money was sold,—and that, too, on credit and at a bargain,—I take to be matter of demonstration. For what but a dealer in this article was that Æolus who supplied Ulysses with motive power for his fleet in bags? What that Ericus, king of Sweden, who is said to have kept the winds in his cap? What, in more recent times, those Lapland Nornas who traded in favorable breezes? All which will appear the more clearly when we consider, that, even to this day, *raising the wind* is proverbial for raising money, and that brokers and banks were invented by the Venetians at a later period.

And now for the improvement of this digression. I find a parallel to Mr. Sawin's fortune in an adventure of my own. For, shortly after I had first broached to myself the before-stated natural-historical and archæological theories, as I was passing, *hæc negotia penitus mecum revolvens*, through one of the obscure suburbs of our New England metropolis, my eye was attracted by these words upon a sign-board,—CHEAP CASH-STORE. Here was at once the confirmation of my speculations, and the substance of my hopes. Here lingered the fragment of a happier past, or stretched out the first tremulous organic filament of a more fortunate future. Thus glowed the distant Mexico to the eyes of Sawin, as he looked through the dirty pane of the recruiting-office window, or speculated from the summit of that mirage-Pisgah which the imps of the bottle are so cunning in raising up. Already had my Alnaschar-fancy (even during that first half-believing glance) expended in various useful directions the funds to be obtained by pledging the manuscript of a proposed volume of discourses. Already did a clock ornament the tower of the Jaalam meeting-house, a gift appropriately, but modestly, commemorated in the parish and town records, both, for now many years, kept by myself. Already had my son Seneca completed his course at the University. Whether, for the moment, we may not be considered as actually lording it over those

Baratarias with the viceroyalty of which Hope invests us, and whether we are ever so warmly housed as in our Spanish castles, would afford matter of argument Enough that I found that sign-board to be no other than a bait to the trap of a decayed grocer. Nevertheless, I bought a pound of dates (getting short weight by reason of immense flights of harpy flies who pursued and lighted upon their prey even in the very scales), which purchase I made, not only with an eye to the little ones at home, but also as a figurative reproof of that too frequent habit of my mind, which, forgetting the due order of chronology, will often persuade me that the happy sceptre of Saturn is stretched over this Astræa-forsaken nineteenth century.

Having glanced at the ledger of Glory under the title *Sawin, B.*, let us extend our investigations, and discover if that instructive volume does not contain some charges more personally interesting to ourselves. I think we should be more economical of our resources, did we thoroughly appreciate the fact, that, whenever Brother Jonathan seems to be thrusting his hand into his own pocket, he is, in fact, picking ours. I confess that the late *muck* which the country has been running has materially changed my views as to the best method of raising revenue. If, by means of direct taxation, the bills for every extraordinary outlay were brought under our immediate eye, so that, like thrifty housekeepers, we could see where and how fast the money was going, we should be less likely to commit extravagances. At present, these things are managed in such a hugger-mugger way, that we know not what we pay for; the poor man is charged as much as the rich; and, while we are saving and scrimping at the spigot, the government is drawing off at the bung. If we could know that a part of the money we expend for tea and coffee goes to buy powder and balls, and that it is Mexican blood which makes the clothes on our backs more costly, it would set some of us athinking. During the present fall, I have often pictured to myself a government official entering my study and handing me the following bill:—

WASHINGTON, Sept. 30, 1848.

REV. HOMER WILBUR to Uncle Samuel, Dr.

To his share of work done in Mexico on partnership account, sundry jobs, as below.	
" killing, maiming, and wounding about 5,000 Mexicans, ...	$2.00
" slaughtering one woman carrying water to wounded, ...	.10
" extra work on two different Sabbaths (one bombardment and one assault) whereby the Mexicans were prevented from defiling themselves with the idolatries of high mass, .	3.50
" throwing an especially fortunate and Protestant bombshell into the Cathedral at Vera Cruz, whereby several female Papists were slain at the altar, ...	.50
" his proportion of cash paid for conquered territory, ...	1.75
" do. do. for conquering do. .	1.50
" manuring do. with new superior compost called "American Citizen,"	.50
" extending the area of freedom and Protestantism, ...	.01
" glory, ...	.01
	$9.87

Immediate payment is requested.

N. B. Thankful for former favors, U. S. requests a

continuance of patronage. Orders executed with neatness and despatch. Terms as low as those of any other contractor for the same kind and style of work.

I can fancy the official answering my look of horror with,—"Yes, Sir, it looks like a high charge, Sir; but in these days slaughtering is slaughtering." Verily, I would that every one understood that it was; for it goes about obtaining money under the false pretence of being glory. For me, I have an imagination which plays me uncomfortable tricks. It happens to me sometimes to see a slaughterer on his way home from his day's work, and forthwith my imagination puts a cocked-hat upon his head and epaulettes upon his shoulders, and sets him up as a candidate for the Presidency. So, also, on a recent public occasion, as the place assigned to the "Reverend Clergy" is just behind that of "Officers of the Army and Navy" in processions, it was my fortune to be seated at the dinner-table over against one of these respectable persons. He was arrayed as (out of his own profession) only kings, court-officers, and footmen are in Europe, and Indians in America. Now what does my over-officious imagination but set to work upon him, strip him of his gay livery, and present him to me coatless, his trowsers thrust into the tops of a pair of boots thick with clotted blood, and a basket on his arm out of which lolled a gore-smeared axe, thereby destroying my relish for the temporal mercies upon the board before me!—H. W.]

No. IX.

A THIRD LETTER FROM B. SAWIN, ESQ.

[UPON the following letter slender comment will be needful. In what river Selemnus has Mr. Sawin bathed, that he has become so swiftly oblivious of his former loves? From an ardent and (as befits a soldier) confident wooer of that coy bride, the popular favor, we see him subside of a sudden into the (I trust not jilted) Cincinnatus, returning to his plough with a goodly-sized branch of willow in his hand; figuratively returning, however, to a figurative plough, and from no profound affection for that honored implement of husbandry, (for which, indeed, Mr. Sawin never displayed any decided predilection,) but in order to be gracefully summoned therefrom to more congenial labors. It would seem that the character of the ancient Dictator had become part of the recognized stock of our modern political comedy, though, as our term of office extends to a quadrennial length, the parallel is not so minutely exact as could be desired. It is sufficiently so, however, for purposes of scenic representation. An humble cottage (if built of logs, the better) forms the Arcadian background of the stage. This rustic paradise is labelled Ashland, Jaalam, North Bend, Marshfield, Kinderhook, or Bâton Rouge, as occasion demands. Before the door stands a something with one handle (the other painted in proper perspective), which represents, in happy ideal vagueness, the plough. To this the defeated candidate rushes with delirious joy, welcomed as a father by appropriate groups of happy laborers, or from it the successful one is torn with difficulty, sustained alone by a noble sense of public duty. Only I have observed, that, if the scene be laid at Bâton Rouge or Ashland, the laborers are kept carefully in the background, and are heard to shout from behind the scenes in a singular tone resembling ululation, and accompanied by a sound not unlike vigorous clapping. This, however, may be artistically in keeping with the habits of the rustic population of those localities. The precise connection between agricultural pursuits and statesmanship I have not been able, after diligent inquiry, to discover. But, that my investigations may not be barren of all fruit, I will mention one curious statistical fact, which I consider thoroughly established, namely, that no real farmer ever attains practically beyond a seat in General Court, however theoretically qualified for more exalted station.

It is probable that some other prospect has been opened to Mr. Sawin, and that he has not made this great sacrifice without some definite understanding in regard to a seat in the cabinet or a foreign mission. It may be supposed that we of Jaalam were not untouched by a feeling of villatic pride in beholding our townsman occupying so large a space in the public eye. And to me, deeply revolving the qualifications necessary to a candidate in these frugal times, those of Mr. S. seemed peculiarly adapted to a successful campaign. The loss of a leg, an arm, an eye, and four fingers, reduced him so nearly to the condition of a *vox et præterea nihil*, that I could think of nothing but the loss of his head by which his chance could have been bettered. But since he has chosen to baulk our suffrages, we must content ourselves with what we can get, remembering *lactucas non esse dandas, dum cardui sufficiant.*—H. W.]

I SPOSE you recollect thet I explained my gennle views
In the last billet thet I writ, 'way down frum Veery Cruze,
Jest arter I'd a kind o' ben spontanously sot up
To run unanimously fer the Presidential cup;
O' course it worn't no wish o' mine, 'twuz ferflely distressin',
But poppiler enthusiasm gut so almighty pressin'
Thet, though like sixty all along I fumed an' fussed an' sorrered,
There didn't seem no ways to stop their bringin' on me forrerd:
Fact is, they udged the matter so, I couldn't help admittin'
The Father o' his Country's shoes no feet but mine 'ould fit in,
Besides the savin' o' the soles fer ages to succeed,
Seein' thet with one wannut foot, a pair 'd be more 'n I need;
An', tell ye wut, them shoes 'll want a thund'rin sight o' patchin',
Ef this 'ere fashion is to last we've gut into o' hatchin'
A pair o' second Washintons fer every new election,—
Though, fur ez number one's consarned, I don't make no objection.

I wuz agoin' on to say thet wen at fust I saw
The masses would stick to't I wuz the Country's father-'n-law,
(They would ha' hed it *Father*, but I told 'em 't wouldn't du,

Coz thet wuz sutthin' of a sort they couldn't split
in tu,
An' Washinton hed hed the thing laid fairly to his
door,
Nor darsn't say 'tworn't his'n, much ez sixty year
afore,)
But 'taint no matter ez to thet; wen I wuz nomer-
nated,
'Tworn't natur but wut I should feel consid'able
elated,
An' wile the hooraw o' the thing wuz kind o' noo
an' fresh,
I thought our ticket would ha' caird the country
with a resh.

Sence I've come hum, though, an' looked round, I
think I seem to find
Strong argimunts ez thick ez fleas to make me
change my mind;
It's clear to any one whose brain ain't fur gone in
a phthisis,
Thet hail Columby's happy land is goin' thru a
crisis,
An' 'twouldn't noways du to hev the people's mind
distracted
By bein' all to once by sev'ral pop'lar names
attackted;
'Twould save holl haycartloads o' fuss an' three
four months o' jaw,
Ef some illustrous paytriot should back out an'
withdraw;
So, ez I aint a crooked stick, jest like—like ole (I
swow,
I dunno ez I know his name)—I'll go back to my
plough.

Wenever an Amerikin distinguished politishin

Begins to try et wut they call definin' his posishin,
Wal, I, fer one, feel sure he aint gut nothin' to define;
It's so nine cases out o' ten, but jest that tenth is mine;
And 'taint no more'n is proper 'n' right in sech a sitooation
To hint the course you think 'll be the savin' o' the nation;
To funk right out o' p'lit'cal strife aint thought to be the thing,
Without you deacon off the toon you want your folks should sing;
So I edvise the noomrous friends thet's in one boat with me
To jest up killock, jam right down their hellum hard a lee,
Haul the sheets taut, an', laying out upon the Suthun tack,
Make fer the safest port they can, wich, *I* think, is Ole Zack.

Next thing you'll want to know, I spose, wut argimunts I seem
To see thet makes me think this ere'll be the strongest team;
Fust place, I've ben consid'ble round in bar-rooms an' saloons
Agethrin' public sentiment, 'mongst Demmercrats and Coons,
An' 'taint ve'y offen thet I meet a chap but wut goes in
Fer Rough an' Ready, fair an' square, hufs, taller, horns, an' skin;
I don't deny but wut, fer one, ez fur ez I could see,
I didn't like at fust the Pheladelphy nomernee:

I could ha' pinted to a man thet wuz, I guess, a peg
Higher than him,—a soger, tu, an' with a wooden leg;
But every day with more an' more o' Taylor zeal I'm burnin',
Seein' wich way the tide thet sets to office is aturnin';
Wy, into Bellers's we notched the votes down on three sticks,—
'Twuz Birdofredum *one*, Cass *aught*, an' Taylor *twenty-six*,
An' bein' the on'y canderdate thet wuz upon the ground,
They said 'twuz no more'n right thet I should pay the drinks all round;
Ef I'd expected sech a trick, I wouldn't ha' cut my foot
By goin' an' votin' fer myself like a consumed coot;
It didn't make no diff'rence, though; I wish I may be cust,
Ef Bellers wuzn't slim enough to say he wouldn't trust!

Another pint thet influences the minds o' sober jedges
Is thet the Gin'ral hezn't gut tied hand an' foot with pledges;
He hezn't told ye wut he is, an' so there aint no knowin'
But wut he may turn out to be the best there is agoin';
This, at the on'y spot thet pinched, the shoe directly eases,
Coz every one is free to 'xpect percisely wut he pleases:
I want free-trade; you don't; the Gin'ral isn't bound to neither;—

I vote my way; you, yourn; an' both air sooted to a T there.
Ole Rough an' Ready, tu, 's a Wig, but without bein' ultry
(He's like a holsome hayinday, thet's warm, but isn't sultry);
He's jest wut I should call myself, a kin' o' *scratch*, ez 'tware,
Thet aint exacly all a wig nor wholly your own hair;
I've ben a Wig three weeks myself, jest o' this mod'rate sort,
An' don't find them an' Demmercrats so different ez I thought;
They both act pooty much alike, an' push an' scrouge an' cus;
They're like two pickpockets in league fer Uncle Samwell's pus;
Each takes a side, an' then they squeeze the old man in between 'em,
Turn all his pockets wrong side out an' quick ez lightnin' clean 'em;
To nary one on'em I'd trust a secon'-handed rail
No furder off 'an I could sling a bullock by the tail.

Webster sot matters right in thet air Mashfiel' speech o' his'n;—
"Taylor," sez he, "aint nary ways the one thet I'd a chizzen,
Nor he aint fittin' fer the place, an' like ez not he aint
No more'n a tough ole bullethead, an' no gret of a saint;
But then," sez he, "obsarve my pint, he's jest ez good to vote fer

Ez though the greasin' on him worn't a thing to hire Choate fer;
Aint it ez easy done to drop a ballot in a box
Fer one ez't is fer t'other, fer the bulldog ez the fox?"
It takes a mind like Dannel's, fact, ez big ez all ou' doors,
To find out thet it looks like rain arter it fairly pours;
I 'gree with him, it aint so dreffle troublesome to vote
Fer Taylor arter all,—it's jest to go an' change your coat;
Wen he's once greased, you'll swaller him an' never know on't, scurce,
Unless he scratches, goin' down, with them 'ere Gin-'ral's spurs.
I've ben a votin' Demmercrat, ez reg'lar ez a clock,
But don't find goin' Taylor gives my narves no gret 'f a shock;
Truth is, the cutest leadin' Wigs, ever sence fust they found
Wich side the bread gut buttered on, hev kep' a edgin' round;
They kin' o' slipt the planks frum out th' ole platform one by one
An' made it gradooally noo, 'fore folks know'd wut wuz done,
Till, 'fur'z I know, there aint an inch thet I could lay my han' on,
But I, or any Demmercrat, feels comf'table to stan' on,
An' ole Wig doctrines act'lly look, their occ'pants bein' gone,
Lonesome ez staddles on a mash without no hay-ricks on.

I spose it's time now I should give my thoughts
upon the plan,
Thet chipped the shell at Buffalo, o' settin' up ole
Van.
I used to vote fer Martin, but, I swan, I'm clean
disgusted,—
He aint the man thet I can say is fittin' to be
trusted;
He aint half antislav'ry 'nough, nor I aint sure, ez
some be,
He'd go in fer abolishin' the Deestrick o' Columby;
An', now I come to recollect, it kin' o' makes me
sick'z
A horse, to think o' wut he wuz in eighteen thirty-six.
An' then, another thing;—I guess, though mebby I
am wrong,
This Buff'lo plaster aint agoin' to dror almighty
strong;
Some folks, I know, hev gut th' idee thet No'thun
dough 'll rise,
Though, 'fore I see it riz an' baked, I wouldn't
trust my eyes;
'Twill take more emptins, a long chalk, than this
noo party's gut,
To give sech heavy cakes ez them a start, I tell ye
wut.
But even ef they caird the day, there wouldn't be
no endurin'
To stan' upon a platform with sech critters ez Van
Buren;—
An' his son John, tu, I can't think how thet 'ere chap
should dare
To speak ez he doos; wy, they say he used to cuss
an' swear!
I spose he never read the hymn thet tells how down
the stairs
A feller with long legs wuz throwed thet wouldn't
say his prayers.

This brings me to another pint: the leaders o' the party
Aint jest sech men ez I can act along with free an' hearty;
They aint not quite respectable, an' wen a feller's morrils
Don't toe the straightest kin' o' mark, wy, him an' me jest quarrils.
I went to a free soil meetin' once, an' wut d'ye think I see?
A feller was aspoutin' there thet act'lly come to me,
About two year ago last spring, ez nigh ez I can jedge,
An' axed me ef I didn't want to sign the Temprunce pledge!
He's one o' them that goes about an' sez you hedn't ough' ter
Drink nothin', mornin', noon, or night, stronger 'an Taunton water.
There's one rule I've ben guided by, in settlin' how to vote, ollers,—
I take the side thet *isn't* took by them consarned teetotallers.

Ez fer the niggers, I've ben South, an' thet hez changed my mind;
A lazier, more ongrateful set you couldn't nowers find.
You know I mentioned in my last thet I should buy a nigger,
Ef I could make a purchase at a pooty mod'rate figger;
So, ez there's nothin' in the world I'm fonder of 'an gunnin',
I closed a bargin finally to take a feller runnin'.
I shou'dered queen's-arm an' stumped out, an' wen I come t' th' swamp,

'Tworn't very long afore I gut upon the nest o' Pomp;
I come acrost a kin' o' hut, an', playin' round the door,
Some little woolly-headed cubs, ez many'z six or more.
At fust I thought o' firin', but *think twice* is safest ollers;
There aint, thinks I, not one on 'em but's wuth his twenty dollars,
Or would be, ef I hed 'em back into a Christian land,—
How temptin' all on 'em would look upon an auction-stand!
(Not but wut *I* hate Slavery in th' abstract, stem to starn,—
I leave it ware our fathers did, a privit State consarn.)
Soon'z they see me, they yelled an' run, but Pomp wuz out ahoein'
A leetle patch o' corn he hed, or else there aint no knowin'
He wouldn't ha' took a pop at me; but I hed gut the start,
An' wen he looked, I vow he groaned ez though he'd broke his heart;
He done it like a wite man, tu, ez nat'ral ez a pictur,
The imp'dunt, pis'nous hypocrite! wus 'an a boy constrictur.
"You can't gum *me*, I tell ye now, an' so you needn't try,
I 'xpect my eye-teeth every mail, so jest shet up," sez I.
"Don't go to actin' ugly now, or else I'll jest let strip,
You'd best draw kindly, seein' 'z how I've gut ye on the hip;

Besides, you darned ole fool, it aint no gret of a disaster
To be benev'lently druv back to a contented master,
Ware you hed Christian priv'ledges you don't seem quite aware of,
Or you'd ha' never run away from bein' well took care of;
Ez fer kin' treatment, wy, he wuz so fond on ye, he said
He'd give a fifty spot right out, to git ye, 'live or dead;
Wite folks aint sot by half ez much; 'member I run away,
Wen I wuz bound to Cap'n Jakes, to Mattysqumscot bay;
Don' know him, likely? Spose not; wal, the mean ole codger went
An' offered—wut reward, think? Wal, it worn't no *less* 'n a cent."

Wal, I jest gut 'em into line, an druv 'em on afore me,
The pis'nous brutes, I'd no idee o' the ill-will they bore me;
We walked till som'ers about noon, an' then it grew so hot
I thought it best to camp awile, so I chose out a spot
Jest under a magnoly tree, an' there right down I sot;
Then I unstrapped my wooden leg, coz it begun to chafe,
An' laid it down 'long side o' me, supposin' all wuz safe;
I made my darkies all set down around me in a ring,
An' sot an' kin' o' ciphered up how much the lot would bring;

But, wile I drinked the peaceful cup of a pure heart an' mind,
(Mixed with some wiskey, now an' then,) Pomp he snaked up behind,
An' creepin' grad'lly close tu, ez quiet ez a mink,
Jest grabbed my leg, and then pulled foot, quicker 'an you could wink,
An', come to look, they each on 'em hed gut behin a tree,
An Pomp poked out the leg a piece, jest so ez I could see,
An' yelled to me to throw away my pistils an' my gun,
Or else thet they'd cair off the leg, an' fairly cut an' run.
I vow I didn't b'lieve there wuz a decent alligatur
Thet hed a heart so destitoot o' common human natur;
However, ez there worn't no help, I finally give in
An' heft my arms away to git my leg safe back agin.
Pomp gethered all the weapins up, an' then he come an' grinned,
He showed his ivory some, I guess, an' sez, "You're fairly pinned;
Jest buckle on your leg agin, an' git right up an come,
'Twun't du fer fammerly men like me to be so long from hum."
At fust I put my foot right down an' swore I wouldn't budge.
"Jest ez you choose," sez he, quite cool, "either be shot or trudge."
So this black-hearted monster took an' act'lly druv me back
Along the very feetmarks o' my happy mornin track,

An' kep' me pris'ner 'bout six months, an' worked me, tu, like sin,
Till I hed gut his corn an' his Carliny taters in;
He made me larn him readin', tu, (although the crittur saw
How much it hut my morril sense to act agin the law,)
So'st he could read a Bible he'd gut; an' axed ef I could pint
The North Star out; but there I put his nose some out o' jint,
Fer I weeled roun' about sou'west, an', lookin' up a bit,
Picked out a middlin' shiny one an' tole him thet wuz it.
Fin'lly, he took me to the door, an', givin' me a kick,
Sez,—"Ef you know wut's best fer ye, be off, now, double-quick;
The winter-time's a comin' on, an', though I gut ye cheap,
You're so darned lazy, I don't think you're hardly wuth your keep;
Besides, the childrin's growin' up, an' you aint jest the model
I'd like to hev 'em immertate, an' so you'd better toddle!"

Now is there any thin' on airth'll ever prove to me
Thet renegader slaves like him air fit fer bein' free?
D'you think they'll suck me in to jine the Buff'lo chaps, an' them
Rank infidels thet go agin the Scriptur'l cus o' Shem?
Not by a jugfull! sooner'n thet, I'd go thru fire an' water;

Wen I hev once made up my mind, a meet'nhus aint sotter;
No, not though all the crows thet flies to pick my bones wuz cawin',—
I guess we're in a Christian land,—
Yourn,
BIRDOFREDUM SAWIN.

[Here, patient reader, we take leave of each other, I trust with some mutual satisfaction. I say *patient*, for I love not that kind which skims dippingly over the surface of the page, as swallows over a pool before rain. By such no pearls shall be gathered. But if no pearls there be (as, indeed, the world is not without example of books wherefrom the longest-winded diver shall bring up no more than his proper handful of mud), yet let us hope that an oyster or two may reward adequate perseverance. If neither pearls nor oysters, yet is patience itself a gem worth diving deeply for.

It may seem to some that too much space has been usurped by my own private lucubrations, and some may be fain to bring against me that old jest of him who preached all his hearers out of the meeting-house save only the sexton, who, remaining for yet a little space, from a sense of official duty, at last gave out also, and, presenting the keys, humbly requested our preacher to lock the doors, when he should have wholly relieved himself of his testimony. I confess to a satisfaction in the self act of preaching, nor do I esteem a discourse to be wholly thrown away even upon a sleeping or unintelligent auditory. I cannot easily believe that the Gospel of Saint John, which Jacques Cartier ordered to be read in the Latin tongue to the Canadian savages, upon his first meeting with them, fell altogether upon stony ground. For the earnestness of the preacher is a sermon appreciable by dullest intellects and most alien ears. In this wise did Episcopius convert many to his opinions, who yet understood not the language in which he discoursed. The chief thing is, that the messenger believe that he has an authentic message to deliver. For counterfeit messengers that mode of treatment which Father John de Plano Carpini relates to have prevailed among the Tartars would seem effectual, and, perhaps, deserved enough. For my own part, I may lay claim to so much of the spirit of martyrdom as would have led me to go into banishment with those clergymen whom Alphonso the Sixth of Portugal drave out of his kingdom for refusing to shorten their pulpit eloquence. It is possible, that, having been invited into my brother Biglow's desk, I may have been too little scrupulous in using it for the venting of my own peculiar doctrines to a congregation drawn together in the expectation and with the desire of hearing him.

I am not wholly unconscious of a peculiarity of mental organization which impels me, like the railroad-engine with its train of cars, to run backward for a short distance in order to obtain a fairer start. I may compare myself to one fishing from the rocks when the sea runs high, who, misinterpreting the suction of the undertow for the biting of some larger fish, jerks suddenly, and finds that he has *caught bottom*, hauling in upon the end of his line a trail of various *algæ*, among which, nevertheless, the naturalist may haply find somewhat to repay the disappointment of the angler. Yet have I conscientiously endeavored to adapt myself to the impatient temper of the age, daily degenerating more and more from the high standard of our pristine New England. To the catalogue of lost arts I would mournfully add also that of listening to two-hour sermons. Surely we have been abridged into a race of pigmies. For, truly, in those of the old discourses yet subsisting to us in print, the endless spinal column of divisions and subdivisions can be likened to nothing so éxactly as to the vertebræ of the saurians, whence the theorist may conjecture a race of Anakim proportionate to the withstanding of these other monsters. I say Anakim rather than Nephelim, because there seem reasons for supposing that the race of those whose heads (though no giants) are constantly enveloped in clouds (which that name imports) will never become extinct. The attempt to vanquish the innumerable *heads* of one of those aforementioned discourses may supply us with a plausible interpretation of the second labor of Hercules, and his successful experiment with fire affords us a useful precedent.

But while I lament the degeneracy of the age in this regard, I cannot refuse to succumb to its influence. Looking out through my study-window, I see Mr. Biglow at a distance busy in gathering his Baldwins, of which, to judge by the number of barrels lying about under the trees, his crop is more abundant than my own,—by which sight I am admonished to turn to those orchards of the mind wherein my labors may be more prospered, and apply myself diligently to the preparation of my next Sabbath's discourse.—H. W.]

GLOSSARY.

A.

Act'lly, *actually.*
Air, *are.*
Airth, *earth.*
Airy, *area.*
Aree, *area.*
Arter, *after.*
Ax, *ask.*

B.

Beller, *bellow.*
Bellowses, *lungs.*
Ben, *been.*
Bile, *boil.*
Bimeby, *by and by.*
Blurt out, *to speak bluntly.*
Bust, *burst.*
Buster, *a roistering blade;* used also as a general superlative.

C.

Caird, *carried.*
Cairn, *carrying.*
Caleb, *a turncoat.*
Cal'late, *calculate.*
Cass, *a person with two lives.*
Close, *clothes.*
Cockerel, *a young cock.*
Cocktail, *a kind of drink;* also, *an ornament peculiar to soldiers.*
Convention, *a place where people are imposed on; a juggler's show.*
Coons, *a cant term for a now defunct party;* derived, perhaps, from the fact of their being commonly *up a tree.*
Cornwallis, *a sort of muster in masquerade;* supposed to have had its origin soon after the Revolution, and to commemorate the surrender of Lord Cornwallis. It took the place of the old Guy Fawkes procession.
Crooked stick, *a perverse, froward person.*
Cunnle, *a colonel.*
Cus, *a curse;* also, *a pitiful fellow.*

D.

Darsn't, used indiscriminately, either in singular or plural number, for *dare not, dares not*, and *dared not.*
Deacon off, *to give the cue to*, derived from a custom, once universal, but now extinct, in our New England Congregational churches. An important part of the office of deacon was to read aloud the hymns *given out* by the minister, one line at a time, the congregation singing each line as soon as read.
Demmercrat, leadin', *one in favor of extending slavery; a free-trade lecturer maintained in the custom-house.*

Desput, *desperate*.
Doos, *does*.
Doughface, *a contented lickspittle;* a common variety of Northern politician.
Dror, *draw*.
Du, *do*.
Dunno, dno, *do not* or *does not know*.
Dut, *dirt*.

E.

Eend, *end*.
Ef, *if*.
Emptins, *yeast*.
Env'y, *envoy*.
Everlasting, an intensive, without reference to duration.
Ev'y, *every*.
Ez, *as*.

F.

Fence, *on the;* said of one who halts between two opinions; a trimmer.
Fer, *for*.
Ferfle, ferful, *fearful;* also an intensive.
Fin', *find*.
Fish-skin, used in New England to clarify coffee.
Fix, *a difficulty, a nonplus*.
Foller, folly, *to follow*.
Forrerd, *forward*.
Frum, *from*.
Fur, *far*.
Furder, *farther*
Furrer, *furrow*. Metaphorically, *to draw a straight furrow* is to live uprightly or decorously.
Fust, *first*.

G.

Gin, *gave*.
Git, *get*.
Gret, *great*
Grit, *spirit, energy, pluck*.
Grout, *to sulk*.
Grouty, *crabbed, surly*.
Gum, *to impose on*.
Gump, *a foolish fellow, a dullard*.
Gut, *got*.

H.

Hed, *had*.
Heern, *heard*.
Hellum, *helm*.
Hendy, *handy*.
Het, *heated*.
Hev, *have*.
Hez, *has*.
Holl, *whole*.
Holt, *hold*.
Huf, *hoof*.
Hull, *whole*.
Hum, *home*.
Humbug, *General Taylor's anti-slavery*.
Hut, *hurt*.

I.

Idno, *I do not know*.
In'my, *enemy*.
Insines, *ensigns;* used to designate both the officer who carries the standard, and the standard itself.
Inter, intu, *into*.

J.

Jedge, *judge*.
Jest, *just*.
Jine, *join*.
Jint, *joint*.
Junk, *a fragment of any solid substance*.

K.

Keer, *care*.
Kep', *kept*.

Killock, *a small anchor.*
Kin', kin' o', kinder, *kind, kind of.*

L.

Lawth, *loath.*
Less, *let's, let us.*
Let daylight into, *to shoot.*
Let on, *to hint, to confess, to own.*
Lick, *to beat, to overcome*
Lights, *the bowels.*
Lily-pads, *leaves of the water-lily.*
Long-sweetening, *molasses.*

M.

Mash, *marsh.*
Mean, *stingy, ill-natured.*
Min', mind.

N.

Nimepunce, *ninepence, twelve and a half cents.*
Nowers, *nowhere.*

O.

Offen, *often.*
Ole, *old.*
Ollers, olluz, *always.*
On, *of;* used before *it* or *them*, or at the end of a sentence, as, *on't, on'em, nut ez ever I heerd on.*
On'y, *only.*
Ossifer, *officer* (seldom heard).

P.

Peaked, *pointed.*
Peek, *to peep.*
Pickerel, *the pike, a fish.*
Pint, *point.*
Pocket full of rocks, *plenty of money.*
Pooty, *pretty.*
Pop'ler, *conceited, popular.*
Pus, *purse.*
Put out, *troubled, vexed.*

Q.

Quarter, *a quarter-dollar.*
Queen's arm, *a musket.*

R.

Resh, *rush.*
Revelee, *the réveille.*
Rile, *to trouble.*
Riled, *angry; disturbed*, as the sediment in any liquid.
Riz, *risen.*
Row, a long row to hoe, *a difficult task.*
Rugged, *robust.*

S.

Sarse, *abuse, impertinence.*
Sartin, *certain.*
Saxon, *sacristan, sexton.*
Scaliest, *worst.*
Scringe, *cringe.*
Scrouge, *to crowd.*
Sech, *such.*
Set by, *valued.*
Shakes, great, *of considerable consequence.*
Shappoes, *chapeaux, cocked-hats.*
Sheer, *share.*
Shet, *shut.*
Shut, *shirt.*
Skeered, *scared.*
Skeeter, *mosquito.*
Skooting, *running*, or *moving swiftly.*
Slarterin', *slaughtering.*
Slim, *contemptible.*

Snaked, *crawled like a snake;* but *to snake any one out* is to track him to his hiding-place; *to snake a thing out* is to snatch it out.
Soffies, *sofas.*
Sogerin', *soldiering;* a barbarous amusement common among men in the savage state.
Som'ers, *somewhere.*
So'st, *so as that.*
Sot, *set, obstinate, resolute.*
Spiles, *spoils; objects of political ambition.*
Spry, *active.*
Staddles, *stout stakes driven into the salt marshes,* on which the hay-ricks are set, and thus raised out of the reach of high tides.
Streaked, *uncomfortable, discomfited.*
Suckle, *circle.*
Sutthin', *something.*
Suttin, *certain.*

T.

Take on, *to sorrow.*
Talents, *talons.*
Taters, *potatoes.*
Tell, *till.*
Tetch, *touch.*
Tetch tu, *to be able;* used always after a negative in this sense.
Tollable, *tolerable.*
Toot, used derisively for *playing on any wind instrument.*
Thru, *through.*
Thundering, a euphemism common in New England, for the profane English expression *devilish.* Perhaps derived from the belief, common formerly, that thunder was caused by the Prince of the Air, for some of whose accomplishments consult Cotton Mather.
Tu, *to, too;* commonly has this sound when used emphatically, or at the end of a sentence. At other times it has the sound of *t* in *tough,* as, *Ware ye goin' tu? Goin' ta Boston.*

U.

Ugly, *ill-tempered, intractable.*
Uncle Sam, *United States;* the largest boaster of liberty and owner of slaves.
Unrizzest, applied to dough or bread; *heavy, most unrisen,* or *most incapable of rising.*

V.

V-spot, *a five-dollar bill.*
Vally, *value.*

W.

Wake snakes, *to get into trouble.*
Wal, *well;* spoken with great deliberation, and sometimes with the *a* very much flattened, sometimes (but more seldom) very much broadened.
Wannut, *walnut,* (*hickory.*)
Ware, *where.*
Ware, *were.*
Whopper, *an uncommonly large lie;* as, that General Taylor is in favor of the Wilmot Proviso.
Wig, *Whig;* a party now dissolved.
Wunt, *will not.*
Wus, *worse.*
Wut, *what.*
Wuth, *worth;* as, *Antislavery perfessions 'fore 'lection ain't wuth a Bungtown copper.*
Wuz *was,* sometimes *were.*

Y.

Yaller, *yellow.*
Yeller, *yellow.*
Yellers, *a disease of peach-trees.*

Z.

Zach, Ole, *a second Washington, an antislavery slaveholder, a humane buyer and seller of men and women, a Christian hero generally.*

INDEX.

D.

G.

H.

I.

J.

K.

L.

M.

N.

O.

Q.

R.

S.

T.

Z.

THE UNHAPPY LOT OF MR. KNOTT.

1850.

THE UNHAPPY LOT OF MR. KNOTT.

PART I.

SHOWING HOW HE BUILT HIS HOUSE AND HIS WIFE MOVED INTO IT.

MY worthy friend, A. Gordon Knott,
From business snug withdrawn,
Was much contented with a lot
That would contain a Tudor cot
'Twixt twelve feet square of garden-plot,
And twelve feet more of lawn.

He had laid business on the shelf
To give his taste expansion,
And, since no man, retired with pelf,
The building mania can shun,
Knott, being middle-aged himself,
Resolved to build (unhappy elf!)
A mediæval mansion.

He called an architect in counsel;
"I want," said he, "a—you know what.
(You are a builder, I am Knott,)
A thing complete from chimney-pot
Down to the very grounsel;
Here's a half-acre of good land;

Just have it nicely mapped and planned
And make your workmen drive on;
Meadow there is, and upland too,
And I should like a water-view,
D' you think you could contrive one?
(Perhaps the pump and trough would do,
If painted a judicious blue?)
The woodland I've attended to;"
(He meant three pines stuck up askew,
Two dead ones and a live one.)
"A pocket-full of rocks 'twould take
To build a house of free-stone,
But then it is not hard to make
What now-a-days is *the* stone;
The cunning painter in a trice
Your house's outside petrifies,
And people think it very gneiss
Without inquiring deeper;
My money never shall be thrown
Away on such a deal of stone,
When stone of deal is cheaper."

And so the greenest of antiques
Was reared for Knott to dwell in;
The architect worked hard for weeks
In venting all his private peaks
Upon the roof, whose crop of leaks
Had satisfied Fluellen;
Whatever any body had
Out of the common, good or bad,
Knott had it all worked well in,
A donjon-keep, where clothes might dry,
A porter's lodge that was a sty,
A campanile slim and high,
Too small to hang a bell in;
All up and down and here and there,
With Lord-knows-whats of round and square

Stuck on at random every where,—
It was a house to make one stare,
  All corners and all gables;
Like dogs let loose upon a bear,
Ten emulous styles *staboyed* with care,
The whole among them seemed to tear,
And all the oddities to spare
  Were set upon the stables.

Knott was delighted with a pile
  Approved by fashion's leaders;
(Only he made the builder smile,
By asking, every little while,
Why that was called the Twodoor style,
  Which certainly had *three* doors ?)
Yet better for this luckless man
If he had put a downright ban
  Upon the thing *in limine;*
For, though to quit affairs his plan,
Ere many days, poor Knott began
Perforce accepting draughts, that ran
  All ways—except up chimney;
The house, though painted stone to mock,
With nice white lines round every block,
  Some trepidation stood in,
When tempests (with petrific shock,
So to speak,) made it really rock,
  Though not a whit less wooden;
And painted stone, howe'er well done,
Will not take in the prodigal sun
Whose beams are never quite at one
  With our terrestrial lumber;
So the wood shrank around the knots,
And gaped in disconcerting spots,
And there were lots of dots and rots
  And crannies without number,
Wherethrough, as you may well presume,

The wind, like water through a flume,
  Came rushing in ecstatic,
Leaving, in all three floors, no room
  That was not a rheumatic;
And, what with points and squares and rounds
  Grown shaky on their poises,
The house at nights was full of pounds,
Thumps, bumps, creaks, scratchings, raps—till
    —"Zounds!"
Cried Knott, "this goes beyond all bounds,
I do not deal in tongues and sounds,
Nor have I let my house and grounds
  To a family of Noyeses!"

But, though Knott's house was full of airs,
  He had but one—a daughter;
And, as he owned much stocks and shares,
Many who wished to render theirs
Such vain, unsatisfying cares,
And needed wives to sew their tears,
  In matrimony sought her;
They vowed her gold they wanted not,
  Their faith would never falter,
They longed to tie this single Knott
  In the Hymenæal halter;
So daily at the door they rang,
  Cards for the belle delivering,
Or in the choir at her they sang,
Achieving such a rapturous twang
  As set her nerves ashivering.

Now Knott had quite made up his mind
  That Colonel Jones should have her;
No beauty he, but oft we find
Sweet kernels 'neath a roughish rind,
So hoped his Jenny'd be resigned
  And make no more palaver;

Glanced at the fact that love was blind,
That girls were ratherish inclined
  To pet their little crosses,
Then nosologically defined
The rate at which the system pined
In those unfortunates who dined
Upon that metaphoric kind
  Of dish—their own proboscis.

But she, with many tears and moans,
  Besought him not to mock her,
Said 'twas too much for flesh and bones
To marry mortgages and loans,
That fathers' hearts were stocks and stones
And that she'd go, when Mrs. Jones,
  To Davy Jones's locker;
Then gave her head a little toss
That said as plain as ever was,
If men are always at a loss
  Mere womankind to bridle—
To try the thing on woman cross,
  Were fifty times as idle;
For she a strict resolve had made
  And registered in private,
That either she would die a maid,
Or else be Mrs. Doctor Slade,
  If woman could contrive it;
And, though the wedding-day was set,
  Jenny was more so, rather,
Declaring, in a pretty pet,
That, howsoe'er they spread their net,
She would out-Jennyral them yet,
  The colonel and her father.

Just at this time the Public's eyes
  Were keenly on the watch, a stir
Beginning slowly to arise

About those questions and replies,
Those raps that unwrapped mysteries
  So rapidly at Rochester,
And Knott, already nervous grown
By lying much awake alone,
And listening, sometimes to a moan,
  And sometimes to a clatter,
Whene'er the wind at night would rouse
The gingerbread-work on his house,
Or when some hasty-tempered mouse,
Behind the plastering, made a towse
  About a family matter,
Began to wonder if his wife,
A paralytic half her life,
  Which made it more surprising,
Might not to rule him from her urn,
Have taken a peripatetic turn
  For want of exorcising.

This thought, once nestled in his head,
Ere long contagious grew, and spread
Infecting all his mind with dread,
Until at last he lay in bed
And heard his wife, with well-known tread,
Entering the kitchen through the shed,
  (Or was't his fancy, mocking ?)
Opening the pantry, cutting bread,
And then (she'd been some ten years dead)
  Closets and drawers unlocking ;
Or, in his room (his breath grew thick)
He heard the long-familiar click
Of slender needles flying quick,
  As if she knit a stocking ;
For whom ?—he prayed that years might flit
  With pains rheumatic shooting,
Before those ghostly things she knit
Upon his unfleshed sole might fit,

He did not fancy it a bit,
  To stand upon that footing;
At other times, his frightened hairs
  Above the bedclothes trusting,
He heard her, full of household cares,
(No dream entrapped in supper's snares,
The foal of horrible nightmares,
But broad awake, as he declares,)
Go bustling up and down the stairs,
Or setting back last evening's chairs,
  Or with the poker thrusting
The raked-up sea-coal's hardened crust—
And—what! impossible! it must!
He knew she had returned to dust,
And yet could scarce his senses trust,
Hearing her as she poked and fussed
  About the parlor, dusting!

Night after night he strove to sleep
  And take his ease in spite of it;
But still his flesh would chill and creep,
And, though two night-lamps he might keep,
  He could not so make light of it.
At last, quite desperate, he goes
And tells his neighbors all his woes,
  Which did but their amount enhance;
They made such mockery of his fears
That soon his days were of all jeers,
  His nights of the rueful countenance;
"I thought most folks," one neighbor said,
"Gave up the ghost when they were dead,"
Another gravely shook his head,
  Adding, "from all we hear, it's
Quite plain poor Knott is going mad—
For how can he at once be sad
  And think he's full of spirits?"
A third declared he knew a knife

Would cut this Knott much quicker,
"The surest way to end all strife,
And lay the spirit of a wife,
Is just to take and lick her!"
A temperance man caught up the word,
"Ah, yes," he groaned, "I've always heard
Our poor friend somewhat slanted
Tow'rd taking liquor over-much;
I fear these spirits may be Dutch,
(A sort of gins, or something such,)
With which his house is haunted;
I see the thing as clear as light—
If Knott would give up getting tight,
Naught farther would be wanted:"
So all his neighbors stood aloof
And, that the spirits 'neath his roof
Were not entirely up to proof,
Unanimously granted.

Knott knew that cocks and sprites were foes,
And so bought up, Heaven only knows
How many, though he wanted crows
To give ghosts caws, as I suppose,
To think that day was breaking;
Moreover what he called his park,
He turned into a kind of ark
For dogs, because a little bark
Is a good tonic in the dark,
If one is given to waking;
But things went on from bad to worse,
His curs were nothing but a curse,
And, what was still more shocking,
Foul ghosts of living fowl made scoff
And would not think of going off
In spite of all his cocking.

Shanghais, Bucks-counties, Dominiques,
Malays (that didn't lay for weeks,)

Polanders, Bantams, Dorkings,
(Waiving the cost, no trifling ill,
Since each brought in his little bill,)
By day or night were never still,
But every thought of rest would kill
With cacklings and with quorkings;
Henry the Eighth of wives got free
By a way he had of axing;
But poor Knott's Tudor henery
Was not so fortunate, and he
Still found his trouble waxing;
As for the dogs, the rows they made,
And how they howled, snarled, barked and bayed,
Beyond all human knowledge is;
All night, as wide awake as gnats,
The terriers rumpused after rats,
Or, just for practice, taught their brats
To worry cast-off shoes and hats,
The bull-dogs settled private spats,
All chased imaginary cats,
Or raved behind the fence's slats
At real ones, or, from their mats,
With friends, miles off, held pleasant chats,
Or, like some folks in white cravats,
Contemptuous of sharps and flats,
Sat up and sang dogsologies.
Meanwhile the cats set up a squall,
And, safe upon the garden-wall,
All night kept cat-a-walling,
As if the feline race were all,
In one wild cataleptic sprawl,
Into love's tortures falling.

PART II.

SHOWING WHAT IS MEANT BY A FLOW OF SPIRITS.

At first the ghosts were somewhat shy,
Coming when none but Knott was nigh,
And people said 'twas all their eye,
(Or rather his) a flam, the sly
  Digestion's machination;
Some recommended a wet sheet,
Some a nice broth of pounded peat,
Some a cold flat-iron to the feet,
Some a decoction of lamb's-bleat,
Some a southwesterly grain of wheat;
Meat was by some pronounced unmeet,
Others thought fish most indiscreet,
And that 'twas worse than all to eat
Of vegetables, sour or sweet,
(Except, perhaps, the skin of beet,)
  In such a concatenation:
One quack his button gently plucks
And murmurs "biliary ducks!"
  Says Knott, "I never ate one;"
But all, though brimming full of wrath,
Homœo, Allo, Hydropath,
Concurred in this—that tother's path
  To death's door was the straight one.
Still, spite of medical advice,
The ghosts came thicker, and a spice
  Of mischief grew apparent;
Nor did they only come at night,
But seemed to fancy broad daylight,
Till Knott, in horror and affright,

His unoffending hair rent;
Whene'er with handkerchief on lap,
He made his elbow-chair a trap,
To catch an after-dinner nap,
The spirits, always on the tap,
Would make a sudden *rap*, *rap*, *rap*,
The half-spun cord of sleep to snap,
(And what is life without its nap
But threadbareness and mere mishap ?)
As 'twere with a percussion cap
The trouble's climax capping;
It seemed a party dried and grim
Of mummies had come to visit him,
Each getting off from every limb
Its multitudinous wrapping;
Scratchings sometimes the walls ran round,
The merest penny-weights of sound;
Sometimes 'twas only by the pound
They carried on their dealing,
A thumping 'neath the parlor floor,
Thump-bump-thump-bumping o'er and o'er,
As if the vegetables in store,
(Quiet and orderly before,)
Were all together pealing;
You would have thought the thing was done
By the spirit of some son of a gun,
And that a forty-two-pounder,
Or that the ghost which made such sounds
Could be none other than John Pounds,
Of Ragged Schools the founder.

Through three gradations of affright,
The awful noises reached their height;
At first they knocked nocturnally,
Then, for some reason, changing quite,
(As mourners, after six months' flight,
Turn suddenly from dark to light,)

Began to knock diurnally,
And last, combining all their stocks,
(Scotland was ne'er so full of Knox,)
Into one Chaos (father of Nox,)
Nocte pluit—they showered knocks,
And knocked, knocked, knocked eternally
Ever upon the go, like buoys,
(Wooden sea-urchins,) all Knott's joys,
They turned to troubles and a noise
That preyed on him internally.

Soon they grew wider in their scope;
Whenever Knott a door would ope,
It would ope not, or else elope
And fly back (curbless as a trope
Once started down a stanza's slope
By a bard that gave it too much rope—)
Like a clap of thunder slamming;
And, when kind Jenny brought his hat,
(She always, when he walked, did that,)
Just as upon his head it sat,
Submitting to his settling pat—
Some unseen hand would jam it flat,
Or give it such a furious bat
That eyes and nose went cramming
Up out of sight, and consequently,
As when in life it paddled free,
His beaver caused much damning;
If these things seem o'er-strained to be,
Read the account of Doctor Dee,
'Tis in our college library;
Read Wesley's circumstantial plea,
And Mrs. Crowe, more like a bee,
Sucking the nightshade's honeyed fee,
And Stilling's Pneumatology;
Consult Scot, Glanvil, grave Wie-
rus, and both Mathers; further, see

Webster, Casaubon, James First's trea-
tise, a right royal Q. E. D.
Writ with the moon in perigee,
Bodin de Demonomanie—
(Accent that last line gingerly)
All full of learning as the sea
Of fishes, and all disagree,
Save in *Sathanas apage!*
Or, what will surely put a flea
In unbelieving ears—with glee,
Out of a paper (sent to me
By some friend who forgot to P...
A...Y...,—I use cryptography
Lest I his vengeful pen should dree—
His P...O...S...T...A...G...E...)
  Things to the same effect I cut,
About the tantrums of a ghost,
Not more than three weeks since, at most,
  Near Stratford, in Connecticut.

Knott's Upas daily spread its roots,
Sent up on all sides livelier shoots,
And bore more pestilential fruits;
The ghosts behaved like downright brutes,
They snipped holes in his Sunday suits,
Practised all night on octave flutes,
Put peas (not peace) into his boots,
  Whereof grew corns in season,
They scotched his sheets, and, what was worse,
Stuck his silk night-cap full of burs,
Till he, in language plain and terse,
(But much unlike a Bible verse,)
  Swore he should lose his reason.

The tables took to spinning, too,
Perpetual yarns, and arm-chairs grew
  To prophets and apostles;

One footstool vowed that only he
Of law and gospel held the key,
That teachers of whate'er degree
To whom opinion bows the knee
Wern't fit to teach Truth's a. b. c.
And were (the whole lot) to a T.
  Mere fogies all and fossils;
A teapoy, late the property
  Of Knox's Aunt Keziah,
(Whom Jenny most irreverently
Had nicknamed her aunt-tipathy)
With tips emphatic claimed to be
  The prophet Jeremiah;
The tins upon the kitchen-wall,
Turned tinntinnabulators all,
And things that used to come at call
  For simple household services,
Began to hop and whirl and prance,
Fit to put out of countenance
The *Commis* and *Grisettes* of France
  Or Turkey's dancing Dervises.

Of course such doings, far and wide,
With rumors filled the country-side,
And (as it is our nation's pride
To think a Truth not verified
Till with majorities allied,)
Parties sprung up, affirmed, denied,
And candidates with questions plied
Who, like the circus-riders, tried
At once both hobbies to bestride,
And each with his opponent vied
  In being inexplicit.
Earnest inquirers multiplied;
Folks, whose tenth cousins lately died,
Wrote letters long, and Knott replied
All who could either walk or ride,

Gathered to wonder or deride,
  And paid the house a visit;
Horses were at his pine-trees tied,
Mourners in every corner sighed,
Widows brought children there that cried,
Swarms of lean Seekers, eager-eyed,
(People Knott never could abide,)
Into each hole and cranny pried
With strings of questions cut and dried
From the Devout Inquirer's Guide,
For the wise spirits to decide—
  As, for example, is it
True that the damned are fried or boiled?
Was the Earth's axis greased or oiled?
Who cleaned the moon when it was soiled?
How baldness might be cured or foiled?
  How heal diseased potatoes?
Did spirits have the sense of smell?
Where would departed spinsters dwell?
If the late Zenas Smith were well?
If Earth were solid or a shell?
Were spirits fond of Doctor Fell?
Did the bull toll Cock-Robin's knell?
What remedy would bugs expel?
If Paine's invention were a sell?
Did spirits by Webster's system spell?
Was it a sin to be a belle?
Did dancing sentence folks to hell?
If so, then where most torture fell—
  On little toes or great toes?
If life's true seat were in the brain?
Did Ensign mean to marry Jane?
By whom, in fact, was Morgan slain?
Could matter ever suffer pain?
What would take out a cherry-stain?
Who picked the pocket of Seth Crane,
Of Waldo precinct, State of Maine?

Was Sir John Franklin sought in vain?
Did primitive Christians ever train?
What was the family-name of Cain?
Them spoons, were they by Betty ta'en?
Would earth-worm poultice cure a sprain
Was Socrates so dreadful plain?
What teamster guided Charles's wain?
Was Uncle Ethan mad or sane,
And could his will in force remain?
If not, what counsel to retain?
Did Le Sage steal Gil Blas from Spain?
Was Junius writ by Thomas Paine?
Were ducks discomforted by rain?
How did Britannia rule the main?
Was Jonas coming back again?
Was vital truth upon the wane?
Did ghosts, to scare folks, drag a chain?
Who was our Huldah's chosen swain?
Did none have teeth pulled without payin'
  Ere ether was invented?
Whether mankind would not agree,
If the universe were tuned in C.?
What was it ailed Lucindy's knee?
Whether folks eat folks in Feejee?
Whether *his* name would end with T.?
If Saturn's rings were two or three,
And what bump in Phrenology
  They truly represented?
These problems dark, wherein they groped,
Wherewith man's reason vainly coped,
Now that the spirit-world was oped,
In all humility they hoped
  Would be resolved *instanter;*
Each of the miscellaneous rout
Brought his, or her, own little doubt,
And wished to pump the spirits out,
Through his, or her, own private spout,
  Into his, or her decanter.

PART III.

WHEREIN IT IS SHOWN THAT THE MOST ARDENT SPIRITS ARE MORE ORNAMENTAL THAN USEFUL.

Many a speculating wight
Came by express-trains, day and night,
To see if Knott would "sell his right,"
Meaning to make the ghosts a sight—
 What they called a "meenaygerie;"
One threatened, if he would not "trade,"
His run of custom to invade,
(He could not these sharp folks persuade
That he was not, in some way, paid,)
 And stamp him as a plagiary,
By coming down, at one fell swoop,
With THE ORIGINAL KNOCKING TROUPE,
 Come recently from Hades,
Who (for a quarter-dollar heard)
Would ne'er rap out a hasty word
Whence any blame might be incurred
 From the most fastidious ladies;
The late lamented Jesse Soule
To stir the ghosts up with a pole
And be director of the whole,
 Who was engaged the rather
For the rare merits he'd combine,
Having been in the spirit line,
Which trade he only did resign,
With general applause, to shine,
Awful in mail of cotton fine,
 As ghost of Hamlet's father!
Another a fair plan reveals
Never yet hit on, which, he feels,

To Knott's religious sense appeals—
" We'll have your house set up on wheels,
  A speculation pious;
For music, we can shortly find
A barrel-organ that will grind
Psalm-tunes—an instrument designed
For the New England tour—refined
From secular drosses, and inclined
To an unworldly turn, (combined
  With no sectarian bias;)
Then, travelling by stages slow,
Under the style of Knott & Co.,
I would accompany the show
As moral lecturer, the foe
Of Rationalism; you could throw
The rappings in, and make them go
Strict Puritan principles, you know,
(How *do* you make 'em? with your toe?)
And the receipts which thence might flow,
  We could divide between us;
Still more attractions to combine,
Beside these services of mine,
I will throw in a very fine
(It would do nicely for a sign)
  Original Titian's Venus."
Another offered handsome fees
If Knott would get Demosthenes,
(Nay, his mere knuckles, for more ease,)
To rap a few short sentences;
Or if, for want of proper keys,
  His Greek might make confusion,
Then just to get a rap from Burke,
To recommend a little work
  On Public Elocution.
Meanwhile, the spirits made replies
To all the reverent *whats* and *whys*,
Resolving doubts of every size,

And giving seekers grave and wise,
Who came to know their destinies,
  A rap-turous reception;
When unbelievers void of grace
Came to investigate the place,
(Creatures of Sadducistic race,
With grovelling intellects and base,)
They could not find the slightest trace
  To indicate deception;
Indeed, it is declared by some
That spirits (of this sort) are glum,
Almost, or wholly, deaf and dumb,
And (out of self-respect) quite mum
To sceptic natures cold and numb,
Who of *this* kind of Kingdom Come
  Have not a just conception;
True, there were people who demurred
That, though the raps no doubt were heard
  Both under them and o'er them,
Yet, somehow, when a search they made,
They found Miss Jenny sore afraid,
Or Jenny's lover, Doctor Slade,
Equally awe-struck and dismayed,
Or Deborah, the chamber-maid,
Whose terrors, not to be gainsaid,
In laughs hysteric were displayed,
  Was always there before them;
This had its due effect with some
Who straight departed, muttering, Hum!
  Transparent hoax! and Gammon!
But these were few: believing souls
Came, day by day, in larger shoals,
As the ancients to the windy holes
'Neath Delphi's tripod brought their doles,
  Or to the shrine of Ammon.

The spirits seemed exceeding tame,

Call whom you fancied, and he came;
The shades august of eldest fame
  You summoned with an awful ease;
As grosser spirits gurgled out
From chair and table with a spout,
In Auerbach's cellar once, to flout
The senses of the rabble rout,
Where'er the gimlet twirled about
  Of cunning Mephistophiles—
So did these spirits seem in store,
Behind the wainscot or the door,
Ready to thrill the being's core
Of every enterprising bore
  With their astounding glamour;
Whatever ghost one wished to hear,
By strange coincidence, was near
To make the past or future clear,
  (Sometimes in shocking grammar,)
By raps and taps, now there, now here—
It seemed as if the spirit queer
Of some departed auctioneer
Were doomed to practise by the year
  With the spirit of his hammer;
Whate'er you asked was answered, yet
One could not very deeply get
Into the obliging spirits' debt,
Because they used the alphabet
  In all communications,
And new revealings (though sublime)
Rapped out, one letter at a time,
  With boggles, hesitations,
Stoppings, beginnings o'er again,
And getting matters into train,
Could hardly overload the brain
  With too excessive rations,
Since just to ask *if two and two*
Really make four? or, *How d'ye do?*

And get the fit replies thereto
In the tramundane rat-tat-too,
  Might ask a whole day's patience.

'Twas strange ('mongst other things) to find
In what odd sets the ghosts combined,
  Happy forthwith to thump any
Piece of intelligence inspired,
The truth whereof had been inquired
  By some one of the company;
For instance, Fielding, Mirabeau,
Orator Henley, Cicero,
Paley, John Zisca, Marivaux,
Melancthon, Robertson, Junot,
Scaliger, Chesterfield, Rousseau,
Hakluyt, Boccaccio, South, De Foe,
Diaz, Josephus, Richard Roe,
Odin, Arminius, Charles *le gros*,
Tiresias, the late James Crow,
Casabianca, Grose, Prideaux,
Old Grimes, Young Norval, Swift, Brissot,
Maimonides, the Chevalier D'O,
Socrates, Fenelon, Job, Stow,
The inventor of *Elixir pro*,
Euripides, Spinoza, Poe,
Confucius, Hiram Smith, and Fo,
Came (as it seemed, somewhat *de trop*)
With a disembodied Esquimaux,
To say that it was so and so,
  With Franklin's expedition;
One testified to ice and snow,
One that the mercury was low,
One that his progress was quite slow,
One that he much desired to go,
One that the cook had frozen his toe,
(Dissented from by Dandolo,
Wordsworth, Cynaegirus, Boileau,

La Hontan, and Sir Thomas Roe,)
One saw twelve white bears in a row,
One saw eleven and a crow,
With other things we could not know
(Of great statistic value, though)
  By our mere mortal vision.

Sometimes the spirits made mistakes,
And seemed to play at ducks and drakes
With bold inquiry's heaviest stakes
  In science or in mystery;
They knew so little (and that wrong)
Yet rapped it out so bold and strong,
One would have said the entire throng
  Had been Professors of History;
What made it odder was, that those
Who, you would naturally suppose,
Could solve a question, if they chose,
As easily as count their toes,
  Were just the ones that blundered;
One day, Ulysses happening down,
A reader of Sir Thomas Browne
  And who (with him) had wondered
What song it was the Sirens sang,
Asked the shrewd Ithacan—*bang! bang!*
With this response the chamber rang,
  "I guess it was Old Hundred."
And Franklin, being asked to name
The reason why the lightning came,
  Replied, "Because it thundered."

On one sole point the ghosts agreed,
One fearful point, than which, indeed,
  Nothing could seem absurder;
Poor Colonel Jones they all abused,
And finally downright accused
  The poor old man of murder;

'Twas thus; by dreadful raps was shown
Some spirit's longing to make known
A bloody fact, which he alone
Was privy to, (such ghosts more prone
  In Earth's affairs to meddle are;)
Who are you? with awe-stricken looks,
All ask: his airy knuckles he crooks,
And raps, "I *was* Eliab Snooks,
  That used to be a peddler;
Some on ye still are on my books!"
Whereat, to inconspicuous nooks,
(More fearing this than common spooks,)
  Shrank each indebted meddler;
Further the vengeful ghost declared
That while his earthly life was spared,
About the country he had fared,
  A duly licensed follower
Of that much-wandering trade that wins
Slow profit from the sale of tins
  And various kinds of hollow-ware;
That Colonel Jones enticed him in,
Pretending that he wanted tin,
There slew him with a rolling-pin,
Hid him in a potatoe-bin,
  And (the same night) him ferried
Across Great Pond to t'other shore,
And there, on land of Widow Moore,
Just where you turn to Larkin's store,
  Under a rock him buried;
Some friends (who happened to be by)
He called upon to testify
That what he said was not a lie,
  And that he did not stir this
Foul matter, out of any spite
But from a simple love of right;—
  Which statements the Nine Worthies,
Rabbi Akiba, Charlemagne,

Seth, Colley Cibber, General Wayne,
Cambyses, Tasso, Tubal-Cain,
The owner of a castle in Spain,
Jehanghire, and the Widow of Nain,
(The friends aforesaid) made more plain
  And by loud raps attested;
To the same purport testified
Plato, John Wilkes, and Colonel Pride
Who knew said Snooks before he died,
  Had in his wares invested,
Thought him entitled to belief
And freely could concur, in brief,
  In every thing the rest did.

Eliab this occasion seized,
(Distinctly here the spirit sneezed,)
To say that he should ne'er be eased
Till Jenny married whom she pleased,
  Free from all checks and urgin's,
(This spirit dropt his final g's)
And that, unless Knott quickly sees
This done, the spirits to appease,
They would come back his life to tease,
As thick as mites in ancient cheese,
And let his house on an endless lease
To the ghosts (terrific rappers these
And veritable Eumenides)
  Of the Eleven Thousand Virgins!

Knott was perplexed and shook his head,
He did not wish his child to wed
  With a suspected murderer,
(For, true or false, the rumor spread.)
But as for this roiled life he led,
"It would not answer," so he said,
  "To have it go no furderer."

At last, scarce knowing what it meant,
Reluctantly he gave consent
That Jenny, since 'twas evident
That she *would* follow her own bent,
  Should make her own election ·
For that appeared the only wa,
These frightful noises to allay
Which had already turned him gray
  And plunged him in dejection.

Accordingly, this artless maid
Her father's ordinance obeyed,
And, all in whitest crape arrayed,
(Miss Pulsifer the dresses made
And wishes here the fact displayed
That she still carries on the trade,
The third door south from Bagg's Arcade,)
A very faint "I do" essayed
And gave her hand to Hiram Slade,
From which time forth, the ghosts were laid,
  And ne'er gave trouble after;
But the Selectmen, be it known,
Dug underneath the aforesaid stone,
Where the poor peddler's corpse was thrown,
And found thereunder a jaw-bone,
Though, when the crowner sat thereon,
He nothing hatched, except alone
  Successive broods of laughter;
It was a frail and dingy thing,
In which a grinder or two did cling,
  In color like molasses,
Which surgeons, called from far and wide,
Upon the horror to decide,
  Having put on their glasses,
Reported thus—" To judge by looks,
These bones, by some queer hooks or crooks,
May have belonged to Mr. Snooks,

But, as men deepest-read in books
   Are perfectly aware, bones,
If buried, fifty years or so,
Lose their identity and grow
   From human bones to bare bones."

Still, if to Jaalam you go down,
You'll find two parties in the town,
One headed by Benaiah Brown,
   And one by Perez Tinkham ;
The first believe the ghosts all through
And vow that they shall never rue
The happy chance by which they knew
That people in Jupiter are blue,
And very fond of Irish stew,
Two curious facts which Prince Lee Boo
Rapped clearly to a chosen few—
   Whereas the others think 'em
A trick got up by Doctor Slade
With Deborah the chamber-maid
   And that sly cretur Jinny,
That all the revelations wise,
At which the Brownites made big eyes,
Might have been given by Jared Keyes,
   A natural fool and ninny,
And, last week, didn't Eliab Snooks
Come back with never better looks,
As sharp as new-bought mackerel hooks,
   And bright as a new pin, eh ?
Good Parson Wilbur, too, avers
(Though to be mixed in parish stirs
Is worse than handling chestnut-burs)
That no case to his mind occurs
Where spirits ever did converse
Save in a kind of guttural Erse,
   (So say the best authorities ;)
And that a charge by raps conveyed,

Should be most scrupulously weighed
  And searched into, before it is
Made public, since it may give pain
That cannot soon be cured again,
And one word may infix a stain
  Which ten cannot gloss over,
Though speaking for his private part,
He is rejoiced with all his heart
  Miss Knott missed not her lover.

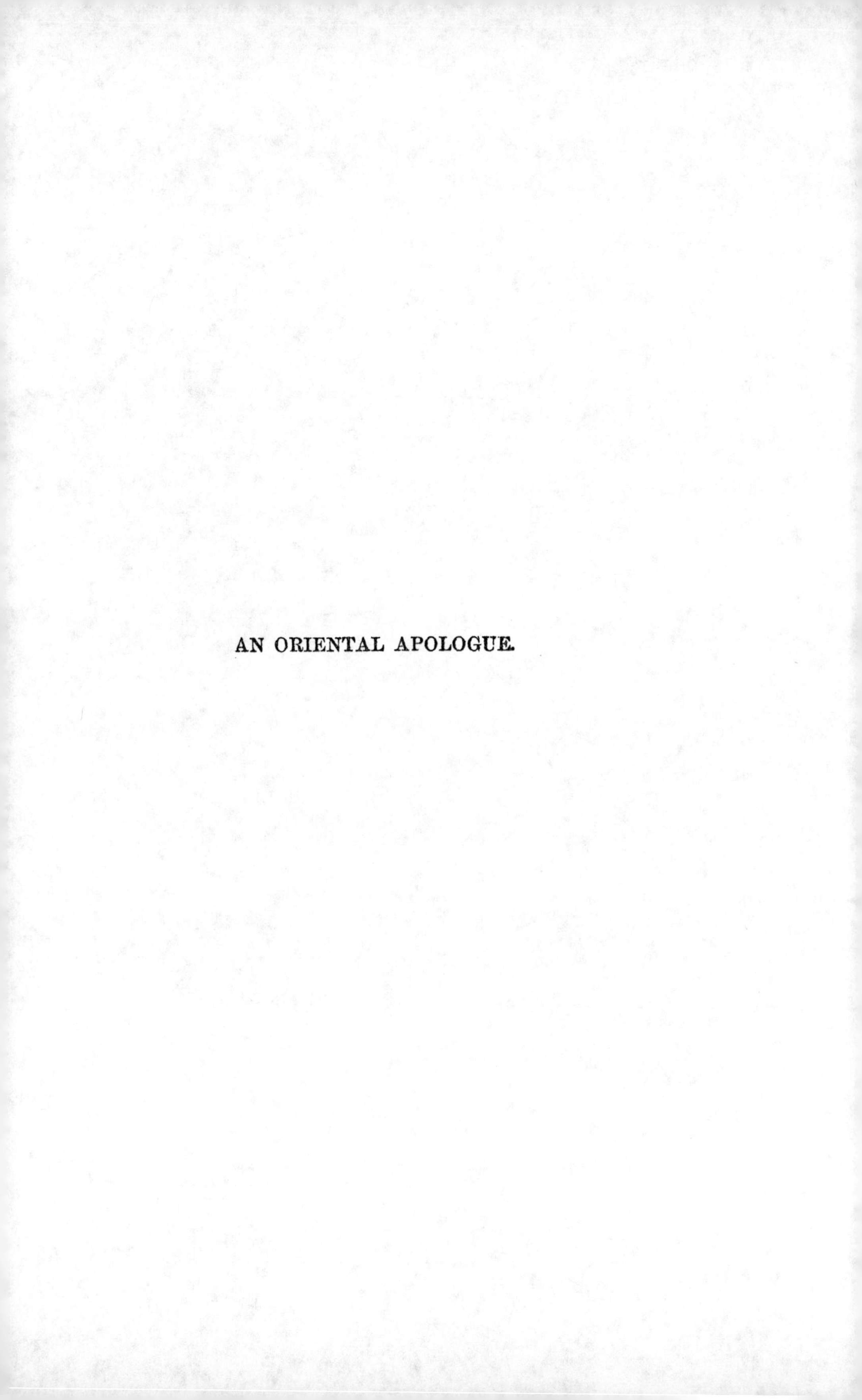

AN ORIENTAL APOLOGUE.

AN ORIENTAL APOLOGUE.

I.

SOMEWHERE in India, upon a time,
(Read it not Injah, or you spoil the verse)
There dwelt two saints whose privilege sublime
It was to sit and watch the world grow worse,
Their only care (in that delicious clime)
At proper intervals to pray and curse;
Pracrit the dialect each prudent brother
Used for himself, Damnonian for the other.

II.

One half the time of each was spent in praying
For blessings on his own unworthy head,
The other half in fearfully portraying
Where certain folks would go when they were dead;
This system of exchanges—there's no saying
To what more solid barter 'twould have led,
But that a river, vext with boils and swellings
At rainy times, kept peace between their dwellings.

III.

So they two played at wordy battledore
And kept a curse forever in the air,
Flying this way or that from shore to shore;

No other labor did this holy pair,
Clothed and supported from the lavish store
Which crowds lanigerous brought with daily care;
They toiled not neither did they spin; their bias
Was tow'rd the harder task of being pious.

IV.

Each from his hut rushed six score times a day,
Like a great canon of the Church full-rammed
With cartridge theologic, (so to say,)
Touched himself off, and then, recoiling, slammed
His hovel's door behind him in a way
That to his foe said plainly—*you'll* be damned;
And so like Potts and Wainwright, shrill and strong
The two D—D'd each other all day long.

V.

One was a dancing Dervise, a Mohammedan,
The other was a Hindoo, a gymnosophist;
One kept his whatd'yecallit and his Ramadan,
Laughing to scorn the sacred rites and laws of his
Transfluvial rival, who, in turn, called Ahmed an
Old top, and, as a clincher, shook across a fist
With nails six inches long, yet lifted not
His eyes from off his navel's mystic knot.

VI.

"Who whirls not round six thousand times an hour
Will go," screamed Ahmed, "to the evil place;
May he eat dirt, and may the dog and Giaour
Defile the graves of him and all his race;
Allah loves faithful souls and gives them power
To spin till they are purple in the face;
Some folks get you know what, but he that pure is
Earns Paradise and ninety thousand houries."

VII.

"Upon the silver mountain, South by East,
Sits Brahma fed upon the sacred bean;
He loves those men whose nails are still increased,
Who all their lives keep ugly, foul and lean;
'Tis of his grace that not a bird or beast
Adorned with claws like mine was ever seen;
The suns and stars are Brahma's thoughts divine
Even as these trees I seem to see are mine."

VIII.

"Thou seem'st to see, indeed!" roared Ahmed back
"Were I but once across this plaguy stream,
With a stout sapling in my hand, one whack
On those lank ribs would rid thee of that Dream!
Thy Brahma-blasphemy is ipecac
To my soul's stomach; could'st thou grasp the scheme
Of true redemption, thou would'st know that Deity
Whirls by a kind of blessed spontaneity.

IX.

"And this it is which keeps our earth here going
With all the stars."—"O, vile! but there's a place
Prepared for such; to think of Brahma throwing
Worlds like a juggler's balls up into Space!
Why, not so much as a smooth lotos blowing
Is e'er allowed that silence to efface
Which broods around Brahma, and our earth, 'tis known,
Rests on a tortoise, moveless as this stone."

X.

So they kept up their banning amebean,
When suddenly came floating down the stream
A youth whose face like an incarnate pæan
Glowed, 'twas so full of grandeur and of gleam;
"If there *be* gods, then, doubtless, this must be one,"
Thought both at once, and then began to scream,
"Surely, whate'er immortals know, thou knowest,
Decide between us twain before thou goest!"

XI.

The youth was drifting in a slim canoe
Most like a huge white waterlily's petal,
But neither of our theologians knew
Whereof 'twas made; whether of heavenly metal
Unknown, or of a vast pearl split in two
And hollowed, was a point they could not settle;
'Twas good debate-seed, though, and bore large fruit
In after years of many a tart dispute.

XII.

There were no wings upon the stranger's shoulders
And yet he seemed so capable of rising
That, had he soared like thistledown, beholders
Had thought the circumstance noways surprising;
Enough that he remained, and, when the scolders
Hailed him as umpire in their vocal prize-ring,
The painter of his boat he lightly threw
Around a lotos-stem, and brought her to.

XIII.

The strange youth had a look as if he might
Have trod far planets where the atmosphere,

(Of nobler temper) steeps the face with light,
Just as our skins are tanned and freckled here;
His air was that of a cosmopolite
In the wide universe from sphere to sphere;
Perhaps he was (his face had such grave beauty)
An officer of Saturn's guards off duty.

XIV.

Both saints began to unfold their tales at once,
Both wished their tales, like simial ones, prehensile,
That they might seize his ear; *fool! knave!* and *dunce!*
Flew zigzag back and forth, like strokes of pencil
In a child's fingers; voluble as duns,
They jabbered like the stones on that immense hill
In the Arabian Nights; until the stranger
Began to think his ear-drums in some danger.

XV.

In general those who nothing have to say
Contrive to spend the longest time in doing it;
They turn and vary it in every way,
Hashing it, stewing it, mincing it, *ragouting* it;
Sometimes they keep it purposely at bay,
Then let it slip to be again pursuing it;
They drone it, groan it, whisper it and shout it,
Refute it, flout it, swear to't, prove it, doubt it.

XVI.

Our saints had practised for some thirty years;
Their talk, beginning with a single stem,
Spread like a banyan, sending down live piers,
Colonies of digression, and, in them,
Germs of yet new migrations; once by the ears,
They could convey damnation in a hem,
And blow the pinch of premise-priming off
Long syllogistic batteries, with a cough.

XVII.

Each had a theory that the human ear
A providential tunnel was, which led
To a huge vacuüm, (and surely here
They showed some knowledge of the general head,)
For cant to be decanted through, a mere
Auricular canal or raceway to be fed
All day and night, in sunshine and in shower,
From their vast heads of milk-and-water-power.

XVIII.

The present being a peculiar case,
Each with unwonted zeal the other scouted,
Put his spurred hobby through its very pace,
Pished, pshawed, poohed, horribled, bahed, jeered, sneered, flouted,
Sniffed, nonsensed, infideled, fudged, with his face
Looked scorn too nicely shaded to be shouted,
And, with each inch of person and of vesture,
Contrived to hint some most disdainful gesture.

XIX.

At length, when their breath's end was come about,
And both could, now and then, just gasp "impostor!"
Holding their heads thrust menacingly out,
As staggering cocks keep up their fighting posture,
The stranger smiled and said, "Beyond a doubt
'Tis fortunate, my friends, that you have lost your
United parts of speech, or it had been
Impossible for me to get between.

XX.

"Produce! says Nature,—what have you produced?
A new straitwaistcoat for the human mind;
Are you not limbed, nerved, jointed, arteried, juiced
As other men? yet, faithless to your kind,
Rather like noxious insects you are used
To puncture life's fair fruit, beneath the rind
Laying your creed-eggs whence in time there spring
Consumers new to eat and buzz and sting.

XXI.

"Work! you have no conception how 'twill sweeten
Your views of Life and Nature, God and Man;
Had you been forced to earn what you have eaten,
Your heaven had shown a less dyspeptic plan;
At present your whole function is to eat ten
And talk ten times as rapidly as you can;
Were your shape true to cosmogonic laws,
You would be nothing but a pair of jaws.

XXII.

"Of all the useless beings in creation
The earth could spare most easily you bakers
Of little clay gods, formed in shape and fashion
Precisely in the image of their makers;
Why, it would almost move a saint to passion,
To see these blind and deaf, the hourly breakers
Of God's own image in their brother men,
Set themselves up to tell the how, where, when,

XXIII.

"Of God's existence; one's digestion's worse—
So makes a god of vengeance and of blood;
Another—but no matter, they reverse
Creation's plan, out of their own vile mud
Pat up a god, and burn, drown, hang, or curse
Whoever worships not; each keeps his stud
Of texts which wait with saddle on and bridle
To hunt down atheists to their ugly idol.

XXIV.

"This, I perceive, has been your occupation;
You should have been more usefully employed;
All men are bound to earn their daily ration,
Where States make not that primal contract void
By cramps and limits; simple devastation
Is the worm's task, and what he has destroyed
His monument; creating is man's work
And that, too, something more than mist and murk."

XXV.

So having said, the youth was seen no more,
And straightway our sage Brahmin, the philosopher,
Cried, "That was aimed at thee, thou endless bore,
Idle and useless as the growth of moss over
A rotting tree-trunk!" "I would square that score
Full soon," replied the Dervise, "could I cross over
And catch thee by the beard! Thy nails I'd trim
And make thee work, as was advised by him."

XXVI.

"Work? Am I not at work from morn till night
Sounding the deeps of oracles umbilical
Which for man's guidance never come to light,
With all their various aptitudes, until I call?"
"And I, do I not twirl from left to right
For conscience sake? Is that no work? Thou silly gull,
He had thee in his eye; 'twas Gabriel
Sent to reward my faith, I know him well."

XXVII.

"'Twas Vishnu, thou vile whirligig!" and so
The good old quarrel was begun anew;
One would have sworn the sky was black as sloe,
Had but the other dared to call it blue;
Nor were the followers who fed them slow
To treat each other with their curses, too,
Each hating 'tother (moves it tears or laughter?)
Because he thought him sure of hell hereafter.

XXVIII.

At last some genius built a bridge of boats
Over the stream, and Ahmed's zealots filed
Across, upon a mission to (cut throats
And) spread religion pure and undefiled;
They sowed the propagandist's wildest oats,
Cutting off all, down to the smallest child,
And came back, giving thanks for such fat mercies,
To find their harvest gone past prayers or curses.

XXIX.

All gone except their saint's religious hops,
Which he kept up with more than common flourish
But these, however satisfying crops
For the inner man, were not enough to nourish

The body politic, which quickly drops
Reserve in such sad junctures, and turns currish;
So Ahmed soon got cursed for all the famine
Where'er the popular voice could edge a damn in.

XXX.

At first he pledged a miracle quite boldly,
And, for a day or two, they growled and waited;
But, finding that this kind of manna coldly
Sat on their stomachs, they ere long berated
The saint for still persisting in that old lie,
Till soon the whole machine of saintship grated,
Ran slow, creaked, stopped, and, wishing him in Tophet,
They gathered strength enough to stone the prophet.

XXXI.

Some stronger ones contrived, (by eating leather,
Their weaker friends, and one thing or another,)
The winter months of scarcity to weather;
Among these was the late saint's younger brother,
Who, in the spring, collecting them together,
Persuaded them that Ahmed's holy pother,
Had wrought in their behalf, and that the place
Of Saint should be continued to his race.

XXXII.

Accordingly 'twas settled on the spot
That Allah favored that peculiar breed;
Beside, as all were satisfied, 'twould not
Be quite respectable to have the need
Of public spiritual food forgot;
And so the tribe, with proper forms decreed
That he, and, failing him, his next of kin,
Forever for the people's good should spin.

END OF VOLUME II.

www.ingramcontent.com/pod-product-compliance
Lightning Source LLC
LaVergne TN
LVHW020227110826
845151LV00003B/841

9781425531652